SIMON

solar thermal technologies for buildings

THE STATE OF THE ART

solar thermal technologies for buildings
THE STATE OF THE ART

EDITOR **M. Santamouris**

JAMES
X
JAMES

Published by James & James (Science Publishers) Ltd
8–12 Camden High Street, London, NW1 0JH, UK

A catalogue record for this book is available from the British Library.

ISBN 1 902916 47 6

Typeset by Saxon Graphics Ltd, Derby

Printed in the UK by The Cromwell Press

Cover image: Christian Richters

Contents

Editorial note

The present book is the first of a new series, *Buildings, Energy and Solar Technology (BEST)*, to be published by James and James (Science Publishers) and for which I have the honor to be the Series Editor.

The new series aims mainly to prepare and publish new high-quality educational and application books reporting the state of art in the field of solar energy and energy-efficient buildings. Emphasis will be given to original works resulting from research and development programmes. We would like to believe that the proposed titles will contribute greatly to improving knowledge on the topic, will promote solar energy and energy-efficient buildings in the market and will assist the educational community to train students and professionals better in this topic.

We are proud to present you the first book of the new series, entitled *Solar thermal technologies for buildings – the state of the art*.

The book includes 10 original contributions from highly recognized experts, covering most of the areas of solar thermal technologies as applied to buildings. Most of the papers were initially prepared for and presented at a thematic Workshop organized in Athens in the frame of the ENERBUILT programme of the Directorate for Science, Research and Development of the European Commission. The programme was coordinated by Professor O. Lewis of the Energy Research Centre of the University of Dublin. The assistance of the European Commission and in particular of Mr G. Deschamps, the manager of the programme, and also of the ENERBUILT network, is highly appreciated.

The first chapter of the book presents a very complete and in-depth description of the state of the art of passive solar heating technologies prepared by Dr K. Voss and V. Wittwer of the Fraunhofer Institute. It is organized around four main sections: the first section presents the physical fundamentals of passive solar heating, and the second section summarizes the very important results of a recent European project, SolGain, on the quantification of passive solar heating in the existing building stock. The third section illustrates the state of the art of passive solar heating in high-performance housing as given by an analysis of demonstration buildings within recent IEA activity. Finally, the fourth section focuses on future perspectives for related materials and technologies with strategic importance for the subject of passive solar heating.

The second chapter focuses on active solar technologies for buildings and is prepared by Professor A. M. Papadopoulos of Aristotle University Thessaloniki. It presents in a very comprehensive way the technological developments in the field and the market situation, and proposes specific actions for future developments.

The third chapter is written by Professor M. G. Hutchins of Oxford Brookes University. It provides an excellent review of the advances made in the field of spectrally selective materials for solar thermal conversion and use in the building envelope with emphasis on transparent glazing. The content reports advances achieved in a selection of recent European research projects and also identifies some important areas where future work remains a priority.

The fourth chapter focuses on advanced control systems for solar and energy-efficient buildings and represents collaborative work between Professor G. Guarracino of Ecole Nationale TPE, Professor D. Kolokotsa of the Technical Educational Institute of Crete and Dr V. Geros of the University of Athens. It gives a very detailed description of the principles and technologies used to control buildings better, and new ideas on smart buildings are presented.

The fifth chapter deals with the use of IT systems for the environmental and the energy quality of buildings, considering design, planning and monitoring. Prepared by Professor J. A. Clarke of the University of Strathclyde, it gives an excellent presentation of very interesting ideas and developments in this very promising field.

The sixth chapter deals with natural ventilation for buildings and is prepared by C. Ghiaus, F. Allard, Y. Mansouri, J. Axley from the University of La Rochelle. The paper presents in a very detailed way the existing developments on the field of natural ventilation while focusing on all aspects related to the application of natural ventilation techniques in the urban environment.

The seventh chapter of the book is prepared by Professors S. Álvarez and J. L. Molina of the University of Seville. It deals with hybrid cooling techniques for buildings and in particular with evaporative, earth and radiative cooling techniques, and roof solutions are also presented. It gives a very important description of the state of the art on this critical topic and presents the latest developments together with suggestions for future research actions.

Thermal comfort in buildings is the subject of the eighth chapter, prepared by Dr F. Nicol. It presents in an excellent way many recent developments in this field, with emphasis on the adaptive comfort approach, and provides results from recent projects.

The ninth chapter is prepared by Professor S. Hassid of Technion University and deals with passive cooling techniques for buildings. The author presents the main developments in this important field, describes some of the latest achievements and suggests future research actions.

Finally, the last chapter is a contribution from the editor of the book and deals with the integration of solar and other energy-efficient technologies in the urban context.

I would like to believe that this book will be useful to all scientists, engineers, researchers and other professionals working on the field of solar and energy-efficient buildings.

M. Santamouris

1 Passive solar heating of buildings

Karsten Voss and Volker Wittwer

Fraunhofer Institute for Solar Energy Systems, ISE, Heidenhofstrasse 2D, D-79110 Freiburg, Germany
Tel: +49 (0)761 4588 5135; fax: +49 (0)761 4588 9000; e-mail: karsten.voss@ise.fhg.de

1.1 Introduction

Based on the information obtained in the EU SolGain project, the passive solar gains to cover the heat demand of the existing European housing stock have been determined. It is obvious that these gains meet 10–15% of the total heat demand. A comparison with official (supply side) energy statistics shows that the value of passive solar gains is not considered and therefore the solar contribution is not counted in its true dimensions. For example, the EUROSTAT energy statistics state that the German value for the use of solar energy (value = total energy supply from renewables without energy from wind, hydroelectricity and biomass) is 7 kWh/year/person, whereas the SolGain calculation determined the utilized passive solar gains in residential buildings to be 922 kWh/year/person. Considering the heating systems in buildings and their related energy sources, total savings of CO_2 emissions by passive solar energy utilization in the EU countries have been estimated as 360 kg/year/person (= 140 Mt/year for the whole of Europe). The economic value of the saved energy is ~€45/person (= M€16,500).

In the heating-dominated climates of Europe, there is a strong trend to lower the space heating demand of new buildings. As more than one third of the end energy demand of these European countries is related to buildings, mainly for space heating, this is a direct consequence of a strategy to reduce the global energy consumption and the related CO_2 emissions. Components for passive solar energy utilization have to be adapted to the new class of high-performance buildings with rising performance needs (U values, solar control function, ...). Therefore, materials research is strongly related to the topic of passive solar energy utilization. For the same reason, research on new and advanced energy supply systems for high-performance housing is strongly recommended.

After this Introduction, the remainder of the chapter is organized into four sub-sections. Physical fundamentals of passive solar heating are covered in the second subsection. The third subsection summarizes the results of a European project on the quantification of passive solar heating in the existing building stock. The fourth subsection illustrates the state of the art of passive solar heating in high-performance housing as given by an analysis of demonstration buildings within an ongoing IEA activity. The final section focuses on future perspectives for related materials and technologies with strategic importance for the subject of passive solar heating.

1.2 The theory of passive solar heating

Equation (1.1) describes the basic building energy balance in a stationary state, identical with that used in the European calculation code EN 832, *Thermal Performance of Buildings – Calculation of Energy Use for Heating* (CEN, 1988). The heat losses due to transmission (Q_T) and ventilation (Q_V) are covered by utilized gains from solar (Q_S) or internal (Q_I) sources and the heat delivered by the heating system (Q_H). The utilization factor (η) takes into account that passive solar and internal gains are – as opposed to the heat delivered by the heating system – not controlled according to the heat demand.

$$(Q_T + Q_V) = \eta(Q_I + Q_S) + Q_H \tag{1.1}$$

The simplification to a stationary energy balance can be applied with minor error as long as the effect of changes in the energy content of the building can be neglected for the time period considered. As

- the change of indoor air temperature is limited due to thermal comfort requirements (19–21°C within the heating season) and

- the thermal mass of buildings is limited due to practicability and economy

appropriate periods for buildings according to experience are one or a few days, depending on the construction (heavy, moderate, light).

In the absence of solar radiation ($Q_S = 0$) and internal gains ($Q_I = 0$), the remaining heat demand to be covered by the heating system is directly proportional to the temperature difference between indoor (T_I) and ambient air (T_A), [see Equation (1.2)]. The proportionality factor is the combined building heat loss coefficient (H), summarizing the effects of transmission (H_T) and ventilation (H_V).

$$Q_H = (Q_T + Q_V) = H (T_i - T_A) = H(T_i - T_A) \tag{1.2}$$

The amount of passive solar gains depends on climatic parameters and the properties, the size and the orientation of the solar aperture of a building. The utilization factor is influenced slightly by the building construction and mainly by the ratio of gains compared to the losses (Figure 1.1). The change in utilization factor is illustrated in Figure1.1 by the changing slope of the heat demand curve with changing solar gains at various levels of heat losses. Almost 100% of the gains are utilized at high losses and

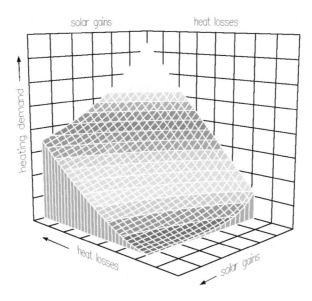

solar gains   heat losses

heating demand

heat losses

solar gains

Figure 1.1 *The space heating demand for a building as a function of the heat losses (transmission, ventilation) and the passive solar gains (transparency) of the building envelope. Qualitative results of a parameter study using dynamic building simulation. Internal gains are kept constant. Climatic data refer to Freiburg, Germany (Luther* et al, *1996)*

small solar gains, whereas in buildings with extremely low heat losses increased solar gains do not end up in a remarkable change in heat demand.

1.3 Passive solar contributions today – the SolGain results

The main goal of the EC-funded research project named 'SolGain', which finished at the end of 2001, was to obtain reliable information about the impact of passive solar energy utilization on the space heating demand of the residential building stock (Eurec, 2001). Broad and substantial information on passive solar gains in Europe's building stock was not available from completed investigations. Initial steps had been taken, e.g. with studies such as *Passive Solar Energy as a Fuel* published in 1990 (European Commission, 1990) The basic passive solar technology covered by the investigation is the use of windows (direct solar gain). Scenarios for future developments also include advanced technologies, such as energy-efficient windows and solar mass walls using transparent insulation (indirect solar gain).

The contribution of passive solar gains is missing in all national and European energy statistics. The reason for this is that the energy statistics consider only the supply side. Passive gains reduce the demand. Calculation codes for the space heating demand of buildings calculate the demand by considering solar gains as part of the building energy balance [see Equation (1.1)].

Within the SolGain project, the passive solar gains of the residential building stock have been determined. The aim was to quantify the overall benefits of passive solar energy utilization to cover the space heating demand. The commercial building sector was not included to keep a strong focus and a clear methodology concentrating on space heating. The calculations have been performed for Belgium, Finland, Germany, Greece, Ireland, Norway and the UK.

The calculations underline that passive solar heating plays a very important role for the heat balance of residential buildings. Depending on the location, the building standard and other factors, the so-called solar fraction, varies from 10% to 18% of the total space heating requirement (see Table 1.1). The total space heat requirement is the sum of heat demand, usable internal loads and usable solar gains. The solar fraction is defined as the ratio of the solar gains to the total space heating requirements [see Equation (1.3)].

$$f_{sol} = Q_S/Q_{tot} = Q_S/[Q_H + \eta \, (Q_I + Q_S)] \tag{1.3}$$

The time period considered is the heating season according to EN 832. The annual contribution is even higher, since the heating season would be much longer if no solar gains were available. Example calculations show that the total usable solar contribution is about double that within the heating season.

Defined and consistent boundary conditions for the calculations have been the main difference from previous studies. A comparison with the study *Passive Solar Energy as a Fuel* (European Commission, 1990) showed differences of factors of 2–3 in the calculated total solar gains.

To obtain comparable information on the environmental (CO_2 emission reduction) and economic impact of passive solar gains, the values are related to the number of inhabitants or to the net floor area in the countries considered.

The estimated average yearly economic savings due to passive solar gains in Europe are €46/person or €1.2/m², which means about M€17,108 for the whole of Europe (Figure 1.2). [It was assumed that the European average equals the average of the participant countries. The upscaled value is calculated by multiplying the average per capita of the participating countries by the total population of Europe (372 million).]

Table 1.1 *The effect of passive solar gain utilization in the existing building stock in terms of energy and emission savings (Eurec, 2001). The data summary takes into account the total amount of residential buildings within the various countries*

Country	Solar fraction (%)	Total solar gains (TWh)	Total savings (M€)	Total CO_2 reduction (Mt)
Norway	10	4.4	295	0.4
Finland	18	8.6	541	2.4
UK	15	57	2631	22.5
Ireland	11	2.0	128	1.2
Germany	13	76	3230	26
Belgium	12	13	646	4.4
Greece	18	8.9	567	3.3

The estimated average saved CO_2 emissions due to the solar gains are 345 kg/person/year or 9 kg/m²/year. For the whole of Europe this means about 128 Mt/year.

Comparison with official energy statistics shows that the value of passive solar gains is not presented in its true dimensions. For example, the energy statistics state that the German value for the use of solar energy is 7 kWh/year/person, whereas we calculated within this project a utilized passive solar gain in residential buildings of 922 kWh/year/person.

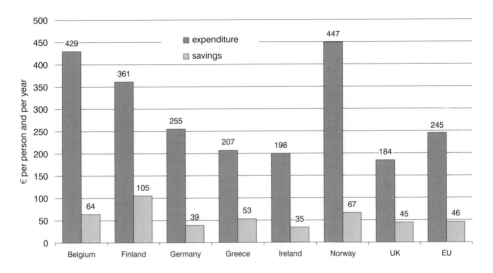

Figure 1.2 *Heating expenditure per person and related savings due to passive solar gains (Eurec, 2001)*

Some selected renovation strategies have been evaluated; e.g. for Germany, three scenarios have been analysed:

● Scenario 'as usual': no political influence on the renovation rate, the renovation is as usual. Today's emissions due to space heating are about 170 × 10⁶ t/year. This will be reduced by 'usual' renovation activities to 119 × 10⁶ t/year in 2030. There will be almost no change in the solar fraction (13% → 14%).

● Scenario 'improved': owing to a political action plan intended mainly to stimulate insulation activities, the emissions can be reduced to 74 × 10⁶ t/year in 2030. The solar fraction will rise to 17% in 2030. The reason for this is the increasing importance of solar gains relative to the losses. The absolute solar gains are lower.

● Scenario 'solar improved': as for the scenario 'improved' plus additional use of transparent insulation materials (ref. 1.5.2.1). In this scenario, the emissions can be reduced to 65 × 10⁶ t/year in 2030. The solar fraction will rise to 25% in 2030.

1.4 High-performance housing – solar gains in buildings with low heat loads

Advanced low-energy houses have been designed and monitored in many countries during the last decade (Krapmeier and Drössler, 2001; Voss, 2002). Since 2001, selected examples have been under comparative investigation within the framework of an International Energy Agency (IEA) activity under the topic 'Sustainable Solar Housing' (on the internet at http: //www.iea-shc.org/). One focus is on the performance evaluation of built examples. Some of the examples here have been chosen to document trends in passive solar heating in high-performance housing of today (Voss, 2002).

1.4.1 The methodology

Measured data for the space heating consumption of buildings (daily average heat consumption related to square metres of net heated floor area) have been analysed on a daily basis and plotted in a diagram versus daily average ambient temperature. The utilization of passive solar gains can be observed by sorting the measured data according to the daily solar radiation intensity.

According to the theory and Equation (1.1), the heat demand in the absence of solar gains and constant indoor temperature is a linear function of the ambient temperature. Solar gains should decrease the heat consumption below this linear correlation. The degree of solar energy utilization can be detected by the scatter of the data points: the greater is the difference between the measured data points and a regression line through the points in the low solar radiation class (line in Figure 1.4), the more intense the utilization of passive solar energy has been. Utilized solar gains can be quantified by summarizing the daily difference in heat demand measured and calculated with the linear regression through the data points in the low radiation class.

The separation into three radiation classes was developed by analysing the long-term meteorological data in Freiburg, Germany, for all days with ambient temperatures below 12°C (= heating days) (Figure 1.3). Although solar radiation on a vertical surface oriented towards the South might be more characteristic for high-performance housing, radiation on the horizontal plane was chosen owing to better availability in most of the monitoring projects. The classification was such that 25% of the data are in each of the high and low radiation classes and 50% are in the average class. The intention is to detect the extreme deviations from the average, without ending up with too few data in the extreme classes.

1.4.2 Four examples

Figure 1.4 shows the diagrams for three apartment buildings in Germany and one in Switzerland. Measurement results for the heat supply to the apartment buildings use data for the whole building. An advantage over terraced or detached houses is the fact

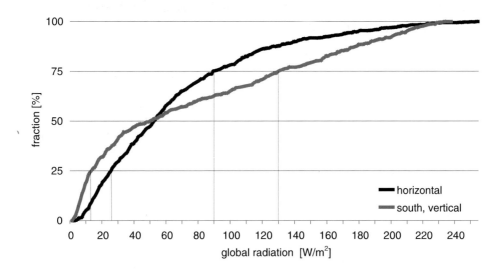

Figure 1.3 *Cumulative distribution of daily average solar radiation on the basis of measurements for Freiburg, Germany, between 1998 and 2001. The distribution relates only to days with ambient temperature below 12°C (= heating season): 25% of the days show a radiation intensity below 25 W/m². Only 25% of the days exceed a radiation intensity of 90 W/m²*

that a statistically significant number of nearly identical units is averaged, so that the behaviour of individual occupants is not as significant.

As the Gundelfingen solar house (third from the top) is the only one of the four that does not have a direct ventilation heat recovery system (heat recovery by heat pump instead), heat losses by ventilation are high. As a result, the slope of the regression line plotted is larger than those for the other three cases. In the absence of solar radiation, the measured daily heat demands are higher. On days with high solar radiation, the measured heat demand is reduced to almost the same level as determined by the houses with ventilation heat recovery. The Gundelfingen house is the one with the highest scatter of measured data points, indicating the high significance of passive solar gains for the success of the energy-saving concept. The building is equipped with transparent insulation on the South facade (Voss and Ufheil, 2002).

Although the calculated losses of the Kassel house are lower than those in Freiburg, the measured performance is almost identical. Both houses do not react very sensitively to solar gains owing to shading (Freiburg) and facade orientation (Kassel).

As the visible collectors of the Winterthur house are part of the supply side and the window sizes are not very large, passive solar gains are not very significant. Higher passive solar gains would not have been successful as they would decrease the utilization of the active gains by the air collector system (no heat storage included).

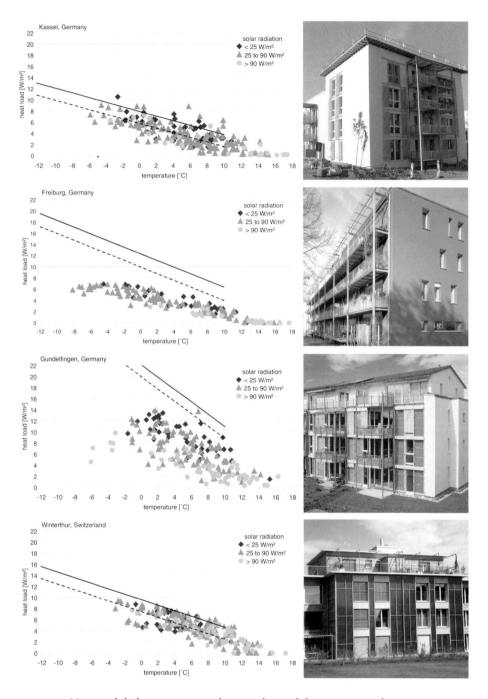

Figure 1.4 *Measured daily average space heating demand data versus outdoor air temperature. Sources of measurements are as follows: Kassel, Passive House Institute, Kassel, Germany; Freiburg and Gundelfingen, Fraunhofer ISE, Freiburg, Germany; Winterthur, Armena, Switzerland*

1.4.3 The shortened heating season

Increasing insulation and market penetration of mechanical ventilation systems with heat recovery shorten the time when active heat supply is needed (heating season). Reduced losses together with passive solar gains shift the temperature to start heating (the so-called balance temperature) from 15°C in the past to about 12°C or even lower in high performance housing (Figure 1.5).

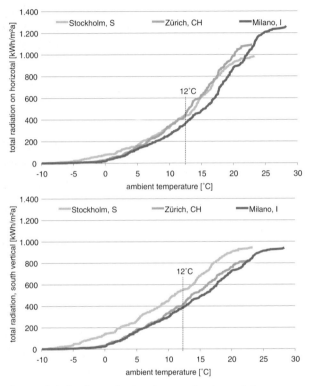

Figure 1.5 *Cumulative global solar radiation (top, on horizontal; bottom, on South vertical) versus ambient temperature for three characteristic locations in Europe*

1.4.4 Lessons learned

Low space heating demands in the central and northern European climates are primarily based on thermal insulation to reduce losses and improve thermal comfort. In cases where architectural considerations are favourable to a concept of passive solar gains, these gains need a remaining demand to be covered. Direct ventilation heat recovery should not be combined with an increased passive solar strategy as the solar gain utilization decreases drastically. Indirect heat recovery via a heat pump may allow an efficient energy supply, which is time shifted in relation to the occurrence of solar gains. This example underlines how building projects can benefit from an integrated system perspective instead of optimizing the demand or supply sides separately. The heat supply has to be adapted to the low loads (~10 W/m²) of high-performance buildings (see Section 1.6).

Extreme concepts for loss reduction (high levels of insulation, direct ventilation heat recovery) are not compatible with extreme passive solar approaches. Low heat loads increase the tendency for an uncomfortably fast increase in indoor air temperatures. Solar gain control becomes a very important task (see Section 1.5.1.3).

1.5 Related materials and technologies

1.5.1 Advanced glazing

1.5.1.1 Reduce thermal losses

Mainly for the central and northern European climates, reducing the transmission losses of the building envelope has proven to be very successful in terms of thermal comfort and energy saving (Krapmeier and Drössler, 2001). In addition to a number of advantages of low U value constructions, one weakness identified relates to the loss of space due to increased insulation thickness of external walls. This weakness might be overcome by introducing vacuum insulation systems into building practice (Fricke, 1988). Owing to the increasing use of ventilation heat recovery techniques, transmission losses again dominate by far the total thermal losses with ~60–80%. About half of these losses are due to the windows, not taking their solar gains into account.

The increasing market for ventilation heat recovery systems and the increased insulation thickness for opaque envelope components underline the weakness of the windows, although dramatic improvements have been achieved over the past decade (see Figure 1.6). The progress mainly benefits from coating technology, allowing for cost-effective, significant improvements. Current developments of window manufac-

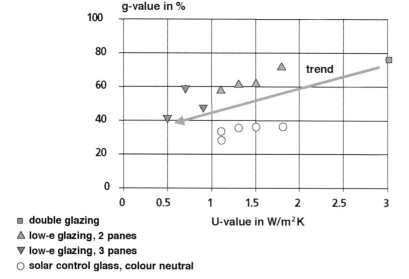

- ◫ **double glazing**
- △ **low-e glazing, 2 panes**
- ▽ **low-e glazing, 3 panes**
- ○ **solar control glass, colour neutral**

Figure 1.6 *The development of glazing properties over the past decade. U value, heat loss coefficient; g value, total solar energy transmittance*

turers have led to frames with improved thermal properties. Whole window U values of 0.8 W/m² K represent state-of-the-art technology (Schnieders, 2001).

Further developments might concentrate on:

- optimized low-e coatings: spectral optimization to further improve the spectral selectivity.

- vacuum glazing technology: technical solutions for spacers and edge technology for low thermal losses. Without such improvements, the overall properties will not exceed the best currently available glazing (triple glazing, two coatings, gas fill). Vacuum glazing could be useful in applications needing light-weight, high-performance glazing.

- frame technology: frames combining narrow profile widths with low U values, e.g. for application with the vacuum glazing of tomorrow.

1.5.1.2 Increase solar gains

Applying multiple glazing to decrease heat losses increases the optical losses by reflection. Anti-reflective coating of glass offers a significant transmittance increase as shown in Figure 1.7 (Gombert *et al*, 1998). One option for suitable surface finishing is coating with a porous sol gel. The long-term stability of such coatings is currently under investigation. A coating could be positioned on the outside surface of a multiple glazing. Direct contact with the environment (rainwater, dust, …) increases the needs for long-term stability.

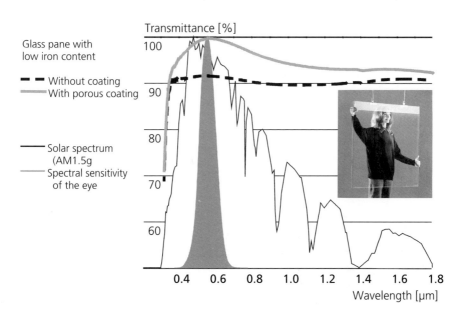

Figure 1.7 *Example for the change in spectral transmittance due to anti-reflective coating on glass with low iron content*

Further developments might concentrate on:

- accelerated ageing to test and improve the lifetime of the coatings with respect to contact with environmental conditions and conditions in the gap of a multiple glazing unit

- increasing and testing the scratch resistance capability.

1.5.1.3 Control solar gains

Reducing the heat demand by passive solar gains has been proved to be a successful option. The architectural quality of buildings with glass is one strong argument for the high market penetration. To be successful in terms of thermal and visual comfort, optimized solar control is a major issue for such buildings.

Passive solar gain control might benefit from new developments for splitting the incident radiation according to the incident angle due to the special properties of microstructured films on glass or double glazing inlays. The basic idea of angle-selective glazing is to create high reflectance of solar radiation incident at high solar altitudes and yet high transmittance of radiation incident at near-horizontal angles. In this way, visual contact with the outside can be provided while excessive heat gains and glare due to direct sunlight are reduced. A technical solution might be a microscopic structure in the form of inclined columns on the glass surface. Such structures are already on the market, e.g. in the form of plastic or metallic inlays for double glazing units. Market penetration is limited owing to high manufacturing costs. Micro-structuring, in principle, offers interesting cost-reduction opportunities and the advantage of improved visual contact compared with large-scale structures.

Active solar control might be achieved by standard solutions such as Venetian blinds, etc., but new options are under investigation or in the pilot application phase (Figure 1.8). Although these activities are mainly focusing on the commercial building sector (making buildings fit for low-energy cooling by reducing external heat loads), spin-offs for the housing sector are sure to come. Current prototypes of gaschromic, heat-mirror glazing (triple pane system) achieve switching from 46 to 13% in the solar heat gain coefficient at U values around 1 W/m^2 K (Fraunhofer, 1999; Wilson and Georg, 2002) (Figure 1.9).

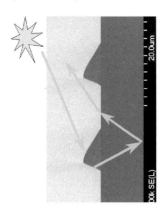
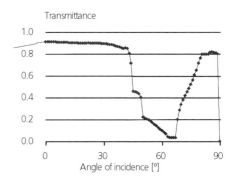

Figure 1.8 *Example and transmittance properties of a typical microstructured surface*

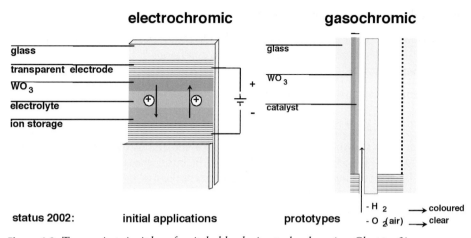

Figure 1.9 *Two main principles of switchable glazing technology (see Chapter 3)*

It is essential for the housing application that the glazing-integrated solar gain control does not reduce the insulation properties which are already state of the art (U value <1.1 W/m^2 K for advanced double glazing).

Further developments might concentrate on:

● microstructures: upscaling of microstructured areas using improved holographic lithography technologies; development of new miniaturized daylighting structures and also downscaling of existing macroscopic systems to a microscopic level; combined systems of dielectric and switchable components

● switchable glazing: bringing switchable glazing based on electrochromism and gasochromism from pilot application to the market; coating optimization with respect to switching and insulation properties; whole system optimization and cost reduction.

1.5.1.4 Multifunctional systems

Windows are necessary parts of buildings and important elements in architecture. In addition to daylighting and passive solar heating, further opportunities could be investigated, such as the following:

● Advanced PV glazing: new solar cell technologies, the so-called 'dye solar cells', might offer a chance to combine generation of solar electricity in facades with window properties. Dye solar cells are electrochemical cells which offer interesting properties such as transparency and low-cost production. Production is done by screen printing, which allows for special design features with respect to architectural considerations. In particular, the technology might by combinable with the coating technology of switchable glazing. The development of dye solar cells is in a very early stage concerning industrial production. Prototypes are available.

● Window collectors: using double glazing technology might give a suitable platform to produce so-called 'window collectors'.

1.5.2 Solar gains on opaque building elements

1.5.2.1 Transparent insulation

Transparent or translucent insulation (TI) of opaque building walls and daylighting elements today has a niche market of about 15,000 to 20,000 m²/year (1999) (source: Industrial Foundation), mainly in Switzerland, Austria and Germany, which certainly can be developed further. Costs are still high in most systems. Almost no public financial support is given, although the technology applied as solar wall heating can be compared with solar-assisted heating with collectors (Platzer, 2000).

Commercial products include:

● a transparent external insulation and finish system

● sealed double glazing units including capillary structures or a translucent mineral wool

● honeycomb plastic panels incorporating aerogel insulation material

● U-shaped cast-glass elements forming a self-supporting daylighting wall with TI material sandwiched between the elements.

The potential energy savings with passive solar walls cannot be compared with the large resource of the windows as shown in section 1.3 (as areas necessarily will be smaller), but typically useful solar gains in typical housing installations can be 15–30% of the window solar gains, even in a new building according to the new building energy code in Germany. The reduction in the heating energy of such a house due to TI is typically 10–20% depending on the TI system and the ratio of TI area to floor area (5% $A_{TI}/A_{floor} \rightarrow$ 10% reduction in heating). There is, theoretically, a high potential of solar renovation, as the TI system is a retrofit solution.

Technical problems still obstructing successful market development are connected with individual products. Excepting for costs, there are two aspects which often need to be considered:

● fire resistance not good enough for large buildings owing to the use of polymeric materials

● temporary condensation problems with some products.

Generally, costs for the products are too high to give positive payback due to energy savings:

● small manufacture production lines with large fraction of labour in production costs

● active solar shading (for summer) is too expensive

● expensive constructive solutions for the TI elements (costs for TI element as such are often in the range 30–40% of total system costs; other costs are construction, shading device, shading control, adaptation to wall, mounting).

Public funding for passive solar walls is only available in small, specialized programmes (some German cities, credits with reduced interest rates for solar renovations from KfW). Therefore, in most cases the installation of a passive solar wall is not economic in a strong sense.

Further developments might concentrate on:

- Prefabrication: cost benefits might be achievable by prefabrication of complete building elements including transparent insulation. As this is directed mainly towards the market of light-weight constructions, successful integration of phase-change materials might be an important advantage.

- Phase-change material (PCM): the integration of PCM in the absorber allows the application of transparent insulation in combination with light-weight walls, while still keeping a high overall solar–thermal system efficiency.

- TI elements including seasonal solar shading in order to avoid expensive active solar shading.

- Building physics of glazed walls (humidity, dust, long-term stability, …).

1.5.2.2 'Low-e paint'

The tendency to increase the insulation of walls decreases the effect of selective paints on the energy performance. Highly insulated walls do not profit significantly from surface coating, as the total heat transfer is mainly determined by the properties of the insulation layer.

A new field of interest arises from the fact that low temperatures on highly insulated external walls increase the surface humidity, thereby increasing the growth of algae (or corrosion on metal panels). Surface coating is, in principle, able to reduce this effect.

1.5.3 Increased thermal capacity

Advanced heat storage in building materials has been investigated for increased utilization of passive solar gains many times in the past. New successful research results have been presented on building-integrated phase-change materials (PCM) based on micro-encapsulated paraffins (Schossig *et al*, 2002). These materials show very promising properties related to passive cooling (increased summer comfort) and active solar thermal systems (solar air-conditioning systems, hypocausts, advanced heat transfer fluids).

Investigations concerning the potential for reduced heat loads by increased utilization of passive gains due to PCM in the walls and ceilings of buildings did not produce any promising results. Savings predicted by detailed building simulations have been in the range of only a few percent.

1.6 Related energy supply

Intensive research has been done in the past to reduce the space heating demand of new and existing buildings. Many European countries have improved their building codes towards lower boundaries for the maximum allowable heat demands due to the success of research, demonstration and market implementation of low-energy houses.

The energy demand for houses with an extremely low space heating demand tends to be dominated by the head demand for domestic hot water (DHW). This shifts the focus from space heating systems with an additional DHW heating function to DHW systems with additional space heating functions. The strong seasonal variation of the total heat demand is smoothed.

Increased research is recommended on adapted heat supply technology which matches this new trend on the demand side. Advanced electric heat pumps might be one important option, especially considering the trend towards increased efficiency in the power grid. The use of the electricity grid avoids the costs of a second energy carrier such as natural gas or oil. The components of heat pumps are potential mass products with many applications. This allows for attractive system costs as long as the cost of the heat pumps' heat source can be kept low.

Further, new technologies such as fuel cells and micro-turbines might be investigated, especially in the low power range and as part of the strategy toward a 'virtual power grid' (Bühring and Russ, 2002).

1.7 References

Bühring, A and Russ, C, 2002, 'From heat pumps to fuel cell heating systems', presented at the VII World Renewable Energy Congress, Cologne.

CEN, 1998, *Thermal Performance of Buildings – Calculation of Energy Use for Heating*, EN 832, Brussels, European Commission for Standardization (CEN).

Eurec, 2001, *SolGain – Contribution and Potential of Passive Solar Gains in Residential Buildings in the European Union*, Final Report EU Thermie Type B Action, Contract No. STR-1742–98-EU, Freiburg/Brussels, Eurec Agency.

European Commission, 1990, *Passive Solar Energy as a Fuel*, Publication No. EUR 13094 EEC, Brussels, European Commission.

Fraunhofer, 1999, *Swift – Switchable Facade Technology*, EU Contract ENK6-CT1999–00012, Freiburg, Fraunhofer ISE.

Fricke, J, 1988, 'Aerogels', in *Scientific American*, May, 92.

Gombert, A *et al*, 1998, 'Glazing with very high solar transmittance', in *Solar Energy*, 62(3), 177–188.

Krapmeier, H and Drössler, E, 2001, *CEPHEUS – Living Comfort Without Heating*, Vienna, Springer-Verlag.

Luther, J, Voss, K and Wittwer, V, 1996, 'Solar technologies for future buildings', presented at the 4th European Conference on Solar Energy in Architecture and Urban Planning, Berlin.

Platzer, W, 2000, 'Transparent insulation materials and products: a review', in *Advances in Solar Energy*, American Solar Energy Society 14, 33–66.

Schnieders, J, 2001, 'Passivhaus geeignete Fenster', in *Energieeffizientes Bauen*, Vol. 2, 87ff.

Schossig, P, Henning, H-M and Hausmann, T, 2002, 'Phase change materials in wall integrated systems', presented at the 2nd Workshop of IEA ECES Annex 17, Advanced Thermal Energy Storage Techniques, Ljubljana, April

Voss, K, 2002, *Demonstration Buildings – Design, Monitoring and Evaluation*, Working Document of IEA SHCP Task 28/LECBS Annex 38, Freiburg, International Energy Agency.

Voss, K and Ufheil, M, 2002, 'Solarenergienutzung und Energieeffizienz im geschosswohnungsbau', presented at the 12th Symposium Thermische Solarenergie, Staffelstein.

Wilson, H R and Georg, A, 2002, 'Switchable glazing with a large dynamic range in total energy transmittance', in *World Renewable Energy Congress VI, Proceedings*, London, Elsevier Science, 195–200.

2 Active solar heating and cooling of buildings*

Agis M. Papadopoulos

Laboratory of Heat Transfer and Environmental Engineering, Department of Mechanical Engineering, Aristotle University Thessaloniki, 54124 Thessaloniki, Greece Tel: +30 2310 996015; fax: +30 2310 996012; e-mail: agis@eng.auth.gr

2.1 Introduction

Almost 30 years after the first oil crisis, the technical and socio-economic background for renewable energy sources (RES) systems in the building sector is certainly quite different to that of the mid-1970s. Within this rather short time frame, active solar systems (ASS) became the most widespread and certainly the best known type of RES system. They are by now a commonly accepted solution for covering specific energy demands, both in the perception of the final consumer and as an example of a highly developed demonstration instrument for scientific progress in the field of thermal processing. These developments were assisted, to a large extent, by national and international policies, and also by public interest in energy conservation and in the reduction of running costs in the residential and tertiary sector. Still, the development of this branch in the 1990s seems to have moved in two different directions. Some types of ASS, such as the flat-plate collectors for domestic hot water (DHW) production, have evolved into technologically mature, well-selling products in recently expanding European markets, such as in Germany. One could also argue that in other markets, which are already quite mature, the 'conventional wisdom' of autonomous solar hot water systems has reached a degree of expansion that is close to the saturation point of the market, the Greek market being a good example of this situation. In this case, a new technological development is needed to overcome the technical barriers arising in the urban built environment, if one aims at covering a significant percentage of the demand in a solar thermal way.

This paper is dedicated to Michael senior for making it all happen and to Michael junior for making it all worth while.

At the same time, one cannot help but form the impression that the development of other ASS, particularly with respect to space heating and cooling applications, lacks momentum. This may be due to the fact that the academic and industrial communities show less enthusiasm to invest in research on solar thermal systems, at least compared with the 1980s, and focus instead on other RES systems, namely those producing electricity. It may also be true that public interest has become weaker, at least in some countries, shifting from energy conservation to the improvement of comfort conditions, a trend that can be observed in the steeply increasing demand for space cooling by means of air conditioning. The stability of energy costs, as a result of the developments in the world's energy markets, but also of the deregulation of the major European energy markets, has certainly been counter-productive in the sense of conserving energy and promoting RES.

The currently prevailing situation can therefore allow some, admittedly provocatively formulated, questions when it comes to the potential for the further development of solar technologies and their perspectives in the market. One can discuss the willingness of providing substantial support to the development and propagation of energy conservation systems in general, when compared with the support given to electricity production RES systems. One can also question whether the partners involved have become too inert to take the necessary steps towards new methods of utilizing solar energy by means of thermal processes or whether this technology has reached its technical and/or financial limits. Finally, one can equally well discuss whether some of the valid support policies are sensible or just a convenient excuse for not improving the systems' cost–benefit performance.

In that sense and in order to assess the prevailing situation in the field of ASS, one could try to apply the methodological approach of Strength–Weakness–Opportunity–Threat analysis (SWOT analysis), considering the solar systems both as independent technical components and also according to their applications (Tsoutsos, 2002). A brief description of these issues, as they arise from the social–economic boundary conditions, could lead to the key-words presented in Table 2.1. It becomes evident that the major part of these remarks applies to a different extent to the various solar systems types, as well as to the political, social and economic environment of each country and society. There are, however, many critical issues, which at the same time can be regarded as opportunities that apply to the same system throughout the European market and also the European Research Area.

In this line of thought and in order to discuss in detail the currently prevailing conditions and the possible aims for future research and propagation efforts, one needs to consider a system and a possible application separately, but also to consider each system with respect to a specific application. Both approaches will be necessary to deal with the issues of future developments of ASS in the building sector, although for reasons of brevity we shall focus on the requirements and the systems which dominate the European markets.

Table 2.1 *SWOT of the active solar systems' field*

Strength	Weakness	Opportunity	Threat
It is a mature basic technology, at least in some systems and applications	Some systems and applications still achieve poor efficiency	International agreements on the reduction of CO_2 emissions (Kyoto – The Hague)	The varying political support with respect to social trends and reactions
The acquaintance of the public with the technology	There is a high initial cost and/or a technical risk of certain systems, be it perceived or real	The will/trend to go ' green' that can be used as a drive towards sustainable development	The low and stable prices f or conventional energy sources, which make RES systems unattractive
The low initial cost of certain systems, such as the flat-plate collectors	The inadequate technical support with respect to integration in the building and the maintenance of systems	The globalization of technologies and markets	The external cost factors are still, in most cases, ignored
The support schemes and measures that attract household and SMEs	The superfluous support schemes and measures which lead the industry to become inert The lack of a branch-wide labelling and promotion campaign	The tightening of building performance standards and regulations	The traditionalism of a conservative and clustered building industry The legislative and managerial barriers still existing at the national, regional or local level

2.2 Classification of solar systems and current state of the art

According to the methodology widely adopted by the academic community and international organizations such as the IEA, active solar energy systems are classified according to the produced energy form and application, the operating principle or the working medium. The main classes, when considering the applications and the produced energy forms, are presented in Figure 2.1. Solar systems implying electricity production are not within the scope of the analysis presented in this chapter and are, in any case, still not competitive in terms of energy production costs (Kaltschmitt and Wiese, 1997; Trieb *et al*, 1997). Despite the fact that the main theme of this analysis is space heating and cooling, most of these applications are technically based on the systems used for hot water production, whilst the combination is as a rule a financially more solid investment. Hence the whole field is considered in this analysis. A brief description of the current status of the technologies for each application is presented in Table 2.2. Further, a brief description of the current status of the various solar collector types as independent components is presented in Table 2.3.

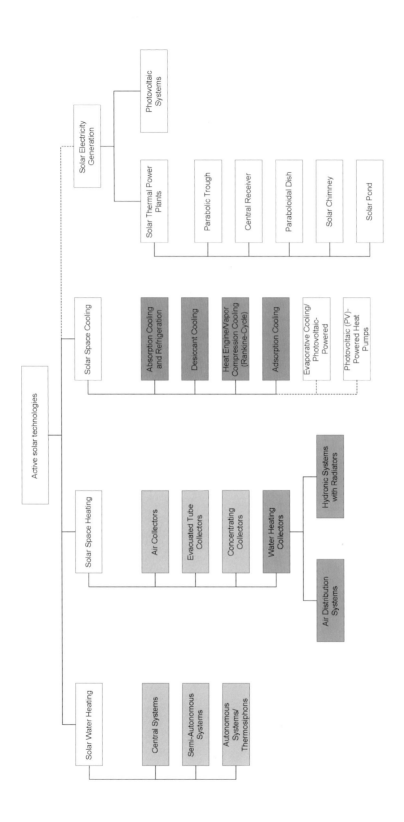

Figure 2.1 *Classification of ASS with respect to the application and the produced energy form*

Table 2.2 *Active solar technologies for domestic hot water, space heating and cooling*

Active solar thermal technologies		
1	Active solar water heating	Solar collectors that utilize solar radiation to heat either water or, in most cases, a working medium, such as a water–glycol antifreeze mixture. In the latter case the water is heated in a heat exchanger acting also as storage vessel. The collectors are as a rule located on the building's roof or close to the building. The collectors used can be flat plated glazed or unglazed or vacuum tube collectors. In some systems an electric pump is used to circulate the working medium through the collectors
1.1	Central systems	There is a collector array, which is common for a building or a whole residential area, which feeds a central storage vessel, that serves all users. In the case of large buildings, housing many users with the same or a similar demand profile, such as multi-storey apartment blocks, hotels and hospitals, the use of a central system is reasonable, as its initial and running costs are significantly lower than those of a corresponding number of autonomous ones. It presupposes, however, the use of efficient storage techniques
1.2	Semi-autonomous systems	The use of semi-autonomous systems, with a common collector field, but separate storage vessels for every user, presents a reasonable proposal for medium-sized buildings, as it ensures autonomy, keeping at the same time the construction costs within a limit
1.3	Autonomous systems – thermosiphons	The autonomous system, in which every single user has his own storage vessel, which is being fed by a respective collector. In smaller buildings or buildings in which the users' profile shows significant differentiation, the autonomous systems are more suitable. They form the major part of the solar systems sold in the market.
2	Active solar space heating	Medium-temperature solar collectors are used for space heating and operate in much the same way as solar water-heating systems, but they have a larger collector array area, larger storage units and more complex control systems. They can also be configured to provide solar water heating and typically provide 30–70% of the residential heating or the combined heating and hot water requirements. Active space-heating systems require more sophisticated design, installation and maintenance techniques
2.1	Water heating collectors	
2.1.1	Air distribution system	The heated water in the storage tank is pumped into a coil located in the return air duct whenever a thermostatic control calls for heat. The controller for the solar system will allow the pumping to occur if the temperature of the solar heated water is above a minimum needed to make a positive contribution to the heating requirement. An auxiliary heater can be used either to add heat to the solar storage tank to maintain a minimum operating temperature or as a conventional burner operating in parallel, heating the fresh air whenever the solar systems is not able to do so
2.1.2	Hydronic system with radiators	The heated water is circulated in series with a boiler into radiators located in the living spaces. As contemporary low-temperature radiators operate effectively at 50–60°C, this is feasible for conventional flat plate solar heating systems. Using the solar system's heated water as the source of water for the boiler will reduce the boiler's conventional energy consumption, if there are controls that enable the system to cover the base load by solar gains and the additional demand by the conventional system

Table 2.2 *continued*

2.2	Air collectors	Transpired air collectors or solar panels, mounted as an exterior cladding on a building's South-facing wall, are used for heating or preheating the fresh air inducted through the ventilation system. A fan is necessary to deliver the heated air into the building. It is an option for commercial and industrial applications that require large quantities of ventilation air, including warehouses and manufacturing plants. In case of smaller residential buildings the panels can operate without any mechanical air circulation, based on buoyancy-driven convection, such as a Trombe wall. The main difficulty is that this system cannot be used for any other purposes, such as hot water production
2.3	Vacuum tube collectors	These collectors consist of rows of parallel transparent glass tubes, each containing an absorber and covered with a selective coating. These collectors are manufactured with a vacuum between the tubes, which helps them achieve extremely high temperatures (70–180°C); they are thus appropriate for commercial and industrial uses
2.4	Concentrating collectors	Concentrating collectors for residential applications are usually parabolic troughs that use mirrored surfaces to concentrate the sun's energy on an absorber tube (called a receiver) containing a heat-transfer fluid
3	Active solar space cooling	Cooling and refrigeration using active solar cooling systems can provide for year-round utilization of collected solar heat, thereby significantly increasing the cost effectiveness and energy contribution of solar installations
3.1	Absorption cooling and refrigeration	Absorption cooling system does not use an electric compressor to pressurise the refrigerant. Instead, it utilizes a heat source, such as a natural gas burner–boiler or a correspondingly dimensioned solar collector, to evaporate the already-pressurized refrigerant from an absorbant/refrigerant mixture. Although absorption coolers require electricity for pumping the refrigerant, the amount is small compared with that consumed by the compressor of a conventional AC system. When used with solar thermal systems, absorption coolers must be adapted to operate at the normal working temperatures for solar collectors (80–120°C). A further option is to produce ice with a solar-powered absorption device, which can then be used for cooling or refrigeration, as well as heat storage, reducing in this way peak energy demands
3.2	Desiccant cooling	These systems improve indoor thermal conditions by removing moisture from the air and hence establishing for the same air temperature lower relative humidity values. The wheel absorbs most of the incoming air's moisture. This heats and dries the air, hence desiccant cooling. The heated air then passes through a rotating heat exchanger wheel, which transfers the heat to the exhaust side of the system. At the same time, the dried air passes through an evaporative cooler, further reducing its temperature. The heated exhaust air continues through an additional heat source (e.g. a solar heat exchanger), raising its temperature to the point that the exhaust air evaporates the moisture collected by the desiccant wheel. The moisture is then discharged outdoors. The various system components require electricity to operate, but they use less than a conventional air conditioner. Most desiccant cooling systems are intended for large applications, such as supermarkets and warehouses. They are also ideal for humid climates
3.4	Heat engine/vapour compression cooling (Rankine cycle)	The Rankine-cycle cooling process uses a vapour compression cycle similar to that of a conventional air conditioner. Solar collectors heat the working fluid, which has a very low vaporization point. The working fluid then drives a Rankine-cycle heat engine. This technology, however, is mainly experimental and is not often used because it needs a large system size to do any meaningful amount of cooling

Table 2.3 *Classification for solar collectors as single components, with respect to the operating principle*

Type of solar collectors		
1	Flat-plate collectors	The most common collector for solar hot water is the flat-plate collector. It is a rectangular box with a transparent cover, installed on a building's roof. Small tubes run through the box, in which circulates fluid – either water or other fluids, such as an antifreeze solution or even air. The tubes are attached to a metallic, black absorber plate, steel or copper, with some sort of selective coating. As heat builds up in the collector, it heats the fluid passing through the tubes. The hot water or liquid goes to a storage tank. If the fluid is not hot water, water is heated by passing it through a coil inside the storage tank, which in that sense acts as a heat exchanger
1.1	Fluid collectors, water heating collectors	In this type of collector the working medium is water or a water–antifreeze solution. These collectors are primarily used for DHW preparation, but they can also be used for space heating. They achieve an average energy yield between 400 and 700 kWh/m^2, depending on the location of installation and their quality
1.2	Air collectors, air heating collectors	Air collectors are simple, flat-plate collectors used primarily for space heating. The absorber plates in air collectors can be metal sheets, layers of screen or non-metallic materials. The air flows past the absorber by natural convection or forced by a fan. Because air has a far smaller specific thermal storage capacity than fluids, air collectors present a significantly lower performance than fluid collector, not exceeding 400 kWh/m^2. In their simplest form they are transpired air collectors, mounted as an exterior cladding on a building's South-facing wall, used for ventilation preheating. These collectors are unglazed. A blower or fan is used to draw air through perforations in the wall to deliver ventilation air into the building. Solar ventilation air preheating systems are generally used in commercial and industrial applications that require large quantities of ventilation air, including warehouses, large manufacturing plants and maintenance hangars. Fairly low-cost systems, easy to integrate in the building's shell, but with low performance and architectural limitations
2	Vacuum-tube collectors water heating collectors	These collectors consist of rows of parallel transparent glass tubes, each containing an absorber and covered with a selective coating. Sunlight enters the tube, strikes the absorber and heats the liquid flowing through the absorber. These collectors are manufactured with a vacuum between the tubes, which helps them achieve extremely high temperatures (75–180°C), so they are appropriate for residential, commercial and industrial uses. Their performance is high, exceeding on average that of the fluid collectors by 30–40%, but their cost is almost correspondingly higher
3	Concentrating collectors	Parabolic-shaped reflectors concentrate solar radiation onto an absorber or receiver, to provide hot water and steam, usually for industrial and commercial applications. Very efficient, particularly when considering their annual performance, but complicated and costly
4	Low-temperature solar collectors	These are systems of low performance and low cost. Unglazed collectors are used to heat or pre-heat water for swimming pools and other similar applications. These simple and cheap collectors typically consist of black plastic or metal tubes through which water is circulated. There is no additional insulation, so temperatures are limited to about 20°C above ambient air temperature. Another form is that of small, insulated water tanks of 100–150 litres, lined with glass on the inside and painted black on the outside, that are mounted on the roof or on the ground and provide DHW

2.3 Aims for the future: the technologies

The discussion of future technological developments can be based on the same two axes mentioned above: one focusing on the solar collectors as independent components and the other on the systems' integration concerning the demands of specific applications.

2.3.1 Components

Considering the main types of solar collectors, it is most probable that the base for future developments in the building sector, with respect to hot water, heating and cooling, will be the flat-plate and vacuum tube collectors.

2.3.1.1 Flat-plate collectors

The use of such systems with a liquid working medium leads in most cases to DHW production at a lower cost than by means of electrical heating, whilst it is about to become competitive with oil- or natural gas-fired systems. The trend of this development is depicted in Figure 2.2. It is therefore only reasonable that they will continue to form the bulk of the solar systems used for most building applications throughout the

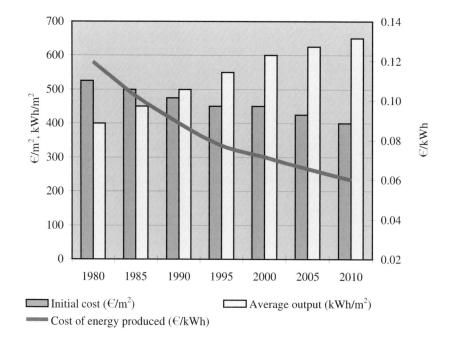

Figure 2.2 *Development of initial cost, average output and energy production costs for hot water production under Greek climatic conditions*

coming decade. The main aim of research has to be cost reduction, by replacing expensive materials such as copper, stainless steel and glass. Polymers and carbonates are the most likely substitutes, with emphasis given to the issues of stability and durability under adverse weather and climatic conditions. A medium-term target of research efforts should be to reduce the initial cost by up to 50%.

Collectors with air as a working medium suffer from both relatively high cost and low performance, to a great extent owing to the lack of economies of scale. Cost reductions should be aimed for by using cheaper materials, but also through an increased use of standardized components, which is still frequently not the case. The use of air as a working medium sets very clear limits on the efficiency achievable. Hence increasing the performance is less of a problem with the collectors as such, but more with the air handling system (fans, ducts, etc.), with respect to each specific building.

2.3.1.2 Vacuum tube collectors

Vacuum tube collectors are the most interesting technology with respect to space heating and cooling, as they can produce the high temperatures that permit high efficiencies. Furthermore, as the inclination of the collector's frame does not influence the slope of the selective surface, they have the significant advantage of not distorting a roof's aesthetics. They can therefore be integrated much more easily in buildings of 'traditional' or 'special' architecture. In that sense, research has to focus on improving their durability and reliability, whilst at the same time reducing the manufacturing costs. In any case, it is interesting to note that in some markets, particularly in China, this type of collector has become fairly popular, covering 35% of the total solar thermal systems' sales. Keeping in mind that sales in the Chinese market reached 15×10^6 m^2 in 1998 and that it is developing at a growth rate of 15% annually, this is an impressive demonstration of the ability to achieve economies of scale (Zhang *et al*, 2001).

With respect to the other types of solar systems, one could mention that concentrating collectors are rather unlikely to play a significant role in active heating and cooling of buildings in the coming decade, owing to their very high initial cost. As far as unglazed collectors are concerned, it is not very likely that they will play an important role in active heating and cooling of buildings in Europe, owing to their very low performance compared with the energy requirements. Still, they are of interest for less developed regions with high and evenly distributed annual solar radiation values, where they could contribute to a significant improvement of living standards at a fairly low initial cost.

2.3.2 Systems' integration and applications

Adopting the systems' integration approach with respect to the main applications of heating and cooling, one can summarize the following arguments.

2.3.2.1 Active solar heating

In most cases solar heating is based on the technology used for active solar water heating. The two main problems for the broader propagation of this technology relate to the need for higher water temperatures and the gap between thermal energy supply and demand, both on a diurnal and on a seasonal basis. The former problem can be dealt with either by means of vacuum tube collectors, provided that their initial cost will be reduced, or by means of low-temperature heating systems, such as floor heating systems.

Medium-temperature solar collectors are certainly the most easily applicable systems to be used for space heating, as they operate in much the same way as indirect solar water-heating systems. Considering the developments in the field of DHW systems, as expressed in terms of their performance, progress has been achieved with respect to the optimum combination of the collector's aperture area and storage volume of the vessels. If one considers the base case (BC) systems of the mid-1990s and the dream case (DC) systems described during this period, then one cannot fail to notice the evolution towards the features of the DC systems, as can be seen in Table 2.4 (Morrison, 2001). The European trend has indeed been clearly towards smaller and more compact systems, always bearing in mind the climatic differences, as can be seen in Table 2.5 (ESIF, 2000).

However, space heating systems require a larger collector array area, and also larger storage units and more complex control systems. On the whole they represent a technological task of more sophisticated design, installation, operation and maintenance.

Such systems can typically cover 30–70% of the residential heating requirements, and also the hot water demand, keeping within a reasonable frame of size and costs. The study of such combined hot water–space heating systems for the favourable Mediterranean climatic conditions, with respect to the size of the building (small,

Table 2.4 *Features of base case (BC) and dream case (DC) systems of the 1990s*

	Canada	Denmark	Germany	The Netherlands	Switzerland	USA
Aperture area BC (m²)	5.60	4.38	6.35	2.84	5.92	2.56
Storage volume BC (l)	273	295	400	115	500	189
Volume/area ratio BC (l/m²)	48.75	67.35	62.99	40.49	84.46	73.83
Aperture area DC (m²)	5.16	3	5.08	2.75	4.48	1.49
Storage volume DC (l)	270	175	300	100	430	138
Volume/area ratio DC (l/m²)	52.33	58.33	59.06	36.36	95.98	92.62

Table 2.5 *European base case systems in 2000*

Features	Southern Europe	Mid-Europe	Northern Europe
Aperture area (m²)	2–4	3–5	4–6
Storage volume per collective surface (l/m²)	100–200	200–300	200–300
Average annual output (kWh/m²)	500–650	400–550	300–450
Initial cost (€/m²)	300–600	400–1000	400–1000
Cost of energy produced (€/kWh)	0.05–0.09	0.07–0.11	0.09–0.14

medium and large) and the heating demand, as a function of the building's thermal insulation and design, lead to the results presented in Figure 2.3. The buildings considered were typical three- to five-storied urban buildings, featuring in DC highly efficient thermal insulation, as imposed or proposed by most contemporary European regulations (Commission of the European Communities, 2001a). In the BC scenario the insulation was average, as was applied in the 1980s, and in the worst case there is no insulation at all, that is in the old buildings (OB) constructed prior to the introduction of regulations. The collector areas needed to achieve a solar fraction of 40% for space heating and 95% for hot water are depicted in the form of curves, referring to the right *y*-axis. This rather conservative approach leads to a marginally acceptable economic feasibility (Papadopoulos *et al*, 2001). However, even so, the surface needed is considerable, especially in the case of larger buildings, whilst the problem of coping with the supply–demand gap, which is strongly linked with the issue of thermal storage, be it short-term or interseasonal, remains to be tackled.

Another option for solar space heating is transpired air collectors or solar air panels. Such systems were introduced during the 1980s, either as autonomous thermosiphonic systems for small residential buildings or in conjunction with the ventilation and air-conditioning systems in commercial buildings. The former type was used with some success in a series of pilot projects in Europe, notably in the Solar Village 3 in Athens, whilst the latter can be met in a series of private and public applications in the USA since the mid-1990s (Kalogirou and Papadopoulos, 1992; DOE, 2001). Although the evaluation of the systems was fairly positive, in terms of both energy performance and economics, their application presupposes suitable buildings or a well thought out

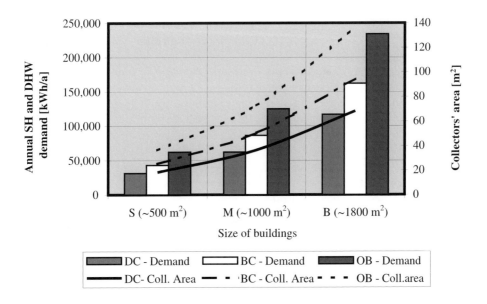

Figure 2.3 *Space heating and hot water demand and the resulting collectors' area needed*

air-handling unit, in order to avoid indoor air quality problems. Both criteria put the solar air collectors at a disadvantage in the typical European urban environment, making the option of water-heating collectors more attractive.

In any case, whether one uses water or air as a working medium, the use of advanced controls that will allow the efficient co-operation of conventional and solar systems is necessary, in order to avoid an overlap of the conventional and the solar systems' operation or phenomena such as the inversion of thermal fluxes. A delicate balance between the building shell's thermal behaviour and the heating system's thermodynamics has to be maintained, in order to achieve the expected efficiencies in practice. In order to achieve this, a high level of scientific expertise is necessary, as the use of even fairly simple computational tools to determine the thermodynamics of a building, presupposes a designer with a solid background in building physics. Furthermore, even when applying sophisticated and widely used software tools for the analysis of a building's energy behaviour, one can expect significant deviations (IEA, 2001).

2.3.2.2 Active solar space cooling

Given the fact that the cooling demand of buildings has become a dominant factor in the electricity balance in most southern European countries, surprisingly little interest has been shown in possible alternatives to the various forms of conventional air conditioning, mainly in the form of split units, that flooded the building sector in the 1990s. Active solar cooling is, in that sense, an attractive option, in order to reduce the sharply increasing peak cooling loads that burden the utilities and create disturbances in the liberalized European markets, with peak loads that increase at annual growth rates of more than 10% in Italy, Greece and Spain (Unander, 2000). At the same time, the solar potential is highest at the same time when the cooling demand is also at its highest, thus offsetting the problem met in the case of solar space heating.

With respect to the possible thermal solar systems, absorption is the most promising option, although in terms of efficiency and cost it is still not competitive with the conventional air-conditioning systems. Currently the main technologies with significant potential are the combinations of flat-plate collectors or vacuum tube collectors, with LiBr–H_2O absorption cycles, the photovoltaic/vapour compression and the photovoltaic/thermoelectric being the next best. Still, the annual efficiency of these systems cannot exceed 10–12%, while the net solar coefficient of performance is currently in the range 0.3–0.6 (Trieb *et al*, 1997; Rannels, 2000). As far as the costs are concerned, the main problem lies within the need for high temperatures, exceeding 100°C, which leads to the adoption of the more expensive types of collectors. Still, as there is reasonable potential for the improvement of the flat-plate collector's performance and for the reduction of the cost of vacuum tube collectors, the case of solar space cooling appears to be the most challenging one for research in the next decade. The aim of improved efficiencies and reduced costs has been, in most cases, the driving force behind developments in the technology of solar systems in the past. The key issue, however, considering the size of urban buildings and the cooling demands that occur, may lie in the principle of autonomous, small-sized solar systems and the question of their feasibility. Larger systems than those currently used for hot water production will be necessary, requiring large collector arrays, not necessarily located on the top of buildings. It is therefore most likely that a significant capacity and an efficient way of storing thermal energy will be needed.

2.3.2.3 A call for thermal storage

For both space heating and cooling, and to a lesser extent for hot water production, thermal storage remains the decisive factor for the successful implementation of solar systems, particularly when it comes to achieving a significant solar fraction. Two aspects are of prime importance: the compactness and the long-term efficiency, both of these aspects applying to short-term diurnal and also to medium- and long-term seasonal storage. The current state of the art is based on storage in the form of sensible heat in water. Water is cheap, abundant and non-toxic and has a relatively high storage density. Still, storage in the form of sensible heat leads inevitably to high losses, even though the performance of thermal insulation materials has been vastly improved over the last decade. Furthermore, the thermal storage properties of water lead to the need for significant masses. This is especially the case when a high solar fraction for space heating is required. A typical small two-storied residential building of 500 m^2, housing four families, requires, even if it is a 'low-energy' house, some 25,000 kWh annually for space heating and an additional 10,000 kWh for hot water. For the favourable climatic conditions in southern Europe and if a solar fraction for space heating of 40% were the aim, the necessary short-term water storage vessel would have a volume of between 2 and 3 m^3, including the thermal insulation layer. The storage capacities needed for the typical buildings of the case studies considered in Section 2.3.2.1 are depicted in Figure 2.4. If the solar fraction were to rise to a minimum of 70% in order for the whole system to become more feasible in terms of economics, the required volume would be almost 5 m^3. One has to keep in mind that these figures are based on the assumption of a very energy-efficient building, with a specific annual heating demand of 50 kWh/m^2 and on short-term storage, which is readily feasible in the Mediterranean area but not always practical in northern Europe. For the same requirements and the less favourable northern European climatic conditions, these volumes can be two to four times larger, whilst in the case of seasonal storage one could easily need some 30 or 40 m^3. It is evident that the space required for such volumes is not easily available in the interior of residential buildings. Furthermore, advanced short-term storage, with its high insulation demands and its controls, leads to initial costs of about €0.8–1/kWh annually, if amortized over the useful lifetime of the system, a figure that doubles for seasonal storage (Fisch *et al*, 1998). Hence, in cases of specific large consumers, such as large hotels, public buildings or industrial applications, large storage volumes may not pose a major problem, but there are clearly limits, in terms of both space and cost, that arise in 'real-world' residential urban buildings, unless one considers the approach of central heating/cooling schemes. Such a solution sets an entirely different aspect for thermal storage, associated with other difficulties mainly in terms of economics, which are beyond the scope of this chapter. Still, the solution of large-scale, centralizing applications probably presents the most interesting option in order to achieve a true impact in the substitution of fossil fuels and the reduction of emissions.

In the long run, high-density, high-efficiency storage materials would make solar energy storage viable for large-scale applications in low-energy houses. This could be

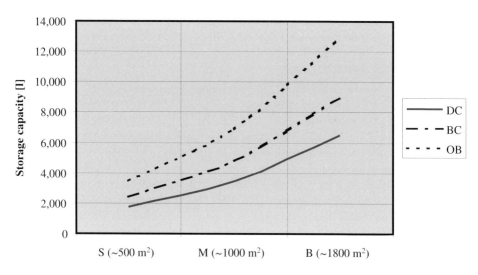

Figure 2.4 *Storage capacities needed to achieve the design performance of the systems*

achieved by sorption, adsorption and absorption, utilizing the latent heat, instead of the sensible heat. Given a storage density of approximately 40 kWh/m³, the storage volume could hence be reduced by a factor of three or even four compared to the conventional water storage capacity, in the form of sensible heat. A comparison of adsorption and absorption is interesting as both approaches present certain advantages and drawbacks, according to the sort of application considered (Berkel, 2000).

Even higher densities are possibly achievable on the basis of energy storage by utilizing the potential of endo/exo-thermic chemical reactions, with the use of the appropriate materials. In theory, the highest storage density and efficiency are achievable by omitting the intermediate thermal step of the process and using photobio/electrochemical reactions. All these options present either technical difficulties, such as the high reaction temperatures, the system's complexity and the presence of gaseous reaction components in the case of thermochemical energy storage, or are still in their infancy, as in the case of photobiochemistry. In that sense they may well be considered as cases for further basic research.

2.4 Aims for the future

2.4.1 The market

At the end of 1999, the total installed surface of solar collectors in the EU reached 8.8×10^6 m², demonstrating a 7.3% increase over the previous year. This figure is perfectly inscribed in the changing scene of the last four years, during which average annual growth reached 6%. This growth rate, however, has not been followed in all European Union countries. The total installed surfaces increased in seven countries between 1996 and 1999: Germany, Austria, Greece, Denmark, the Netherlands, Sweden and Belgium. The opposite trend was monitored during the same period in six other countries: France, Italy, UK, Spain, Portugal and Finland. In those countries, the number of collectors put into service during this period was less than those installed 15 years earlier and had, therefore, reached the end of their useful lifetime. Ireland and Luxembourg registered stagnation in the level of installed surface of collectors, which means that the sales monitored in the market corresponded to the replacement rate of 'first generation' collectors. The annual data for the development of annual installations, showing also the participation of each type of collector, are presented in Table 2.6. The data concerning the cumulative installed surfaces over the last four years are presented in Table 2.7.

The perspectives of thermal solar energy growth in the EU remain good. Taking into consideration the efforts of each country, the surface of solar collector should reach 87×10^6 m^2 by 2010, as can be seen in Table 2.8. This figure should be compared with European Commission targets, which, in its White Paper on renewable energies, announce 100×10^6 m^2 installed in 2010 (Commission of the European Communities, 1997). Projections reveal that this target is behind schedule by approximately 13×10^6 m^2, i.e. the equivalent of one year of installations (Commission of the European Communities, 2001b). On the other hand, for 2003, forecasts are more positive with an estimate of a total surface area of 23,385,700 m^2 vs a target of 15×10^6 m^2 set by the European 'Campaign for Take-off' (ESIF, 2000).

Table 2.6 *Annually installed solar collectors (for 1998 and 1999) per type and country (in thousands of m²)* (Source: EurObserv'ER, 2000)

| | 1998 | | | | 1999 | | | |
	Glazed	Unglazed	Vacuum	Total	Glazed	Unglazed	Vacuum	Total
Germany	337.0	21.9	53.0	411.9	380.0	22.8	60.0	462.8
Greece	153.4	1.0	1.0	155.4	158.0	1.0	1.0	160.0
Austria	163.0	32.3	2.6	197.9	138.8	16.9	2.4	158.1
France	18.5	9.0	0.0	27.5	24.3	8.0	0.0	32.3
Italy	24.6	1.4	1.0	27.0	41.3	2.3	1.5	45.0
The Netherlands	24.4	2.2	0.0	26.6	25.7	2.0	0.0	27.7
Spain	19.6	0.0	0.0	19.6	21.0	0.0	0.0	21.0
Denmark	17.5	0.2	0.0	17.7	15.3	0.3	0.0	15.6
Sweden	7.1	2.6	0.3	10.0	8.8	2.9	0.1	11.8
Portugal	8.0	0.0	0.0	8.0	8.0	0.0	0.0	8.0
Great Britain	5.8	3.2	0.0	9.0	5.8	3.2	0.0	9.0
Belgium	2.0	0.4	0.1	2.5	2.0	0.5	0.1	2.5
Finland	0.8	0.0	0.0	0.8	1.0	0.0	0.0	1.90
Total	781.7	74.2	58.0	913.9	829.8	59.8	65.1	954.7

Table 2.7 *Cumulative installed area of thermal solar collectors in EU countries (in thousands of m²)* (Source: EurObserv'ER, 2000)

	1996	1997	1998	1999
Germany	1515.8	1912.6	2309.5	2750.2
Austria	1400.0	1600.0	1884.0	2020.0
Greece	1900.0	1872.0	1921.0	1975.0
France	690.0	648.5	620.5	579.7
Italy	295.0	280.0	265.0	255.0
Denmark	160.0	187.5	204.7	219.0
The Netherlands	143.0	166.5	190.5	214.2
UK	215.7	206.2	199.0	195.0
Spain	217.7	200.3	189.9	181.0
Portugal	198.7	186.2	173.2	160.2
Sweden	125.3	133.0	140.0	149.0
Finland	84.5	79.0	72.7	67.5
Belgium	37.0	37.0	37.5	38.0
Ireland	1.5	1.5	1.5	1.5
Luxembourg	1.0	1.0	1.0	1.0
Total	6985.2	7511.3	8210.0	8806.3

Table 2.8 *Estimation of collector surfaces to be installed in Europe by 2005 and 2010 (in thousands of m²)* (Source: EurObserv'ER, 2000)

	2005	2010
Germany	17000	55000
Austria	5200	10400
Greece	4860	9800
Holland	–	1360
Spain	–	4500
Italy	–	3000
France	770	1450
Rest of EU	–	1700
Total	27830	87210

2.4.2 A call for sustainable energy policies

Given the fact that solar thermal systems are not commercially exploitable energy-production schemes, like, for example, wind generators, and bearing in mind the points made in the SWOT analysis, there will continue to be a need for policies to promote these systems in the future. There are three major groups of measures that can be taken towards sustainable energy policies, as presented in Figure 2.5, and solar systems are affected by at least two of them: technology support programmes and economic instruments.

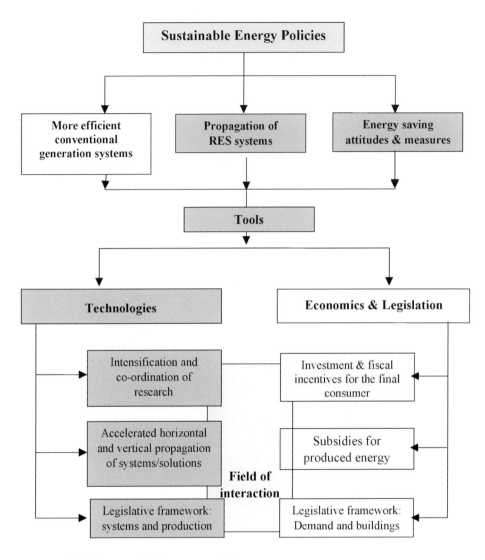

Figure 2.5 *Tools for sustainable energy policies*

Some of the points that could be part of the technological policies are industry product selection tools, development of best practices for solar buildings, guidelines for building associations and decision guidelines for the purchase of solar buildings/products. These points have to form the strategic axis of action for any measures to promote solar thermal systems if it is to become successful, because, as had been proved so far, the influence of research and development projects on the promotion of systems has been rather marginal until now (Focus Marketing Services, 1999; Guery *et al*, 2001). The European Union and the Commission of the European Communities supported during the 1990s a series of actions concerning research and development, and also dissemination and integration (Lewis, 1996). It remains to be seen how the experience and knowledge obtained over these years will be utilized under the new 6th Framework Programme which is about to be launched, in order to achieve the highest possible efficiency.

As far as economics and legislation are concerned, and beyond the conventional measures such as fiscal incentives, one could mention the following actions that could enforce a more environmentally conscious evaluation of solar systems: the quantification and internalization of environmental benefits of solar designs/technologies, the trade-off analysis of environmental issues and solar building strategies, the economic analysis and quantification of CO_2 reductions from solar buildings and the adaptation of a common life-cycle analysis method to evaluate the alternatives (Rabl and Spadaro, 2001).

2.5 Conclusions

Active solar technologies have grown mature over the years, at least in the field of medium-temperature thermal energy conversion. Still, there is significant potential for development in the fields of solar space heating and cooling, which form the bulk of energy consumed in the building sector anyway. In that direction, research effort leads, inevitably, to more efficient, complex and integrated systems. At the same time, costs have to be reduced on the basis of cost per unit of energy produced. This calls for cheaper flat plate and vacuum tube collectors with intelligent and reliable control systems. Furthermore, if one aspires to have a significant impact on the urban built environment, it is necessary to think in the direction of centralized, thermal storage systems. These presuppose significant progress in thermal storage. Finally, one should keep in mind that we face a twofold problem: besides the sophisticated systems needed to cope with rising annual energy demands in European urban buildings, there is always the issue of covering basic energy requirements in less developed and financially weaker regions of the world. In that sense, there is still great need and also a significant market potential for simple, robust and reliable self-contained solar systems, which also have to be state-of-the art, although under different criteria than those discussed in the previous paragraphs. For both aspects, the main technical points of research interest could be summarized as follows:

- development of components such as selective coatings, advanced glazings, polymers and polycarbonates to improve the cost/efficiency ratio of collectors

- development of combined solar water and space heating systems, to achieve better economics

- advanced controls and design and analysis tools to integrate solar technologies more efficiently into buildings

- advanced solar thermal storage techniques, to reduce the necessary installed capacities and achieve better weighted load factors

- building integrated and oriented solar systems and designs, including passive and active solar systems and photovoltaics

- centralized systems, be they at the level of a building, a building block or a residential area.

Simultaneously there are favourable socio-economic boundary conditions, which, if transformed into a flexible but effective framework, could contribute to an accelerated propagation of active solar systems. Developments such as large-scale building renovation projects, urbanization, increased thermal comfort expectations and the creation of buyer groups for solar buildings and/or solar building products, as part of an increasing environmental consciousness, are important. They present the industrial and scientific community with a unique opportunity, not as a result of an energy shock, but as a result of thoughtful evolution.

The main challenge set for the coming decade is the effective interaction between the parties involved, in order to capitalize on these conditions.

2.6 References

Berkel, J, 2000, *Solar Thermal Storage Techniques*, Rhenen, the Netherlands, Entry Technology, 19–29.

Commission of the European Communities, 1997, *Energy for the Future: Renewable Sources of Energy*, White Paper for a Community Strategy and Action Plan, COM(97) 599, Brussels, Commission of the European Communities.

Commission of the European Communities, 2001a, *Communication from the Commission to the Council, the European Parliament, the Economic and Social Committee and the Committee of the Regions on the implementation of the Community Strategy and Action Plan on Renewable Energy Sources (1998–2000)*, COM(2001) 69, Brussels, Commission of the European Communities.

Commission of the European Communities, 2001b, *Proposal for a Directive of the European Parliament and of the Council on the Energy Performance of Buildings*, COM(2001) 226, Brussels, Commission of the European Communities.

DOE, 2001, *Solar Buildings: Transpired Air Collectors*, DOE/GO-102001–1288, Washington, DC, US Department of Energy, National Renewable Energy Laboratory.

ESIF, 2000, *Solar Thermal Systems in Europe: Information Booklet*, Kempten, Germany, European Solar Industry Federation.

EurObserv'ER, 2000, 'Thermal solar barometer, habitat solaire, habitat d'aujourd'hui', in *Systèmes Solaires*, No. 138, July/August, 85–87.

Fisch, M N, Guigas, M and Dalenback, J O, 1998, 'A review of large scale solar heating systems in Europe', in *Solar Energy*, 63(6), 355–366.

Focus Marketing Services, 1999, *Creating a Comprehensive Solar Water-heating Deployment Strategy, Report Prepared for the National Renewable Energy Laboratory, US DOE, Colorado*, Westlake Village, CA, Focus Marketing Services, 6–13.

Guery B, Husson, J-P, Marin, N and Montgolfier, P, 2001, 'Energy policy and energy R&D in EU, convergence or divergence?', in *The Shared Analysis Project, Economic Foundations for Energy Policy*, Essor Europe, Paris, for the European Commission DG Energy, Vol. 10, 143–145.

IEA, 2001, *Solar Heating and Cooling Programme, 2000 Annual Report*, Report IEA/SHC/AR00, Washington, DC, IEA, 15–17.

Kalogirou, K and Papadopoulos, A, 1992, 'Evaluation of the thermosiphonic solar air panel and its potential in Greece', in *Proceedings of 4th National Conference on RES*, Vol. A, Thessaloniki, Institute of Solar Technology (in Greek), 85–91.

Kaltschmitt, M and Wiese, A (eds), 1997, Solarthermische Waermenutzung', in *Erneubare Energien*, Berlin, Springer Verlag, 111–176.

Lewis, J O, 1996, 'Solar building – European Union Research and Development Programmes', in *Solar Energy*, 58(1–3), 127–135.

Morrison, G L, 2001, 'Solar water heating', in Jeffrey Gordon (ed), *Solar Energy, the State of the Art*, London, James and James, 260–272.

Papadopoulos, A M, Kaltschmitt, M, Koroneos, C and Bauen, A (2001) *SEPEDIC: a Guide for the Propagation of RES Systems, Final Report of the ALTENER Project*, XVII/4.1030/7/98–262, financed by CEC/DG TREN, Thessaloniki, Aristotle University.

Rabl, A and Spadaro, J V, 2001, 'The cost of pollution and the benefit of solar energy', in Jeffrey Gordon (ed), *Solar Energy, the State of the Art*, London, James & James, 464–470.

Rannels, J, 2000, 'The DOE office of solar energy technologies; vision for advancing solar technologies in the new millennium', in *Solar Energy*, 69(5), 363–368.

Trieb, F, Langnib, O and Klaib, H, 1997, 'Solar electricity generation – a comparative view of technologies, costs and environmental impact', in *Solar Energy*, 59(1–3), 89–99.

Tsoutsos, T D, 2002, 'Marketing solar thermal technologies: strategies in Europe, experience in Greece', in *Renewable Energy*, 26, 33–46.

Unander, F, 2000, 'Meetings the Kyoto targets in liberalised markets', in *Proceedings of the Conference, IAEE Annual European Energy Conference, Bergen, Norway*.

Zhang, Z, Wang, Q, Zhuang, X, Hamrin, J and Baruch, S, 2001, *Renewable Energy Development in China: the Potential and the Challenges*, Center for Resource Solutions, San Francisco, CA, 41–47.

3 Spectrally selective materials for efficient visible, solar and thermal radiation control

Michael G. Hutchins

Solar Energy Materials Research Laboratory, School of Technology, Oxford Brookes University, Oxford OX3 0BP, UK
Tel: +44 (0)1865 483604; fax: +44 (0)1865 484263; e-mail: mhutchins@brookes.ac.uk

3.1 Introduction

Since the pioneering work of Tabor (1956), the development of thin-film optically selective surfaces has been widely pursued to allow the efficient conversion and control of visible, solar and thermal radiation. Today such materials represent mature technologies which find many applications in e.g. solar thermal collectors, photovoltaics, windows and daylighting. Spectrally selective solar absorber coatings enhance the efficiency of solar thermal systems by maximizing solar gain and minimizing radiative losses from the heated collector surface (Lampert, 1979; Niklasson and Granqvist, 1983). Transparent low thermal emittance (low-e) coated glazings are used in passive solar design in climates where high solar gain and reduced thermal loss are key objectives (Johnson, 1991; Button and Pye, 1993). Solar control coatings, which selectively transmit incident visible light and reflect near-infrared solar radiation, reduce the risk of overheating in buildings whilst preserving good levels of natural daylight (Pulker, 1984; Hill and Nadel, 1999). Angular selective glazing is designed to attenuate radiation coming directly from the sun and which is the main source of glare (Smith *et al*, 1998). Dynamic variable transmittance apertures, such as electrochromic, gasochromic and thermotropic glazing, aim to avoid overheating during peak periods of solar availability, reduce glare problems and allow a greater use of glazing area to enhance solar gain during the heating season (Lampert and Granqvist, 1990; Granqvist, 1995; Georg *et al*, 1998).

Scientific and technical advances in coating design and the progress achieved by industry in producing large-area coatings with excellent uniformity have been matched by improved accuracy and reliability in the measurement of surface optical properties (van Nijnatten, 2000; Roos *et al*, 2001) and the development of simulation tools for component design and calculation of performance (LBL, 1993; van Dijk and Bakker, 1995; Köhl, 2001). Currently, European research and development is focused on providing technical information in forms suitable for use by the manufacturer, designer and architect to aid choice in product selection appropriate to building type, end-use and climate (van Dijk and Hutchins, 2002). Performance rating and energy labelling of window products in Europe are also being investigated (EWRS, 2000).

An overview of advances made in the field of spectrally selective materials for solar thermal conversion and use in the building envelope with an emphasis on transparent glazing is presented. The work was stimulated by advances achieved in a selection of recent European research projects and the aim of identifying some important areas where future work remains a priority.

3.2 Solar thermal conversion

The solar thermal collector converts incident solar radiation into useful heat. Flat plate and evacuated tube collectors are commonly used for applications such as domestic hot water. Concentrating solar collectors are used when higher delivery temperatures are required (Duffie and Beckman, 1980). Three optical properties are relevant for collector performance, i.e. the solar transmittance, τ_s, of the transparent collector cover and the solar absorptance, α_s, and the thermal emittance, ε, of the absorber surface. The useful energy gain of the collector is found by subtracting the thermal losses from the total solar gain. In simplified form the dependence of the collector efficiency, η, on the optical properties of the absorber and cover may be written as

$$\eta = \tau_s \alpha_s - \varepsilon \Delta T^4$$

where ΔT^4 describes the effective temperature difference for radiative exchange. Conduction, convection, collector geometry and heat removal are not considered here. Detailed treatments of collector performance and efficiency are given elsewhere (Duffie and Beckman, 1980).

The solar transmittance, τ_s, is defined as:

$$\tau_s = \frac{\int_{\lambda_1}^{\lambda_2} \tau_\lambda \, G_\lambda \, d\lambda}{\int_{\lambda_1}^{\lambda_2} G_\lambda \, d\lambda}$$

where G_λ is the incident solar spectral irradiation, τ_λ is the spectral transmittance of the material and λ_1 and λ_2 define the short- and long-wavelength limits, respectively, of the solar spectral distribution.

The solar absorptance, α_s, and solar reflectance, ρ_s, are similarly defined:

$$\alpha_s = \frac{\int_{\lambda_1}^{\lambda_2} \alpha_\lambda \, G_\lambda \, d\lambda}{\int_{\lambda_1}^{\lambda_2} G_\lambda \, d\lambda}$$

$$\rho_s = \frac{\int_{\lambda_1}^{\lambda_2} \rho_\lambda\, G_\lambda\, d\lambda}{\int_{\lambda_1}^{\lambda_2} G_\lambda\, d\lambda}$$

where α_λ and ρ_λ are the spectral absorptance and spectral reflectance, respectively.

All spectral and integrated optical properties are thus expressed as fractions in the range of 0 to 1. For light interacting with the material, energy conservation also requires the optical properties of a material to satisfy the relationship

$$\alpha_\lambda + \rho_\lambda + \tau_\lambda = 1$$

Kirchhoff's law (Siegel and Howell, 1972), $\alpha_\lambda = \varepsilon_\lambda$, enables the spectral emittance, ε_λ, to be found from the relationship

$$\varepsilon_\lambda = 1 - (\rho_\lambda + \tau_\lambda)$$

For an infrared opaque sample where $\tau_\lambda = 0$, this relationship reduces to $\varepsilon_\lambda = 1 - \rho_\lambda$.

The spectral emittance, ε_λ, derived from spectral reflectance measurements is convoluted with the Planck blackbody spectral distribution, $E_{b\lambda}$, for the radiative temperature T of operation and normalized to the ideal emitter ($\varepsilon = 1$) to give the total thermal emittance ε.

The thermal emittance is thus expressed as

$$\varepsilon_s = \frac{\int_{\lambda_2}^{\lambda_2'} \varepsilon_\lambda F_{b\lambda}\, d\lambda}{\int_{\lambda_2}^{\lambda_2'} E_{b\lambda}\, d\lambda}$$

where λ_1' and λ_2' are the respective wavelength limits of the blackbody spectral distribution for the temperature of interest.

To maximize the solar collector optical gain, which is a direct function of the $\tau_s\alpha_s$ product, both τ_s and α_s should be as high as possible, i.e. close to unity. The collector must be insulated from its environment to minimize losses from the heated absorber surface. The radiative component of the overall collector heat loss coefficient is minimized through the use of a selective solar absorber surface with low thermal emittance.

3.2.1 Solar absorber coatings

The absorber surface is the central component of the solar collector. This receiver surface serves to absorb the incident solar radiation and convert it into useful heat which is removed from the collector via a heat transfer fluid for subsequent use. The desired optical properties of the spectrally selective solar absorber, i.e. high solar absorptance, α_s, and low thermal emittance, ε, are commonly achieved through a tandem two-component system comprising a short-wavelength absorbing, infrared-transparent upper layer and an infrared-reflective underlayer and/or metallic substrate. The absorber is then both effectively black to the short-wave incident solar radiation and highly reflective at longer thermal wavelengths characteristic of the blackbody temperature of the heated receiver surface. A representative spectral reflectance curve at solar and thermal wavelengths showing the transition from high absorptance at short wavelengths to high reflectance in the infrared is shown in Figure 3.1.

Many surface coating types have been successfully developed. The most popular selective absorbers include black chrome, black nickel, black copper, black cobalt, metal pigmented aluminium oxide and oxidized stainless steel (Seraphin and Meinel, 1976; Driver, 1981; Hutchins *et al*, 1987). Historically, selective absorbers were produced electrochemically but today they are commonly prepared in industry by sputtering (see Figure 3.2). Sputtering allows the preparation of water-free composite coatings within which chemical composition, compositional grading, metal particle size and volume fill-factor can be carefully controlled (Interpane, Lauenföde, Germany) (Wäckelgård and Hultmark, 1998). Such selective absorbers readily achieve $\alpha_s > 0.95$ and $\varepsilon < 0.10$.

The absorbing thin-film layer is usually a metal:dielectric composite often with graded refractive index, increasing with depth. A fine-grained dispersion of sub-micron-sized conducting particles embedded in an infrared-transparent insulating matrix of low dielectric constant is favoured. Examples include Ni: Al_2O_3 (nickel-pigmented aluminium oxide), Cr: CrO_x (black chrome) and Ni: SiO_2 (Farooq *et al*, 1998). Many physical processes may contribute to the high solar absorptance, e.g. plasma resonance of free electrons, resonant scattering by discrete conducting particles, textural discontinuities and surface roughness, interband transitions and interference effects. Figure 3.3 shows the typical surface roughness and grain size distribution of a selective solar absorber.

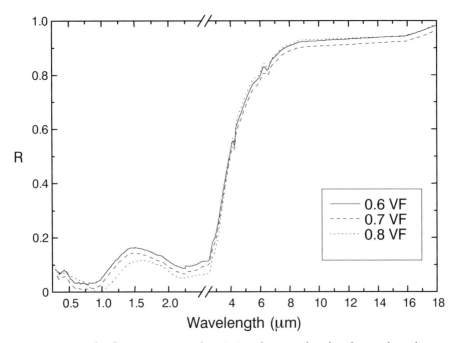

Figure 3.1 *Spectral reflectance curves of Ni: SiO$_2$ selective solar absorber surfaces for different metallic volume fractions (VF) (Farooq et al, 1998)*

Figure 3.2 *Coil coating sputter coater for selective absorbers (Interpane, Lauenföde, Germany)*

The optical properties of the inhomogeneous absorber surface can be described using effective medium theories. Much work was performed using the theories of Maxwell–Garnet (Garnet, 1904) and Bruggeman (Bruggeman, 1935) to clarify the dependency of observed optical properties on surface microstructure, chemical composition, particle size, orientation, etc. In recent years the validity of these models has been questioned and revised effective medium theories have been developed (Smith *et al*, 1998). Coating design based on these approaches allows candidate materials to be evaluated and composition and performance optimized (Farooq and Hutchins, 2002a,b).

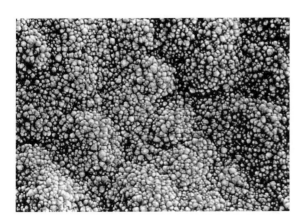

Figure 3.3 *Scanning electron micrograph of a black cobalt selective solar absorber surface with surface roughness dimensions appropriate for absorption of short-wavelength solar radiation (Hutchins et al, 1987)*

Solar absorber surfaces have been successfully produced for many years and are widely used in all solar thermal collector applications. Some areas where further research is necessary or ongoing include spectrally selective paints (Crnjak Orel *et al*, 1996), non-black selective absorbers for facade integration (Crnjak Orel *et al*, 2002), improved absorber geometry and cheaper collector substrate materials and coatings for higher temperature ranges, e.g. process heat supply up to 140°C.

3.2.2 The transparent collector cover

The transparent cover not only serves to protect the collector from the hazards of its environment, wind, rain, pollution, etc., but also to reduce heat losses. Lowering the collector heat transfer coefficient introduces an accompanying reduction of the total incident solar radiation entering the collector equal to the solar transmittance, τ_s, of the cover itself.

Clear float glass is the conventional choice for the collector cover. Polymeric materials which can withstand elevated temperatures and ultraviolet radiation are also used. The solar transmittance τ_s of 6 mm clear float glass is typically ~0.84 which significantly reduces the $\tau_s \alpha_s$ optical gain. The use of water white glass, wherein the iron oxide is removed from the glass and the consequent strong near-infrared absorption band is absent, increases the cover solar transmittance to ~0.90.

Anti-reflection (AR) thin-film layers applied to the glass or cover material surface can be used to increase the transmittance further. The need is for broad-band AR layers that are effective across the whole of the solar spectral range. Conventional multilayers can work well in the visible region but the effect is to increase the near-infrared reflectance. Etching the glass surface by immersion in strong acids can achieve the required optical properties but the process is a disadvantage. Porous surfaces or subwavelength surface-relief grating structures have been shown to be effective ways of achieving broad-band anti-reflecting properties. Subwavelength surface-relief gratings are diffractive optical elements that produce zero-order diffraction (Gombert *et al*, 1998). Examples are porous sol–gel layers produced in a dip-coating process (Nostell *et al*, 1996) and subwavelength grating structures embossed in organically modified sol–gel or acrylic materials (Gombert *et al*, 1998). Figure 3.4 shows the spectral transmittance of glass antireflected with a porous sol-gel coating. Such coatings can increase the transmittance by ~3% for each applied surface.

3.3 Transparent selective coatings for windows

The use of thin-film coatings on glass and other transparent media for glazing purposes, most notably in buildings but also in vehicles, aircraft and satellites, represents the most significant and successful application of selective materials for visible, solar and thermal radiation control.

In many countries, the demands for heating, cooling and lighting in residential and commercial buildings comprise the largest single sector of total energy use. Reduction of energy consumption, the improvement of visual and thermal comfort and the lessening of adverse environmental impacts, by lowering greenhouse gas emissions, are

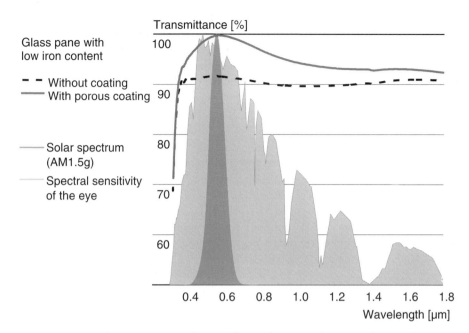

Figure 3.4 *Spectral transmittance of anti-reflective low-iron glass (Gombert* et al, *1998)*

important considerations for the design and operation of 'better' buildings. In these respects the window plays a critical role in determining building energy performance. Advanced glazings, employing selective thin-film coatings, offer the potential to transform the building envelope into a highly efficient energy system, adaptable to the needs of the climate and the end user.

For the characterization of the optical and thermal performance of a window, the three main areas of interest are the thermal transmittance, the solar gain and the visible light transmittance through the window. The quantitative properties of interest are the window overall heat loss coefficient (U value), the total solar energy transmittance (g value) and the visible light transmittance (τ_v).

The total solar energy transmittance, g, is the sum of the direct solar transmittance, τ_s and the secondary fraction, q_i, of the incident solar radiation absorbed in the glazing which subsequently flows inwards through the glazing, i.e. $g = \tau_s + q_i$.

The U value, or thermal transmittance, is defined as the (steady-state) density of heat transfer rate per temperature difference between the environmental temperatures on each side in the absence of solar radiation, in $W/(m^2K)$. For values reported here, the U value is defined for the transparent centre-of-glass part of the glazing. The influences of the edge, spacer and frame are extremely significant but are not considered further in this work (Aschehoug, 1995; Frank and Ghazi Wakili, 1995).

Accurate determination of the optical and radiative properties of advanced glazing materials is necessary to permit product and performance comparison and selection and sizing of the appropriate technologies for specific applications. Total solar energy transmittance and U value may be measured but these properties are commonly calculated from knowledge of the optical properties of the component panes and the glazing construction. To calculate the *g* and *U* values of a window, it is normally necessary to measure the spectral optical properties of each of the component panes, from which the visible and solar transmittance, reflectance of all surfaces and the thermal emittance of all surfaces are derived. To allow reliable estimation of annual solar gain the spectral directional optical properties should also be known. These may be measured directly or derived from near-normal measurements (ECONTROL, Flabeg, Furth im Wald, Germany) (Hutchins *et al*, 2001a).

Transparent spectrally selective coatings on glass and polymeric substrates represent the state-of-the-art of advanced glazing materials for window applications. The worldwide manufacture of low-emittance (low-e) coatings has made available windows with a wide range of different properties. Coatings can be specifically designed and tailored to exhibit optical properties suitable for the intended application and climate. The low-e coatings divide conveniently into two categories: those which transmit a large fraction of solar radiation (high *g* value and high τ_v) and those which selectively transmit the incident solar radiation allowing a high proportion of visible radiation to be transmitted whilst reflecting the unseen near-infrared component (low *g* value and high τ_v).

3.3.1 Spectrally selective low emittance for passive solar gain

High solar transmittance, τ_s, and *g* value combined with low thermal emittance and hence *U* value of e.g. a double-glazed unit (DGU) are achieved by depositing a heavily doped wide-bandgap semiconductor coating such as fluorine-doped tin oxide (SnO_2: F) onto float glass.

This pyrolytic deposition process is performed on-line during production of the float glass and results in a highly durable product of excellent optical homogeneity. These low-e coatings are used when solar gain is not a serious problem, e.g. in residential heating-dominated climates such as northern Europe. The semiconducting nature of the transparent coating places a limit on the infrared reflectance of the material and hence the lowest value of emittance which can be achieved. The thermal emittance is typically in the range $0.10 < \varepsilon < 0.15$ and the centre-of-glass *U* value of an argon-filled DGU is typically ~1.6–1.9 W/(m^2 °C). The spectral optical properties of such a pyrolytic low-emittance coating, K GLASS (Pilkington, St Helens, UK), are shown in Figure 3.5.

3.3.2 Solar control glazing

For many years, the conventional means of reducing glazing solar transmittance was to use body-tinted and/or 'metal'-coated glass producing a reduction in the solar transmittance across the entire solar spectral distribution and severely limiting visible transmittance. In the absence of adequate daylight, the effect was to boost the need for additional interior lighting. Today, the rapid development of the family of solar control coatings, employing silver-based multilayers, provides excellent opportunities to combine daylight provision for natural lighting, solar gain reduction and high thermal resistance in a single window. Such glazings are characterized by high visible transmittance, τ_v, and low solar transmittance, τ_s.

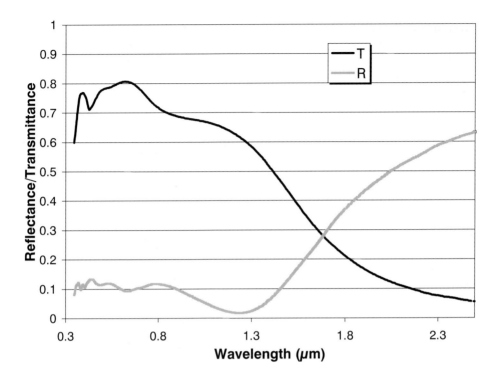

Figure 3.5 *Spectral transmittance and reflectance (coated side) of K GLASS (Pilkington, St Helens, UK). SnO₂: F low-emittance coating on clear float glass for use in heating-dominated applications*

Both single silver and double silver layer coatings are commercially available. Increasing the number of thin-film layers narrows the transmittance bandwidth and sharpens the performance of the optical filter. Such solar gain control coatings are commonly prepared by sputtering multilayer dielectric–metal–dielectric stacks. The degree of selectivity achieved by the coating may be quantified in terms of the τ_v: τ_s ratio. High values of τ_v: $\tau_s \approx 2$ are produced with double silver stacks. Single silver stacks have a broader transmission bandwidth and admit more near-infrared radiation (Hill and Nadel, 1999). The thermal emittance of the double silver coatings may be as low as 0.03; single silver emittance values are higher and typically ~0.07–0.10 (note that τ_v: $\tau_s \approx 2$ is a value approaching the theoretical limit since approximately half of the incident solar radiation lies within the visible range). A comparison of typical spectral optical properties of double and single silver solar control coatings is shown in Figure 3.6. These coatings are ideal for application in a cooling-dominated climate or in heavily glazed facades such as are commonly found in commercial buildings where excessive solar gain can cause significant overheating.

The importance of the coating position in the DGU should be underlined. Solar radiation that is not directly transmitted or reflected by a glazing will be absorbed, causing the glazing temperature to rise. This absorbed solar radiation will be emitted

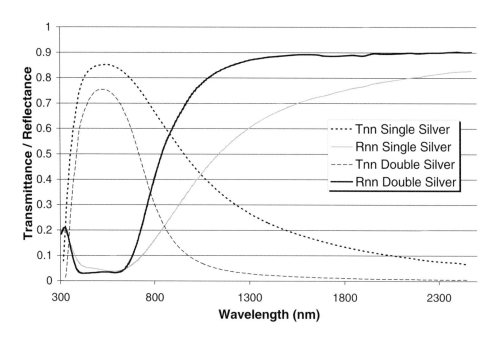

Figure 3.6 *Comparison of the near-normal spectral transmittance and reflectance of single and double silver solar control coatings on glass*

as long-wavelength thermal radiation, some to the outside and some to the inside, the latter being the secondary inward flowing component, q_i, of the total solar energy transmittance, g. Solar control coatings are normally located on Surface 2 (first pane, gap side) of the DGU, whereas low-emittance coatings for passive solar gain are normally placed on Surface 3 (second pane, gap side) of a DGU.

In Table 3.1, the g value, visible transmittance and U value of representative low-e DGU combinations suitable for use in either heating- or cooling-dominated applications are shown.

Table 3.1 *Visible transmittance, total solar energy transmittance and U value of insulating double-glazed units using low-emittance and solar control coatings for heating-dominated and cooling-dominated applications*

Glazing	Gas fill	τ_v	g	U [W/(m² K)]
Clear float single glazing	–	0.90	0.86	6.4
Clear float double-glazed unit (DGU)	Air	0.81	0.76	2.9
DGU, low-e pyrolytic heat mirror (coating on Surface 3) for use in heating-dominated applications	Argon	0.75	0.72	1.9
DGU, low-e sputtered solar control (coating on Surface 2) for use in cooling-dominated applications	Argon	0.66	0.34	1.2

Thermal conductivity and hence the *U* value of double- and triple-glazed units can be reduced by replacing the air in a sealed unit with an inert noble gas. Argon is the most common choice for a substitute gas fill but further reductions in *U* value, with additional cost, can be achieved with krypton and xenon. Optimum gap spacing in the sealed unit is gas dependent.

3.3.3 Evacuated glazing

Transparent selective thin-film coatings find application in vacuum windows or evacuated glazing. The vacuum window is an emerging technology which may compete with conventional gas-filled insulated glazing units. Elimination of gaseous conduction and convection by the use of a vacuum between two glass sheets could lead to a window with high thermal insulation and good optical properties. Radiative heat transfer is minimized through the use of a transparent low-emittance coating on the internal surfaces of one or both of the two glass sheets. Many practical difficulties have to be overcome in order to produce an evacuated glazing unit. These include the method of ensuring a leak-free edge seal, the maintenance of a high vacuum between the glass sheets for the working life of the unit and the withstanding of stresses set up by atmospheric forces.

Large area (1.0×1.0 m^2) evacuated glazings were first produced by the University of Sydney, Australia and represent the state-of-the-art in this technology (Collins and Robinson, 1991; Garrison and Collins, 1995). The basic concept has been commercialized by Nippon Sheet Glass with the product name SPACIA. The two glass sheets are separated by an array of small (~0.3 mm) glass pillars and a fused solder glass edge seal is employed. A schematic representation of this window is shown in Figure 3.7.

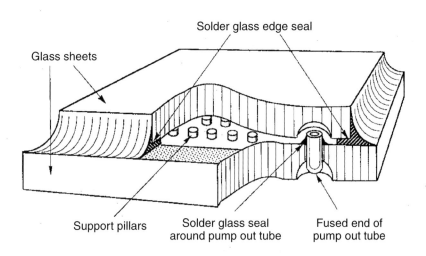

Figure 3.7 *Schematic diagram of the University of Sydney vacuum glazing (Collins and Simko, 1998)*

Pillar conductance and radiative transfer contribute to the heat losses. Only the pyrolytically deposited low-emittance coating, described in Section 3.3.1 above, can withstand the high temperatures necessary for the formation of the fused glass edge seal. The comparatively high thermal emittance of these coatings (~0.15) results in centre-of-glass U values of about 1.0 W/(m^2 °C) (Collins and Simko, 1998). A low-temperature edge seal technique, which would permit the sputtered low-emittance coatings to be used or a reduction in emittance of present pyrolytic coatings to around 0.05, would result in increased thermal resistance and U values of about 0.5 W/(m^2 K) could theoretically be achieved. Research to develop a low-temperature hermetic edge seal using an indium alloy which allows low-temperature sealing has been reported (Griffiths *et al*, 1998). For such a glazing $U_c = 0.36$ W/(m^2 K) and $\tau_v = 0.72$ is predicted for a system with 6 mm panes and a 40 mm pillar separation. Such a glazing would function as a solar gain control product.

3.3.4 Nanoparticle-doped polymeric solar control glazing

The creation of an effective medium of nano-sized particles in a transparent polymeric medium can produce solar gain control properties suitable for glazing applications with the added potential benefit of a flexible system. The dimensions of nanoparticles permit spectrally selective absorption without scattering. Indium tin oxide (ITO) and antimony tin oxide (ATO) are ideal materials for achieving high visible transparency with near-infrared absorption. Nanoparticle-doped polymers employing ITO or ATO nanoparticles in PMMA sheet and polycarbonate foil demonstrate selective solar gain control characteristics and values of $\tau_v = 0.87$ and $\tau_s = 0.62$ are reported for some experimental clear glass laminate glazings (Smith *et al*, 2002).

3.4 Switchable glazing materials

The spectrally selective glazings materials described in Section 3.3 possess fixed or 'static' optical properties. Regulation of solar gain and/or glare through the window is normally provided through the use of blinds or shutters, which in some cases may be integrated with the glazing. Switchable glazing or 'smart windows' introduces the concept whereby the optical properties of the glazing materials themselves can be controlled and varied *in situ* in a reversible way (Lampert and Granqvist, 1990). Smart windows provide a means to avoid overheating during peak periods, reduce glare problems and permit the use of greater glazed areas for increased solar gain and daylight. Integration with the building energy management system can reduce artificial lighting loads and reduce the size of heating, ventilation and air conditioning (HVAC) systems.

Chromogenic materials form the basis of many switchable glazing designs. Photochromic materials darken as the intensity of light increases and may be used for shading applications. Thermochromic materials darken when the temperature exceeds a threshold value and the material undergoes an associated phase change. Electrochromic materials colour by charge injection and electrochromism is a property of many inorganic transition metal oxides. The ability to control the optical properties of an electrochromic device through the application of an external electric field enables the control strategy to be independent of environmental conditions, which is an attractive feature for building applications. There are many other switchable materials, e.g. liquid crystals, metal hydrides and suspended particle devices, but these are not discussed in detail here.

3.4.1 Electrochromic glazing

For building applications, electrochromic tungsten oxide, WO_3, is commonly used as the active material. WO_3 is a transparent thin film. The application of a D.C. electric field drives the injection of ions and electrons into the lattice of the electrochromic material and creates the conditions necessary for a change of colour. In WO_3 the reversible coloration reaction may be written as

$$xM^+ + xe^- + WO_3 \Leftrightarrow M_xWO_3$$

The metal ion M^+ in the coloured tungsten bronze M_xWO_3 may be H^+ but is more commonly Li^+ since this avoids the presence of water in the electrochromic device. In the bleached state the ions are stored in a counter electrode such as vanadium titanium oxide or nickel oxide and are driven from the counter electrode through an ion-conducting medium to the tungsten oxide side of the device when the working electrode is cathodically biased.

A first generation of electrochromic glazings were made available commercially following research with the EU JOULE programme (Gallego *et al*, 1996, 1999) and there are a number of buildings in Germany where this laminated form of the electrochromic window is in use (ECONTROL, Flabeg, Furth im Wald, Germany). Figure 3.8 shows the facade of the Stadt Sparkasse bank in Dresden, the world's first example of an operational electrochromic building.

This first generation of laminated electrochromic devices for building applications employed polymer electrolytes as the ion conducting medium. Such a device normally employs two glass substrates and is assembled from the two respective halves: one employing the active electrochromic layer, e.g. WO_3, and the second the counter electrode or ion storage layer. A schematic representation of a laminated electrochromic window developed within the EU JOULE program by Pilkington and partners (Gallego *et al*, 1999) is shown in Figure 3.9. The device employs amorphous tungsten oxide as the active electrochromic layer and a vanadium–titanium mixed metal oxide as the counter electrode. K GLASS substrates are used for the two transparent conductors. required The spectral transmittance curves of two such devices for both the transparent and coloured states are shown in Figure 3.10.

Current research in electrochromic devices for buildings is addressing the development of the all-solid-state monolithic stack employing an inorganic ion-conducting layer such as Ta_2O_5 (Hutchins *et al*, 2001a) and a transparent conducting low-e top electrode. An all-solid-state monolithic structure, built upon a transparent substrate, would (i) confer low emittance properties to the device through the final layer deposition of a transparent conducting thin film, such as ITO, and (ii) increase the transmittance of the device in its bleached state by eliminating the need for a second glass substrate and thereby increase the dynamic range.

Figure 3.8 *Electrochromic facade of the Stadt Sparkasse, Dresden, Germany (photograph courtesy of Flabeg GmbH, Furth im Wald, Germany)*

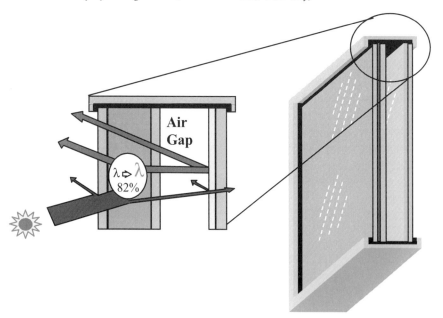

Figure 3.9 *Schematic representation of the structure of a laminated electrochromic device using a polymeric electrolyte in a double glazed unit with low-e coating on Surface 3 for application as a variable-transmission window (Gallego et al, 1996)*

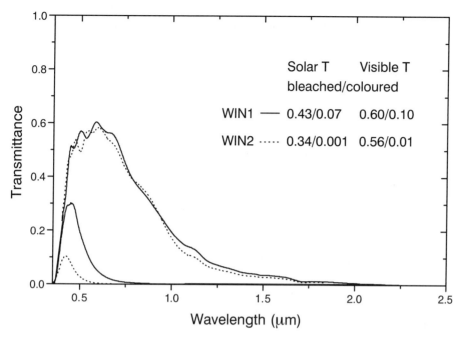

Figure 3.10 *Spectral transmittance of prototype laminated electrochromic variable-transmission windows in the bleached and coloured states (Gallego et al, 1996)*

3.4.2 Thermochromic and thermotropic glazing

The optical properties of thermochromic materials alter when the material undergoes a change of phase, i.e. the transmittance is reduced when the material is heated above a critical temperature and melting or a change in crystal structure occurs. Thermochromism in inorganic compounds such as tungsten-doped vanadium dioxide has been successful in producing films which significantly modulate the near-infrared transmittance and possess transition temperatures in the range 17–65°C.

Promising results have been obtained for thermotropic materials which undergo a reversible change between a homogeneous, transparent state at lower temperatures and a heterogeneous, scattering state at higher temperatures. A thermochromic polymer gel with transition temperatures close to ambient thermal comfort temperatures has been researched extensively by Interpane, Germany (Raicu *et al*, 2002). Above the transition temperature the material becomes more reflective. The laminated thermotropic element can be incorporated with a low-e coated glass to form a variable-transmission, low *U* value glazing unit. The temperature dependence of the spectral transmittance of such a thermotropic material is shown in Figure 3.11 (Ageorges and Hutchins, 1996).

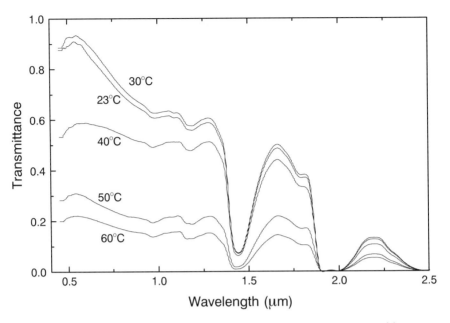

Figure 3.11 *Total hemispherical transmittance spectra of a thermotropic variable-transmittance device at different temperatures (Ageorges and Hutchins, 1996)*

3.4.3 Gasochromic glazing

Gasochromic glazing is a candidate technology for dynamic control of solar energy gain in buildings and such devices are being researched within the EU SWIFT (Switchable Facade Technology) RTD project (SWIFT, 1999). Within the project the performance of both electrochromic and gasochromic switchable glazing technology is being assessed for real application conditions. The reliability, practicability and usability of switchable facades are being tested and integration into building facades and interaction with heating, cooling and lighting systems are being investigated. In addition to materials-related issues, demand assessment and energy/CO_2 reduction potentials due to lighting/heating/cooling are being evaluated, peak load reduction for cooling and lighting systems is being determined and environmental impact over the life cycle of the glazing is being estimated.

Gasochromic glazings, based upon an active layer of tungsten oxide, switch from a highly transparent clear state to a dark-blue, low-transmittance coloured state when hydrogen is inserted into the active WO_3 material. A gasochromic fenestration system consists of three main components: a gasochromic insulating glazing unit (IGU), a gas supply unit and a control unit (Wilson *et al*, 2002). The optically active component of a gasochromic IGU is a film of WO_3, less than 1 μm thick, which is coated with a thin film of a catalyst (Lampert, 1979). It is located on the inner surface of the outer pane of a triple IGU (Figure 3.12). When the gasochromic film is exposed to a low concentration of hydrogen (well below the combustion limit of 3%) in a carrier gas of argon or nitrogen, it colours blue, reducing the visible and total solar energy transmittance

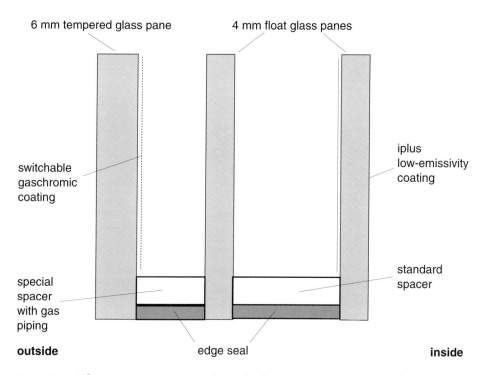

Figure 3.12 *Schematic representation of a triple-glazed gasochromic insulated glazing unit investigated in the EU SWIFT RTD project (SWIFT, 1999)*

values. On exposure to a low concentration of oxygen, the WO_3 film bleaches to the original transparent state. The gas mixture is introduced into the cavity between the outer and middle panes of a triple IGU. The second gas-filled cavity and third pane, which has a low-emittance coating, ensure that the IGU has good thermal insulating properties (low U value). Clear visibility from inside to outside is retained in all switching states. The gas supply unit consists of an electrolyser and a pump, which is connected by pipes to the window in a closed-loop configuration. Ideally, the gas supply unit is integrated into the external building facade. The control unit allows both manual and automatic control. Integration into a bus system allows the glazing to be switched to optimize lighting conditions, thermal comfort and/or building energy consumption.

Within the SWIFT project, double- and triple-glazed gasochromic glazings have been investigated in the laboratory environment and in outdoor test facilities. Spectrophotometric measurements of double- and triple-glazed units together with measurement of the respective constitutent panes allow the derivation of the optical properties of WO_3-coated glass for the bleached and coloured gasochromic states (Table 3.2). The spectral transmittance of a gasochromic triple IGU for the bleached and coloured states is shown in Figure 3.13 and the optical properties of gasochromic tungsten oxide derived from measurements of the component panes are presented in Figure 3.14 (Wilson *et al*, 2002).

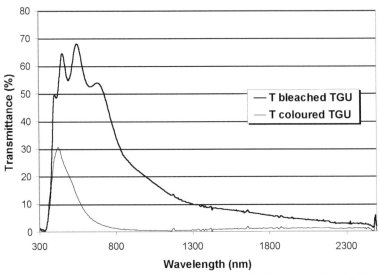

Figure 3.13 *Spectral transmittance of a gasochromic triple-glazed IGU for the bleached and coloured states (Wilson et al, 2002)*

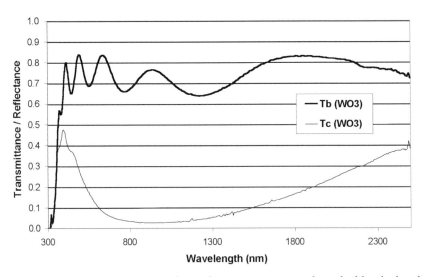

Figure 3.14 *Spectral transmittance of gasochromic tungsten oxide in the bleached and coloured states (Wilson et al, 2002)*

Table 3.2 *Derived integrated solar (s) and visible (v) optical properties of gasochromic WO₃ on clear float glass for the bleached and coloured states [(c) coated surface; (uc) uncoated surface]*

	τ_s	ρ_s (c)	ρ_s (uc)	τ_v	ρ_v (c)	ρ_v (uc)
WO₃ on clear float (bleached)	0.72	0.17	0.14	0.74	0.18	0.17
WO₃ on clear float (coloured)	0.14	0.13	0.08	0.17	0.09	0.07

3.5 Measurement of the optical properties

The impact of glazing choice on the energy performance and thermal comfort of the building in all climates is highly significant. Accurate, reliable and comprehensive measurement of the spectral optical properties of materials is a necessary input for the design process and for characterization procedures such as window energy labelling and performance rating. Historically, the spectral optical properties and calculated integrated visible and solar optical properties of commercially available glazing products were most commonly reported only for near-normal angles of incidence. Measurement of spectral optical properties at oblique angles of incidence was difficult and time consuming. Results from EU-organized inter-laboratory comparisons revealed that commercially available oblique incidence reflectance/transmittance accessories were often unreliable and many measurements were inaccurate (Hutchins and Ageorges, 1993).

For European latitudes, a significant proportion of the annual solar irradiance on a vertical surface is incident at angles in the range 40–70° from the surface normal. Calculations based on near-normal transmittance and reflectance values alone over-estimate annual gain. The need to know the angle-dependant optical properties of glass and window products has increased with the use of advanced glazing materials. Reliable determination of the angle-dependent optical properties of glass and glazing products is therefore essential for the accurate estimation of total solar energy gain in buildings.

3.5.1 Angle-dependent visible and solar properties

The European Union ADOPT project (ADOPT, 1996) has been concerned with the accurate determination of the optical properties of coated glass products, describing reliable procedures for angle-dependent measurements and the development of predictive algorithms to permit accurate angle-dependent performance characterization based upon near-normal values only.

To address the issue of angular dependence and to avoid expensive measurement time, the key glazing parameters may be calculated using a suitable algorithm. If the composition of the coating is known, this can be exactly handled by the Fresnel formalism. This however, is seldom the case. At best the user will know what kind of coating it is, but, without knowing all details, exact Fresnel calculations cannot be performed. From the ADOPT research two new predictive algorithms have been developed and validated. The ADOPT algorithms, which require near-normal input data only, are capable of predicting the angle-dependent transmittance, reflectance and total solar energy transmittance for double- and triple-glazed windows to an accuracy which allows reliable calculation of the annual solar heat gain through windows. The work is pre-normative and the results contribute in part to the current revisions of the ISO 9050 (ISO, 1990) and EN 410 (CEN, 1998a) standards for glass in buildings. Such validated predictive algorithms provide the glass and glazings industry with a simplified tool to permit more comprehensive product performance specification of individual panes and multiple glazed units.

An essential element of the ADOPT project was the inter-laboratory comparison of transmittance and reflectance measurements for commercially available glazings. The intercomparison builds upon earlier EU work performed for the Bureau Commune de Reference of DG XII in 1991 (Hutchins and Ageorges, 1993). Sixteen laboratories participated in the ADOPT inter-comparison. They included representatives of major European glass laboratories, national research institutes and USA-based members of the National Fenestration Rating Council (NFRC). The selected test samples represented major categories of coated glass products used in buildings. The inter-comparison was undertaken to establish the state-of-the-art measurement capability and to provide further data to test the suitability of the predictive algorithms in providing an alternative method for determining angle-dependent properties. Each participant was required to measure the angle-dependent spectral transmittance and reflectance under appropriate polarization conditions for incident wavelengths within the solar spectral distribution. The results are described in full elsewhere (Hutchins *et al*, 2001b). Shown in Figure 3.15a and b are the spectral transmittance and spectral reflectance measured at 60° for s- and p-polarized radiation for two of the five round-robin samples. Data received from nine laboratories are shown.

The ADOPT project considered three different models or algorithms to allow the prediction of the angle-dependent optical properties of coated glass samples from knowledge of near-normal integrated values only (Montecchi *et al*, 1999; Karlsson *et al*, 2001; van Nijnatten, 2001a). Figure 3.16 shows the predicted angle-dependent solar transmittance of the five round-robin samples using the mean near-normal transmittance obtained by the 16 participating laboratories and the algorithm developed by Roos and co-workers (Karlsson *et al*, 2001). Also shown are the seven values of solar transmittance at 60° calculated from the measured data.

The ADOPT round robin showed that all participating laboratories have the capability to measure the near-normal spectral transmittance and reflectance of coated glass samples across the solar spectral region to a reasonable degree of accuracy. Reflectance measurements produce higher levels of uncertainty at near-normal and oblique incidence. Commercially available accessories for angle-dependent measurements were often unreliable but a new generation of variable angle transmittance/reflectance accessories have now been developed directly from the work of the ADOPT project, which remove much of the difficulty associated with angle-dependent measurements and are commercially available (van Nijnatten, 2001b, 2002). Angle-dependent optical properties may now be measured accurately or predicted with the validated algorithms. Comprehensive product optical performance data are now more readily available.

3.5.2 Thermal optical properties measurements

Thermal emittance is a key property in determining the energy-saving capability of glazing. Figure 3.17 shows the dependence of the U value of a double glazing unit on the thermal emittance of the coated glass surface for two different gas fills (van Nijnatten, 2002). Glazing manufacturers in Europe are obliged to determine this property of their coatings according to the standard EN 673 (CEN, 1997). The thermal emittance was traditionally determined from the spectral reflectance measured

(a)

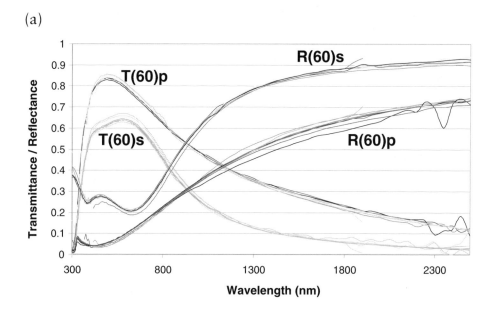

(b)

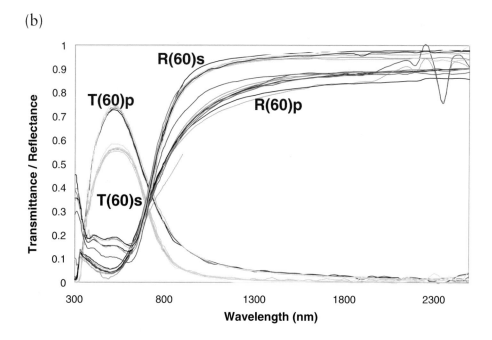

Figure 3.15 *Normal-directional spectral transmittance and reflectance (60° incidence;
s- and p- polarization) of (a) St. Gobain Planiterm Futur single silver solar
control glass and (b) St. Gobain CoolLite SKN 172 double silver solar control
glass*

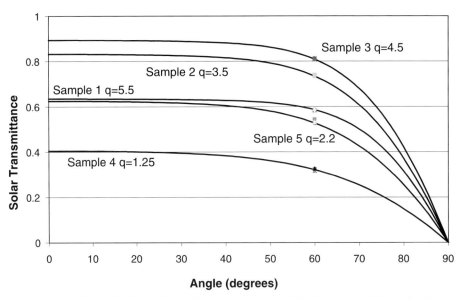

Figure 3.16 *The angle-dependent solar transmittance of the five ADOPT round-robin coated glass samples predicted using the Roos polynomial (Karlsson et al, 2001) based on the mean value of near-normal solar transmittance and category parameter q. The measured values of solar transmittance at 60° of the participating laboratories are also shown*

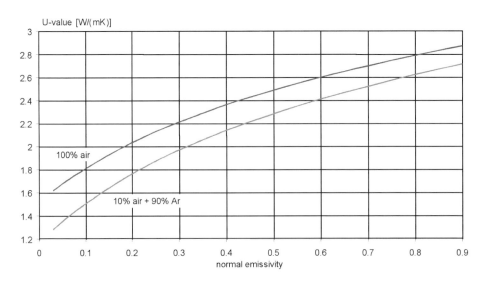

Figure 3.17 *The effect of the coating emissivity on the U value of a double glazing consisting of two 4 mm glass panes separated by a 12 mm gap and the coating on position 3 (second pane, gap-side). The two curves are for different gas compositions (van Nijnatten, 2002)*

using a dispersive (grating) spectrophotometer equipped with a reflectance accessory. In the 1990s, manufacturers of spectrophotometers ceased production of these instruments and completely switched over to producing the more modern and cheaper Fourier transform (FT) spectrometers. For the purpose of the glass industry, however, these new instruments and their accessories proved to be unsuitable. Measurements obtained by different instruments often disagree significantly and the wavelength range that can be measured in a single configuration does not cover the range necessary according to EN 673. The need to address these problems was deepened through the successful development and commercialization of the silver-based solar control glazings where emittance values as low as 0.03 are now attained.

In 2002, the EU GROWTH Programme commenced the Thermes project (THERMES, 2001) with the aim of the solving those problems necessary to obtain a better understanding of the measurements with FT instruments and provide measurement recommendations for the glazing industry. Work is in progress to improve the design of suitable reflectance accessories for FT instruments capable of meeting the needs for accuracy demanded by the glass industry, i.e. high accuracy and precision and an absolute measurement of reflectance. In addition, algorithms are being developed for the extrapolation of reflectance spectra to predict the spectral reflectance of coated glass products which lie outside the normal mgeasurement range of many FT instruments (wavelengths >25 μm) unless the required spectra are obtained by altering the spectrometer optics.

3.5.3 An EU window energy data thematic network (WinDat)

The consolidation of knowledge and data relevant to the design of glazing systems for better buildings in Europe is being addressed in the recently formed EU WinDat RTD Thematic Network (van Dijk and Hutchins, 2002). The aim of WinDat is to make available and distribute widely a free European software tool with high-quality input and output for the calculation of thermal and solar properties of commercial and innovative window systems, on the basis of known component properties (glazings, shading devices, frames and edges, gases, etc.). The software will be an updated version of the Window Information System or WIS, which was developed between 1994 and 1996 by an international team, also with EC funding (WIS, 1994; van Dijk and Bakker, 1995). It is intended that this tool will be collectively supported and used in research, industry, standardization, education and design throughout Europe. It will be used to compare, select and promote innovative windows and window components for the optimum use of renewable energy and maximized energy savings and indoor comfort. One of the unique elements in the software tool is the combination of glazings and shading devices. This makes the tool particularly suited to calculate the thermal and solar performance of complex windows and active facades.

An integral part of WIS is the database of commercially available products and their optical and thermal properties. Components to be included in the updated database include uncoated and coated glazings, spacers for double-glazing units, frames and certain types of shading devices (mainly Venetian blinds and roller blinds). European manufacturers of components or of complete systems are submitting data about their products for inclusion in the database. With this database, users of WIS will be able to calculate the optical and thermal properties of complete fenestrations in accordance with the methods prescribed in European and other international standards (ISO, 1990; CEN, 1997, 1998a). A protocol for defining the data and for quality assurance has been agreed. In collaboration with the Lawrence Berkeley National Laboratory, the US database for glazings (LBL, 1993) used with their programs (Optics 5 and Window 5) will also be accessible. The long-term aim is to ensure that the two databases will be completely compatible in order that a single international glazing library suitable for worldwide use can be established (International Glazing Library, http://windows.lbl.gov/materials/optical_data/default.htm).

To date there is only limited and recent experience with international standardization in respect of the thermal and solar properties of shading products (CEN, 1998b, 2001; ISO, 2001). The WIS algorithms account for free or forced air circulation and associated heat transfer along blinds. These algorithms were used as input for recent international standards in CEN and ISO (CEN, 1998b; ISO, 2001). New data formats are being developed and defined to enable workers to deal with the properties of scattering components in general. The algorithms currently used in WIS for shading devices such as Venetian blinds assume that reflectance and transmittance have two components, one regular (or specular or directional), the other Lambertian diffuse. This approximation was recently adopted in ISO standard ISO/FDIS 15099 (ISO, 2001) and will be used as a basis to introduce other types of shading devices into WIS, e.g. roller blinds and concertina (pleated) blinds and scattering glazings. The best definition of the regular component is being investigated. The permeability to air of roller and concertina blinds also affects the thermal properties. Other additional properties such as backward transmission, as distinct from forward transmission, and slat curvature, are also being considered in the database. In the longer term it is desirable to extend the capabilities of WIS to calculate the spatial distributions of light transmitted and reflected by solar shading devices. This would allow the use of WIS for modelling light-redirecting devices and also make it a useful tool in daylighting evaluations (REVIS, 1998; van Dijk, 2001).

The WinDat Network membership comprises about 40 research and educational organizations, industry, consulting engineers and designers. Together, they represent all interested parties in Europe from research through development to manufacture and distribution The WinDat web site (www.windat.org) is the principal means for exploitation and dissemination of the work. The web site is operational and provides interested third parties with basic information on the network.

3.6 Conclusions

The significant advances made by industry in producing homogeneous large-area thin-film coatings for use as selective absorbers and window coatings for efficient control and conversion of solar and thermal radiation have created numerous and widespread opportunities for the effective use of solar and renewable energy systems. Many technologies have been successfully developed which permit coating performance to be tailored to meet end-user requirements. Issues of building integration, product selection, proper usage and energy performance assessment are of the utmost importance and remain to be more fully developed in future programmes of work.

In buildings, commonly experienced problems concern overheating and bad daylight quality, high energy use for heating, cooling and lighting, and component lifetime. Solar energy can be passively utilized to reduce heating and artificial lighting loads in buildings and to improve the quality of the indoor environment, but solar gains may result in visual discomfort, summer overheating or high cooling loads. Control strategies and devices are needed to influence the solar and light transmittance of the transparent part of the building envelope. Beyond the conventional measures of interior or exterior blinds or shutters, the need is for the development and design of solar facades with improved integrated performance with respect to indoor climate, energy savings and life cycle cost.

Windows can be developed to gain more energy than they lose by increasing the total solar energy transmittance and lowering the thermal transmittance. Innovative solar shading can be developed to stop the overheating of buildings, light-controlling elements can be developed to improve the use of daylight in the buildings and solar facades can be developed to have a better life cycle economy by increasing the durability and the energy savings relative to cost. Proper implementation of windows and solar facades will allow Europe to conserve energy, promote comfort and improve the quality of life and the quality of European products. This requires not only looking at technical barriers, but also at socio-economic issues, building regulations, standards and certification.

Through initiatives and projects such as the WinDat Thematic Network, SWIFT, ADOPT, THERMES and others discussed, European research is providing the combination of improved knowledge of high-performance components, products and techniques, together with expert knowledge on user needs and informatics. The outputs from these projects facilitate the creation of direct lines between product development, performance specification, appreciation in building regulations and other national incentive schemes. These initiatives will promote the use of reliable, clean, efficient and safe building cladding incorporating the functions of renewable energy solar thermal collectors, high-performance windows, efficient solar shading and daylight provision. Proper integration in facades, optimization of design and knowledge dissemination activities throughout Europe will help to reduce both installed peak energy and annual energy demand for heating, cooling and lighting purposes.

3.7 Acknowledgements

I would like to acknowledge the contributions of Professor Svend Svendsen, Technical University of Denmark, Michael Köhl, Dr Werner Platzer and Dr Helen Rose Wilson, Fraunhofer Institute for Solar Energy Systems, Germany, Dick van Dijk, TNO-Bouw, the Netherlands, and Professor Claes Granqvist, Uppsala University, Sweden, for their assistance in presenting this work and Pilkington Technology Management, UK, Flabeg GmbH, Germany, and Interpane, Germany, for the reproduction of figures and photographs. The contributions and support of my long-term associates Professor Arne Roos, Uppsala University, and Dr Peter van Nijnatten, TNO-TPD, Eindhoven, remain invaluable. Much of the work described received financial support from the EU Directorate General for Research and the Directorate General for Energy and

Transport. Finally, I pay special thanks to Professor Mat Santamouris, University of Athens, for his encouragement and patience in the preparation and completion of this work.

3.8 References

ADOPT, 1996, *Angle-dependent Optical Properties Measurements (ADOPT)*, Commission of the European Communities, Standards, Measurement and Testing Programme, DG XII, Contract No. SMT4-CT96–2138, Coordinator University of Uppsala, Uppsala, Sweden.

Ageorges, P and Hutchins, M G, 1996, *Optical Characterization of a Fraunhofer/BASF Thermotropic Device*, Working Document, IEA Solar Heating and Cooling Task 18, T18/B3/UK4/96.

Aschehoug, Ø, 1995, 'Frame and edge-seal technology – an international state-of-the-art review', in *Window Innovations '95*, Ottawa, Ministry of Supply and Services Canada, 82–89.

Bruggeman, D A G, 1935, in *Annalen der Physik (Leipzig)*, 24, 636.

Button, D and Pye, B (eds), 1993, *Glass in Buildings*, Butterworth Architecture.

CEN, 1997, *Glass in Building – Determination of Thermal Transmittance (U Value) – Calculation Method*, EN 673, Brussels, European Commission for Standardization (CEN).

CEN, 1998a, *Glass in Building – Determination of Luminous and Solar Characteristics of Glazing*, EN 410, Brussels, European Commission for Standardization (CEN).

CEN, 1998b, *Solar Energy and Light Transmittance Through Glazing with Parallel Solar Protection Device – Part 2, Reference Calculation Method*, CEN TC89/N129rev9 (draft prEN 13363–2), Brussels, European Commission for Standardization (CEN).

CEN, 2001, 'CEN/STAR workshop on daylighting and glazing', in *Rivista della Staz. Sper. del Vetro*, 1, 12.

Collins, R E and Robinson, S J, 1991, in *Solar Energy*, 47, 27.

Collins, R E and Simko, T M, 1998, in *Solar Energy*, 62, 189.

Crnjak Orel, Z, Leskovesk, N, Orel, B and Hutchins, M G, 1996, in *Solar Energy Materials and Solar Cells*, 40, 197.

Crnjak Orel, Z, Klanjòèek Gunde, M and Hutchins, M G, 2002, 'Non-black spectrally selective solar absorbers', in *Proceedings of the World Renewable Energy Congress VII, Cologne, Germany*, Amsterdam, Elsevier.

Driver, P M, 1981, in *Solar Energy Materials*, 4, 179.

Duffie, J A and Beckman, W A, 1980, *Solar Engineering of Thermal Processes*, New York, Wiley.

EWRS, 2000, (European Window Energy Rating Systems (EWERS)), *EU SAVE Project*, Contract 4.1031/Z/00–030/2000.

Farooq, M, Green, A A and Hutchins, M G, 1998, in *Solar Energy Materials and Solar Cells*, 54, 67.

Farooq, M and Hutchins, M G, 2002a, in *Solar Energy Materials and Solar Cells*, 71, 73.

Farooq, M and Hutchins, M G, 2002b, in *Solar Energy Materials and Solar Cells*, 71, 523.

Frank, T and Ghazi Wakili, K, 1995, 'Linear thermal transmittance of different spacer bars', in *Window Innovations '95*, Ottawa, Ministry of Supply and Services Canada, 253–262.

Gallego, J M, Hutchins, M G, Owen, J R and Anderson, S, 1996, 'The development and use of variable transmission electrochromic glazings', in *4th European Conference Solar Energy in Architecture and Urban Planning*, 545–548.

Gallego, J M, Consigny, M, Owen, J R, Hutchins, M G and Orel, B, 1999, *High Performance Variable Solar Control Glazing (SMARTGLASS) JOULE III Publishable Report*, EU Contract JOE3-CT95–0030.

Garnet, J C M, 1904, in *Philosophical Transactions of the Royal Society (London)*, 203, 385.

Garrison, J D and Collins, R E, 1995, 'Manufacture and cost of vacuum glazing', in *Solar Energy*, 55, 151.

Georg, A, Graf, W, Schweiger, D, Wittwer, V, Nitz, P and Wilson, H R, 1998, in *Solar Energy*, 62, 215.

Gombert, A, Glaubitt, W, Rose, K, Dreibholz, J, Zanke, C, Blasi, B, Heinzel, A, Horbelt, W, Sporn, D, Döll, W, Wittwer, V and Luther, J, 1998, in *Solar Energy*, 62, 177.

Granqvist, C G, 1995, *Handbook of Inorganic Electrochromic Materials*, Amsterdam, Elsevier.

Griffiths, P W, Di Leo, M, Cartwright, P, Eames, P C, Yianoulis, P, Leftheriotis, G and Norton, B, 1998, in *Solar Energy*, 63, 243.

Hill, R J and Nadel, S J, 1999, *Coated Glass Applications and Markets*, BOC Coating Technology.

Hutchins, M G and Ageorges, P, 1993, in *Proceedings of the SPIE*, 2017, 13–24.

Hutchins, M G, Wright, P J and Grebenik, P D, 1987, in *Solar Energy Materials*, 16, 113.

Hutchins, M G, Butt, N S, Topping, A J, Gallego, J M, Milne, P E, Jeffrey, D and Brotherston, I D, 2001a, in *Proceedings of the SPIE*, 4458 (Solar and Switching Materials), 120–127.

Hutchins, M G, Topping, A J, Anderson, C, Olive, F, van Nijnatten, P A, Polato, P, Roos, A and Rubin, M, 2001b, 'Angle-dependent optical properties of coated glass products: results of an inter-laboratory comparison of spectral transmittance and reflectance', in *Thin Solid Films*, 392(2), 269.

ISO, 1990, *Glass in Building: Determination of Light Transmittance, Solar Direct Transmittance, Energy Transmittance and Ultra-violet Transmittance and Related Glazing Factors*, International Standard ISO 9050, ISO/TC 160, Geneva, International Organization for Standardization.

ISO, 2001, *Thermal Performance of Windows, Doors and Shading Devices – Detailed Calculations*, International Standard ISO/FDIS 15099, ISO/TC 163, Geneva, International Organization for Standardization.

Johnson, T E, 1991, *Low-E Glazing Design Guide*, Butterworth Architecture.

Karlsson, J, Rubin, M and Roos, A, 2001, 'Evaluation of some models for the angle-dependent total solar energy transmittance of glazing materials', in *Solar Energy*, 71, 1.

Köhl M, 2001, *Performance, Durability and Sustainability of Advanced Windows and Solar Components for Building Envelopes*, International Energy Agency Solar Heating and Cooling Programme Task 27, Paris, International Energy Agency.

Lampert, C M, 1979, 'Coatings for enhanced photothermal energy collection', in *Solar Energy Materials*, 1, 319.

Lampert, C M and Granqvist, C G (eds), 1990, *Large-area Chromogenics: Materials and Devices for Transmittance Control*, SPIE Optical Engineering Press.

LBL, 1993, *Window 4.1: a PC Program for Analyzing Window Thermal Performance*, LBL Report 32091, Berkeley, CA, Lawrence Berkeley Laboratory, Windows and Daylighting Group.

Montecchi, M, Nichelatti, E and Polato, P, 1999, 'Equivalent models for the prediction of angular glazing properties', in *Rivista della Staz. Sper. del Vetro*, 5, 225.

Niklasson, G A and Granqvist, C G, 1983, in *Journal of Material Science*, 18, 3475.

Nostell, P, Roos, A and Karlsson, B, 1996, in *Proceedings of the SPIE*, (Optical Materials Technology for Energy Efficiency and Solar Energy Conversion).

Pulker, H K, 1984, *Coatings on Glass*, Amsterdam, Elsevier.

Raicu, A, Wilson, H R, Nitz, P, Platzer, W, Wittwer, V and Jahns, E, 2002, in *Solar Energy*, 72, 31.

REVIS, 1998, *Daylighting Products with Redirecting Visual Properties, REVIS*, European Commission JOULE III Programme, Contract JOE3-CT98–0096.

Roos, A, Polato, P, van Nijnatten, P A, Hutchins, M G, Olive, F and Anderson, C, 2001, 'Angular dependent optical properties of low-e and solar control windows – simulations versus measurements', in *Solar Energy*, 69(Suppl.), 15–26.

Seraphin, B O and Meinel, A B, 1976, *Optical Properties of Solids – New Developments*, Amsterdam, North-Holland, Chapter 17.

Siegel, R and Howell, J R, 1972, *Thermal Radiation Heat Transfer*, New York, McGraw-Hill.

Smith, G B, Dligatch, S, Sullivan, R and Hutchins, M G, 1988, in *Solar Energy*, 62, 229–244.

Smith, G B, Radchik, A V, Reuben, A J, Moses, P, Skyrabin, I and Dligatch, S, 1998, in *Solar Energy Materials and Solar Cells*, 54, 387.

Smith, G B, Earp, A, Franklin, J and McCredie, G, 2002, in *Proceedings of the SPIE*, 4458 (Solar and Switching Materials), 10–18.

SWIFT, 1999, *SWIFT, Switchable Facade Technology*, European Commission FP5 Contract No. ENK6-CT-1999–00012, Coordinator Fraunhofer-ISE, Freiburg, Germany.

Tabor, H, 1956, in *Bulletin of the Research Council of Israel*, 5A(2), 119.

THERMES, 2001, *THERMES, Thermal Emissivity of Energy-saving Coatings on Glass – Preservation of the Measurement Infrastructure of the Glazing Industry*, EU Growth Programme Contract G6RD-CT-2001–00658.

van Dijk, H A, 2001, in *Rivista della Staz. Sper. del Vetro*, 1, 65.

van Dijk, H A and Bakker, L, 1995, 'Development of a European Advanced Window Information system (WIS)', in *Window Innovations '95*, Ottawa, Ministry of Supply and Services Canada, 337–346.

van Dijk, H A and Hutchins, M G, 2002, 'WinDat, European RTD Thematic Network on Windows as Renewable Energy Sources for Europe – Window Energy Data Network', presented at the 4th International Conference on Coatings on Glass (ICCG 4), Braunschweig, Germany, November 2002.

van Nijnatten, P A, 2000, 'Measurement techniques for solar energy properties of glazing', in *Proceedings of the World Renewable Energy Conference 2000, Part I*, 171–176.

van Nijnatten, P A, 2001a, 'A pseudo-Fresnel approach for predicting directional optical properties of coated glazing', in *Thin Solid Films*, 392, 282.

van Nijnatten, P A, 2001b, *L631 0200 Directional VW Reflection Set – User Manual*, TNO 2001 (accessory sold by Perkin-Elmer).

van Nijnatten, P A, 2002, 'Measurement and modelling tools for the evaluation of directional optical and thermal radiation properties of glazing', *PhD Thesis*, Oxford Brookes University.

Wäckelgård, E and Hultmark, G, 1998, in *Solar Energy Materials and Solar Cells*, 54, 165.

Wilson, H R, Blessing, R, Hagenström, H, Hutchins, M G, Dvorjetski, D and Platzer, W, 2002, 'The optical properties of gasochromic glazing', presented at the 4th International Conference on Coatings on Glass (ICCG 4), Braunschweig, Germany, November 2002.

WIS, 1994, *Advanced Windows Information System, WIS*, European Commission DGXII Joule Programme, DG XII Contract JOU2-CT94–0373, 1994.

4 Advanced control systems for energy and environmental performance of buildings

Gérard Guarracino
Ecole Nationale TPE, Laboratoire Sciences de l'Habitat, Département Génie Civil Bâtiment, URA CNRS, Rue M. Audin, 69518 Vaulx en Velin Cedex, France

Denia Kolokotsa
Technological Educational Institute of Crete, Department of Natural Resources Engineering, 3 Romanou Str, 73133 Chalepa, Chania, Crete, Greece

Vassilios Geros
National and Kapodistrian University of Athens, Physics Department, Group Buildings, Environmental Studies, Building Physics 5, University Campus, 15784 Athens Greece

Urbanization in recent years has needed to adapt solar techniques to the requirements of urban buildings. This is a priority for solar buildings researchers and designers, and and the main challenge in the design of control systems for energy performance of buildings is to find the balance between implementation costs, operation costs, energy consumption, indoor climate quality, users' satisfaction and contribution to sustainable building.

In fact, the development of a control strategy for a specific building will depend not only on technical parameters such as building type and design, ventilation system, external noise and pollution, solar shading and internal loads, but also on parameters such as user attitude and user expectation.

Current research on energy-efficient buildings has proven that although the design and the facilities including Building Energy and Indoor Environment Management Systems (BEMS) aim to satisfy the thermal and visual comfort plus the air quality demands while minimizing the energy needs, they often do not reach their goals owing to user interference (Oreszczyn, 1993; Lowry, 1996; Foster and Oreszczyn, 2001). The latest trends in designing BEMS incorporate a man–machine interface that collects the users' preferences and adapts the control strategy accordingly (Lowry, 1996). Moreover, technological developments based on artificial intelligence techniques (neural networks, fuzzy logic, genetic algorithms, etc.) offer significant advantages compared with the classical control systems in the incorporation of users' demands, reduction of energy use and improvement of the indoor environment (Kolokotsa *et al*, 2001a,b).

Summarizing the above, a control system must satisfy the following objectives at the zone level:

- to maintain thermal, visual and indoor air quality comfort based on scientific guidelines in the relevant literature (Fanger, 1970, 1972; ASHRAE, 1985, 1989, 1989–1993, 1992; CIBSE, 1994a,b)

- to give priority to passive techniques in order to reach the comfort requirements

- to be flexible, that is, to have the ability to satisfy the different users' preferences (e.g. by using smart cards containing the users' preferences, inserted in a specially designed reader unit that supports the proposed application)

- to achieve a response of the controlled variables without overshootings and oscillations that can cause energy waste.

Another recent trend concerns the integration of various network technologies (LANs, internet, cellular networks, etc.) with building-related services (sensing of various parameters, control of appliances, smart devices, etc). By combining information technologies and services with appliances inside and outside the buildings, this approach aims to integrate concepts optimally adjusted to the specific needs and behaviour of users (Bos and van Leest, 2001). In these kinds of systems buildings are units 'embodied' in a wide network (most suitable is the internet) where the transfer of information is dual, from the 'outdoor environment' to the building and vice versa. The purpose of this integration is to provide services to the end-users and these services can be provided and activated inside or outside the building envelope. The services can be directly coupled to separate appliances or a set of appliances (in order to optimize their performance), or can partially be a miscellaneous service that has no link to appliances or systems. There is a variety of services that can be offered ranging from entertainment to energy-related services. The network services can be classified into five general groups (Aronsson and Tholén, 2000; Smart Homes, 2001a,b):

- *information services* such as news, databases, education, errands, citizen networks, online services, etc.

- *entertainment services* for leisure, such as video on demand, music on demand, TV on demand and online games

- *E-commerce services* providing shopping and financial business transactions

- *communication services* such as IP-telephony (telephony via the internet), picture telephony, videoconferencing, telecommuting (makes home offices possible) and notice boards (public electronic notice boards)

- *telemetric services* include HVAC (heating, ventilation and cooling controlled by the tenant or automatically controlled as one wishes), weather forecast control, monitoring, lighting, reservations, safety/surveillance, alarm, door locking, video surveillance, convenience, etc. The list of available services is endless.

A Service Provider that is a part of the whole system and in most cases is physically located outside the building can provide these services. In a general approach, these integrated systems are composed by the local network, installed inside the building where the appliances are connected, an external network (e.g. internet), a kind of gateway that connects these two networks and the service providers.

4.1 Impact of global control of building in terms of energy performance and sustainable building

Many buildings based on passive solar heating and cooling techniques are being built in Europe, thanks to the promotion of these techniques by European projects. At the same time, a growing interest in building automation systems and more generally in BEMS has been observed. However, when implemented in bioclimatic buildings, these systems are generally applied to the control of active systems only. For the optimum use of the passive elements, solar control or natural ventilation, designers usually rely on occupants' behaviour, operation of shading devices, windows and vent opening. This often results in energy performances and comfort levels poorer than expected.

Moreover, the combined control of active and passive systems, e.g. night ventilation cooling and mechanical cooling or hybrid ventilation, generally requires the use of so-called 'logic control' implemented by various rules in order to determine which of the passive or active systems should be operated.

Many digital controllers offer this possibility to implement logic control rules as well as On–Off or PID control. The problem with not implementing the techniques is therefore not a technological problem, but rather a lack of awareness among building designers and control engineers.

This absence of human action is even more important in public buildings, where customers represent the main occupants and the relationship between indoor climate and user acceptance in user-controlled rooms is not well known.

Research indicates that users are more flexible towards deviations in indoor thermal climate if it is controlled by themselves. Even though users should have the maximum possibility of controlling their own environment, automatic control is needed to support the users in achieving a comfortable indoor climate and to take over during unoccupied periods.

Another important criterion is the number of hours during which comfort temperature limits may be exceeded. A temperature of 26°C is one such limit according to ASHRAE. If this number of hours is <100, then it is usually accepted that auxiliary cooling is not necessary.

The use of automatic control for the control of passive elements and its integration into a BEMS system, when compared with classical manual control as usually implemented, could result in:

- energy savings for the building considered

- improved and satisfactory indoor comfort levels even without auxiliary cooling

- no or limited additional cost within certain conditions.

4.2 Function and control tasks

The control strategy should determine both time and rate control, and thus different control modes in relation to different weather conditions. The actual control strategy should reflect the demands of the building owner, the following needs of the users and the requirements in standards and regulations:

- indoor air quality during occupied and unoccupied hours

- room temperature during occupied hours in summer

- solar shading

- night ventilation during summer

- preheating of ventilation air

- room heating and cooling

- fan assistance and alternating passive and active systems.

Selecting the right control strategy is a difficult task. The final choice depends on many independent parameters such as the type of building, the other parameters and equipment controlled, the building architecture (partitioned or not) and of course global costs.

In order to understand better the requirements of an automatic control system, and and thus its main capabilities and advantages, a short description of the classical architecture of an automatic control system is given below, focusing on the differences from manual control.

An automatic control system is thus composed of:

- *One or more sensors*: necessary to measure the parameters required for the implementation of any control strategy. For natural ventilation control, classical parameters to be measured can include indoor and outdoor temperatures, CO_2 (or air quality) sensors, wind velocity and direction and rain detectors. The selection of the right parameters depends on the control strategy, i.e. control overheating, promote comfort or improve indoor air quality.

- *One or more actuators.*

- *A controller*: the heart of the control system. It is comparable to a personal computer receiving and treating data from the sensors and sending orders to the actuators. The control strategy is stored in the memory of the controller, and continuously implemented at fixed time intervals. Modern controllers are designed with the aim of handling any type of sensors, actuators and control strategies.

- *A supervisor*: implemented in a BEMS, a computer is necessary in order to supervise control decisions from different controllers and possibly override local control decisions, e.g. to decide which windows to open according to wind direction or close all windows in case of fire.

Manual control requires only actuators as additional equipment to the building. Extra investment costs for automatic control are thus for sensors, controllers, supervisor and wiring.

Occupancy detectors could be used to determine whether somebody broke into the building and in this case set off an alarm.

When lighting conditions are also monitored using luxmeters and shading devices also automatically controlled from the same control system, priorities can be set in order to optimize the coupled operation of shading devices and windows.

However, the difficulty in implementing appropriate control strategies increases with the size of the building and the number of parameters to be monitored. This would usually result in extended design, setting and commissioning periods for the control system in complex buildings.

One of the great advantage of automatic control systems is, however, their flexibility. Once the right actuators and sensors have been installed, the control strategy can be modified at any time.

4.3 Requirements for the implementation of automatic control

Many sensors are usually required. The main ones are the following:

- *Temperature sensors*: basic components of a control system, used for measuring indoor and outdoor temperatures. They indicate whether fresh air should be introduced as a cooling means. Most temperature sensors used in control systems are resistance thermometer devices (RTDs). These are based on the variation of some metal's electric resistance, usually platinum or nickel, with temperature. The accuracy of such sensors varies from 0.1°C to 0.5°C. Indoor sensors should be placed several metres away from the window at a position where incoming air has mixed. They should also be protected from direct solar radiation.

- *Carbon dioxide (CO_2) sensors*: used in order to evaluate indoor pollution caused by occupants only. Most of these sensors are based on infrared absorption spectrometry. The main problems with these sensors are their accuracy, from 50 to 100 ppm, while setpoints are typically around 800 ppm, and their cost. Further, these sensors have to be recalibrated at regular periods.

- *Mixed gas sensors (air quality sensors):* used to estimate indoor air quality based on multigas sensing. Their sensitivity can be adjusted by the system manager. Their advantage lies in the fact that they are sensitive to pollutants other than those produced by people such as cigarette smokers. There is, however, a lack of validation on the correlation between these sensors' outputs and actual indoor air pollution. They also require frequent recalibration.

- *Wind speed and wind direction sensors*: essential when natural ventilation is implemented. Wind direction is measured in order to select which openings on which facades should be opened, while wind speed is mostly used in order to adjust openings position and close them if wind is too strong. The most commonly used anemometer is the three-cup anemometer. It measures the horizontal component of the wind speed, whereas a vane anemometer is used to determine wind direction. It is fairly cheap and does not require much maintenance. The three-cup anemometer is, however, not very sensitive to very low wind speeds. Such sensors are usually placed on top of the roof.

● *Rain detectors*: necessary to avoid water ingress into building and should be placed on top of the roof. They are often combined with wind speed and direction sensors so that vents are shut only when both factors introduce a risk. The most commonly used rain detector works by a change of capacitance as the area of moisture on the detector increases. Such sensors are heated in order to dry the detector quickly and to melt and thus detect falling snow.

Other sensors are also found in such control systems:

● *Window security sensors*: they are needed for the detection of intrusion or glass breaking.

● *Solar gain sensors*: their role for natural ventilation control might be to increase ventilation rates in case of high solar radiation.

● *Humidity sensors*: these are sometimes necessary in order to control specific room ventilation rates. However, indoor relative humidity cannot easily be controlled with natural ventilation and humidity sensors will thus not be often used.

Although most manufacturers offer very comparable products, some controllers are sometimes limited by the number of rules or control functions that can be implemented This restriction will in most cases not be a major problem, but should be considered when complex control strategies have to be implemented.

Although defining a general control strategy for any building is almost impossible, there are some common rules and common principles that can be applied to any building. Some basic control strategies can thus be defined:

● *Control based on indoor pollution*: this strategy consists in monitoring an air quality index (i.e. CO_2 or air quality sensor) and open or close windows and vents as follows:

  ● if measured CO_2 concentration is above setpoint, open vents

  ● if measured CO_2 concentration is below setpoint, close vents.

The number of vents to open and/or the opening ratio of each vent (if control is not restricted to simple on–off control) cannot be defined for a general strategy. This will depend on wind conditions, building's shape, rain and differences from one zone to another and logic control will have to be implemented in order to define these parameters.

CO_2 concentration should beside be measured in each room. This is however expensive. If this solution is not possible, at least one CO_2 sensor should be placed on each facade in a representative room, representative for number of occupants or volume, but unnecessary ventilation might occur in unoccupied or partly occupied rooms.

● *Control based on temperatures indoor and outdoor*: this strategy is a 'free cooling strategy'. The aim of such a strategy is to determine whether outdoor air can be used as cooling means or not. There are various ways of achieving this. The problem is to know which action to undertake when the internal temperature is lower than the external temperature. At night, when the building is not occupied, vents should be closed if the external temperature is greater than the internal temperature. During the day, however, the increase in relative velocity could compensate the relative increase of indoor temperature due to ventilation. This is difficult to assess. However, when the outdoor temperature exceeds the indoor temperature by more than 2–3°C, vents should also be closed.

- *Integral control strategy*: in this case, both indoor air quality indices and temperatures are taken into account in the control strategy. Vents, windows or dampers are operated according to the most demanding of the two criteria. This strategy is similar to the temperature-based strategy. The settings of the control strategy depend strongly on the building shape, function and organization.

- *Mixed-mode control strategies*: in bioclimatic buildings, passive systems will not be sufficient for achieving thermal comfort throughout the year. Mechanical cooling systems are therefore necessary. Specific control strategies need to be developed in order to integrate control of passive and active systems. These control strategies are defined as 'mixed-mode control strategies'. They can be integrated into the temperature-based or integral control strategies. The main rules to follow when implementing this strategy are the following:

  - set two temperature setpoints, one at which heating is required (e.g. 21°C) and one at which cooling is required (e.g. 24°C)

  - avoid implementing heating and cooling on the same day

  - define priorities.

Again however, the settings will strongly depend on the building's shape, organization and on its equipment (air handling units, local fan coil units, etc.).

4.4 Communication protocols for the implementation of advanced control systems

A typical centralized commercial BEMS consists of the central station and a number of outstations. The outstation accepts inputs from sensors monitoring the values of variables such as flow and return temperatures of a heating system. Then the inputs are processed and the outstation sends output signals to control items of a plant, i.e. actuators or a valve. The outstation contains a small circuit board, the communication board, which allows it to interface with the central station, usually using modems or a Local Area Network (LAN). As microprocessors become even smaller and cheaper, it has become common practice for computers to be used to control and monitor building facilities, such as heating, ventilation and air conditioning systems (HVACs), fire detection, security control, lights, lifts, etc.

The major issue nowadays in building monitoring and control systems is the *interoperability* and *expandability* of the communication protocols. The lack of standards and the increased competitive pressures led each manufacturer to develop its unique proprietary communications protocol. This resulted in significant difficulties in integrating products made by different manufacturers. Stand-alone energy management systems, lighting control systems and fire detection and suppression systems are now common, but integration of these systems is rare. Even with a single building automation function, e.g. HVAC control, there has been a difficulty. If there is a need to expand or upgrade the control system, a building owner has been forced either to return to the same vendor who installed the existing system, replace it in its entirety, or install a separate independent system because the communication protocols for other products are incompatible (Bushby, 1997). However, it is possible to integrate systems using interfaces referred to as gateways. With a gateway relevant data can be passed from the fire system to the building energy management controlling lights and fans. For a gateway project to work successfully, the manufacturers of the systems involved must be prepared to release details of their protocols. Another issue in gateway use is change control. If alterations are made to one system, how would this affect the system to which it is linked? Moreover, the cost of these integrations and gateways is high, creating marketing problems. It would appear that if manufacturers agree to a common protocol or standards, these problems are resolved.

In the past decade, attempts have been made throughout the world to establish a standard communication protocol. Progress is slow bearing in mind the many different candidates for standards: Profibus, Batibus, EIBus, Echelon, BACnet, etc.

The characteristics of each communication protocol specialized in building automation are analysed below:

- *BACnet*: BACnet was developed over a period of 8 years by ASHRAE (American Society of Heating Refrigeration and Air Conditioning Engineers) Standing Project Committee 135 that included major HVAC manufacturers, consultants and end-users. The protocol was developed specifically to address interoperability and proprietary system concerns in the building automation industry.

   The final version release of the BACnet standard was approved in July 1995 and has now been published as an official ASHRAE standard, ANSI (American National Standards Institute) standard and a European CEN standard.

   BACnet is based on four layers of the Open Systems Interconnection (OSI) model: the Application, Network, Data Link, and Physical layers.

   BACnet can operate on several different types of transport media: RS485 at up to 1 Mbit/s, RS232, ARCnet at 2.5 Mbit/s, Ethernet at 10 Mbit/s or more (commonly used for IT networks in buildings) and LONtalk are included within the standard. Recently, BACnet has been extended to cover transmission over the internet protocol, TCP/IP.

   BACnet uses multiple physical architectures to handle high- and low-speed networks, and also point-to-point connections. BACnet defines Objects of information to be communicated over these physical media and defines Services to handle the flow of Objects between BACnet devices.

   The BACnet protocol can be used by head-end computers, complete sub-systems, general-purpose controllers, application-specific or unitary controllers, and smart sensor/actuator devices. It may be applied to monitoring and controlling HVAC, refrigeration, and other building systems. Currently objects are being added which support the integration of security and fire alarm systems.

- *LONWORKS*: LONWORKS is an open standard networking platform created by Echelon Corporation for network control. The Local Operating Network (LON) is formed by a number of nodes communicating over a variety of media such as twisted pair, power lines, radio frequency, fibre optics, etc., using an event-driven protocol named the LonTalk protocol (Echelon, 1995). The LON nodes are intelligent devices that can be connected with conventional sensors (temperature, humidity, illuminance, etc.), actuators (HVAC, lighting, alarms, etc.) and interfaces (displays, terminals, PCs, etc.) and in addition to the communication protocol can run an application program. The LON network is suitable for distributed control applications and is featured with simple integration of different devices, higher performance due to peer-to-peer communication type and low installation and reconfiguration costs. The media supported ensure the applicability of the system in existing buildings.

  A LonWorks network consists of a number of nodes (sensors, actuators, interfaces) communicating over a number of media using a common protocol. The LonTalk protocol follows the reference model for OSI developed by the International Organization for Standardization (ISO) and provides services at all seven layers of the OSI reference.

  LONWORKS allows free topology connection (ring, bus or star topology and all the combinations of the above).

  A number of LON companies have formed the Lonmark Association to develop a plug and play approach to fixed algorithm design of various types of air conditioning controllers.

- *EIB: European Installation Bus*: European Installation Bus was originally developed by a group of companies led by Siemens. Until the end of 1995, Siemens held the exclusive rights for the bus interface implementation. It is now controlled by the European Installation Bus Association (EIBA). The EIB protocol is one part of an architecture designed to meet the need for control of installation products.

  Installation products are loosely defined as intelligent building control products, such as lighting, blinds and simple HVAC components. The bus is a twisted pair operating at 9600 bit/s and can be used to carry both the signal and power. Recently the standard has been extended to define the operation over Ethernet. The addressing scheme allows up 65,536 nodes. It is designed for systems that have many units on a network requiring little transfer of data, e.g. lighting, fire detectors, room controllers, etc. In the EIB protocol, a device consists of a Bus Coupling Unit (BCU) connected to an Applications Module. The BCU provides the interface to the EIB protocol and in some installations may be powered by the bus.

  A simple set of objects suitable for small devices has been developed. These have been designed for ease of operation with BACnet systems.

  EIB is already widely used in German speaking areas, especially in the fields of lighting and blind control. The European Home Systems Association (EHSA) and Batibus Club International (BCI) have now joined EIBA in a consortium named KONNEX (www.konnex.org) which intends to market a single European field protocol.

● *Batibus*: Batibus was developed in 1988 by Merlin Gerin in France. Primarily it was designed to interconnect field-level devices, such as intelligent sensors, actuators and terminal unit controllers, within a building. In addition to transmitting data, a small amount of power can also be provided over the bus, reducing the need to also run power cables.

  Batibus was designed for commercial, institutional and industrial use. It uses an asynchronous transmission mode that can have 240 addressable points and up to 1000 'nodes' per network. The transport medium is a twisted pair cable either shielded or unshielded with a data rate of 4800 bit/s. The protocol operates in a distributed fashion without a master node. Batibus applications are implemented on standard microprocessors (suppliers including Intel and NEC) that include a serial I/O channel.

  The Batibus Club International (BCI) was founded in 1989 and has a membership from several European countries.

● *EHS*: European Home Systems (EHS) is a comprehensive home communication system developed by European industries with the help of funding from the European Commission. Its aim is to interconnect different kinds of electrical and electronic products and services used within the home.

  EHS is promoted by the EHSA as the future open network technology to be used for home automation applications. The objectives of this technology are to allow integrated communication based on different types of media, to be cost effective for the consumer, and and to provide the means for the type of user friendliness that consumers would expect. The key to such a system is the standardization of the communication protocol of the network which links these products in a home. New products developed by different manufacturers can work alongside previously installed applications. EHS follows the plug and play concept in that products must be easy to install, use, and remove.

  The protocol supports several media such as powerline, coax, twisted pair, infrared and radio frequency.

● *X-10 residential protocol*: X-10 is a powerline carrier protocol designed for the residential market that allows compatible devices to communicate via the 110 V A.C. power wiring within the house. X-10 allows for a maximum of 256 addresses. X-10 and LON are the predominant protocols at the residential level. X-10 is included in this list to show the differences between a powerful scalable protocol and a simple practical protocol that has been developed with a single low-cost target market in mind. Typically, X-10 devices would have very limited options, such as start/stop, and would be programmed from a standard residential PC.

As far as BEMS and Energy Management and Control systems architecture is concerned, the centralized architecture continues to play a significant role (Xie *et al*, 1998). From a technical perspective, centralized control architectures serve with advantage in application systems where time-critical closely coupled synchronization and high data flow are required. When devices and systems are loosely coupled and the synchronization is less time critical, the advantages in adopting distributed control architecture are likely to become apparent. Being physically distributed is perhaps the major feature of such systems, with key advantages derived from simplified wiring, related cost savings and improved maintenance. The distribution of intelligence is in fact very limited as the lack of design tools still prevails. The design paradigms of a distributed control system are simple and not over-sophisticated. This leads to the adoption of the components-based approach (Pu and Moore, 1995). The term 'components' as a design concept is relatively familiar to the software industry as a deviation from object-oriented design. Components in a distributed architecture are the 'smart' sensors and actuators and controllers that aim to transform the simple On–Off operation of micro-switches to a more sophisticated operation, e.g. counting, time delay, response, etc. (Clarke, 1995).

Summarizing, a distributed system must have the following characteristics:

● interface with a broad range of sensors and actuators

● incorporate application programs that blur the distinction between legacy sensors and actuators and intelligent networked devices

● include a design and installation tool that can interconnect everything in the control network

● incorporate software that simplifies hardware configuration and reduces commissioning time

● include an open I/O driver that can be used with a variety of third-party human–machine interface tools.

From the previous analysis, it is obvious that a competitive BEMS should have the following characteristics:

● it must be an advanced open system, respecting common standards

● it should have the possibility to mix and match components from various manufacturers

● it should be easy to install in existing buildings without a major retrofitting effort

● it should possess the possibility of industrial programmable central unit with advanced capabilities

● it should be low cost.

The control strategies for the indoor environment proposed up to now are limited to On–Off and conventional PID methods (Dounis *et al*, 1995, 1996). The difficulty to determine the exact mathematical model lies with the use of trial and error methods to develop the PID strategy for each building. As far as On–Off control in buildings is concerned, the controlled variable swings continuously and thermal comfort is regulated only by the indoor temperature. Moreover, classical PID control does not respond well, with disturbances and modifications required for different buildings. On the other hand, recent research in building-related artificial intelligence topics has shown that 'smart control techniques' such as fuzzy systems and neural networks can contribute to a reduction of energy consumption while maintaining indoor comfort in acceptable margins (Dounis *et al*, 1992). In any case, user preferences were not taken into account in all the above work.

4.5 State of the art in advanced control systems

The aim of a control system is to maintain indoor comfort. Comfort is a very delicate subject and reflects the subjectivity of the users. The main parameters that influence the users' comfort are mentioned elsewhere and are:

● thermal comfort

● visual comfort

● indoor air quality

● acoustic comfort.

Each of the above depends upon a great number of variables. At present, advanced control systems do not take acoustic comfort into account.

The control of the thermal comfort has been limited to temperature and sometimes humidity regulation. Normally thermal comfort depends upon a great number of parameters such as air velocity, mean radiant temperature, people's activity, etc.

Visual comfort, on the other hand, depends upon a number of parameters (subjective and objective), such as the illuminance levels and their spatial distribution, the glare, the colour rendering, the view, etc. (Baker *et al*, 1993; Yener, 1999).

The indoor air quality is mainly influenced by the concentration of pollutants in the controlled space. There is a wide range of indoor pollutants and specific sensors are required to measure each one of them. The CO_2 concentration (measured in ppm) is the most representative controlled variable to measure the indoor air quality, as it reflects the presence of users as well as various sources of pollutants in the building (Dounis *et al*, 1996a).

The conventional control strategies for indoor comfort proposed up to now are limited to On–Off and conventional PID methods (Dounis *et al*, 1996b).

The On–Off control in buildings has shown that the controlled variable swings continuously. Moreover, the On–Off control in thermal comfort means control of indoor temperature only, without taking into account other critical thermal comfort variables.

Classical PID as well as On–Off control have been proved to be energy 'inefficient' (Clarke, 1995; Dounis *et al*, 1996b). The controlled variable creates overshootings and oscillations once the reference signal is reached causing energy waste.

Artificial intelligence has attracted the growing interest of researchers in various scientific and engineering areas. The number and variety of applications of fuzzy logic and neural networks ranges from consumer products and industrial process control to medical instrumentation, information systems and decision support (Lin and Lee, 1996).

Fuzzy logic is based on the way in which the human brain deals with inexact information. Fuzzy systems are structured numerical estimators. They start from formalized insights about the structure of categories that exist in the real world and then formulate fuzzy IF–THEN rules that represent expert knowledge. They combine fuzzy sets with fuzzy rules and they produce complex non-linear behaviour.

Fuzzy sets, introduced by Zadeh (1973) as a mathematical way to represent ambiguity and vagueness, is a generalization of the classical set theory. In a classical (non-fuzzy) set, an element of the universe either belongs to or does not belong to the set. This means that the *membership function* of an element is crisp (either yes or no). A fuzzy set is a generalization of the classical set as it allows the degree of membership of each element to range over the unit interval [0 1]. Therefore, the membership function of a fuzzy set maps each element of the universe of discourse to its range space. One of the most important differences between crisp and fuzzy sets is that the former always have unique membership functions whereas every fuzzy set has an infinite number of membership functions that may represent it. This enables fuzzy systems to be adjusted for maximum utility in a given situation. Fuzzy theory can be applied to fuzzify either basic fields such as probability theory, arithmetic, etc., or artificial intelligence fields such as neural networks, genetic algorithms, etc., to obtain fuzzy neural networks and fuzzy genetic algorithms, respectively.

Fuzziness is often confused with probability. The main difference between fuzzy logic and probability is that fuzziness deals with deterministic plausibility whereas probability concerns the likelihood of non-deterministic and stochastic events. Fuzziness expresses the uncertainty in the definition of phenomena such as 'tall person', 'large room', etc.

The major feature of fuzzy logic is its ability to express the ambiguity in human thinking, subjectivity and knowledge in a comparatively accurate manner.

When is it appropriate to use fuzzy logic? – when the process is concerned with continuous phenomena that are not likely to be broken down into discrete segments; when a mathematical model of the process either does not exist or exists but is too difficult to encode or is too complex to be evaluated fast enough for real-time operation; when ambient noise levels must be dealt with or it is important to use inexpensive sensors and/or low-precision microcontrollers; when the process involves human interaction; finally, when an expert is available to specify the rules underlying the system behaviour and the fuzzy sets that represent the characteristics of each variable. As a result of the above, and and taking into account the comparative study of the artificial intelligence techniques presented in Table 4.1, the use of fuzziness in the indoor comfort control of a building is imposed by the following factors (Dounis *et al*, 1995):

- a fuzzy description of comfort conditions fits naturally to the problem

- the system to be controlled is highly non-linear

- the required expertise to achieve indoor comfort by minimizing the energy use is available in the bibliography and need to be encoded in fuzzy rules and sets.

Table 4.1 *Comparisons of fuzzy systems (FS), neural networks (NN), genetic algorithms (GA) and conventional control theory**

	FS	NN	GA	Control theory
Mathematical model	SG	B	B	G
Learning ability	B	G	SG	B
Knowledge representation	G	B	SB	SB
Expert knowledge	G	B	B	SB
Nonlinearity	G	G	G	B
Optimization ability	B	SG	G	SB
Fault tolerance	G	G	G	B
Uncertainty tolerance	G	G	G	B
Real time operation	G	SG	SB	G

*The fuzzy terms used for grading are good (G), slightly good (SG), slightly bad (SB) and bad (B)

Applications of fuzzy theory in the control of the sustainable building's indoor environment are described below.

● Dounis *et al* (1992) developed a fuzzy control system for the realization of thermal comfort. Natural ventilation is incorporated during the night and the early morning of the summer period to remove the additional thermal load. The inputs of the fuzzy controller are the PMV index and the outdoor temperature and the outputs are the heating system, the cooling system and the window opening (natural ventilation). The fuzzy rules give very good results in both extreme climatological seasons where the maximum and minimum illumination and temperature occur.

● Various techniques for the control of the indoor air quality of natural ventilated buildings were compared by Dounis *et al* (1996b) including On–Off, PID, PI with deadband and fuzzy control. The fuzzy control technique reduces the oscillations of the controlled variable and is proved by simulation results to be the most promising one for the indoor air quality control of naturally ventilated buildings.

● Guillemin and Morel (2001) developed a self-adaptive integrated system for building energy and comfort management. Both artificial and natural lighting controllers have been designed in order to fit the integrated approach. The shading device controller is split into two parts depending on the user presence. When the user is present, priority is given to visual comfort, and when she is absent, priority is given to thermal aspects (heating/cooling energy saving). The artificial lighting controller is used to complete the illuminance in the room up to the level desired by the user, which is learned by the system through the user wishes. Many simulations have allowed comparisons of different variants of the lighting controllers. The models used in the control system are regularly adapted to the measurements. Therefore, the system continuously adapts itself to the environment and the room characteristics. Experiments are performed in the occupied LESO-PB office building to demonstrate that this integrated system leads to 25% lower total energy consumption than a conventional system.

- Miriel and Fermanel (2001) developed a new room thermostat, based on a fuzzy logic function, to improve the performance and thermal comfort of individual forced hot water heating systems equipped with a gas-fired wall boiler, for homes. The improved thermostat assimilates the characteristics of the different parts of the system: boiler, heaters, building, climate, etc. The new thermostat was tested in simulation and good results were obtained. It was then validated experimentally. The experimentation was carried out in a two-storey house and was deemed very satisfactory with respect to thermal comfort, the number of electrovalve changeovers and the robust nature of the fuzzy thermostat.

- Egilegor *et al* (1997) developed a neuro fuzzy control system that regulates the fan coil air flow rate of three zones of a dwelling to improve comfort. The controlled variable used in the PMV index and the TRNSYS simulation program is used to simulate the building. The fuzzy control implemented is a fuzzy PI. The neural network uses as the adaptive parameter an offset of the PMV error and learns to associate a change in the offset with a change of the PMV index mean value. The PMV oscillations are quite strong and while the output of the fuzzy is an analogue signal the fan coils have three discrete flow rates. Moreover, the PMV is calculated taking into account the temperature and humidity of the dwelling's zones.

- So *et al* (1997) applied a self-learning fuzzy controller to an air handling unit (AHU). While PID control for an AHU is a simple and straightforward solution, fuzzy control can be more robust, more energy efficient and faster in responding to changes due to executing expert knowledge. Additionally, the self-learning fuzzy controller has the advantage of being adaptable to changes in the control process and the environment and no system model needs to be assumed beforehand. Therefore, faster response and reduction of the energy consumption of the AHU are achieved.

- A fuzzy controller for the regulation of the indoor temperature of a discontinuously occupied building was compared with a classical controller by Fraisse *et al* (1997). The fuzzy controller combines the variables of thermal comfort (set-point temperature of the occupied space and set-point temperature of the unoccupied one), the programming of occupancy scenarios and the optimization of the restart time of the heating system to regulate the indoor temperature by controlling the supply temperature of the water in the heating system.

- Dexter and Hawkins (1993) presented a fuzzy controller for the mixing box of an AHU, designed by data obtained from computer simulations. The controller uses measurements of the return and fresh air temperatures, together with the pressure drops across the dampers, to calculate the actuator control signals that determine the dampers' position. The performance of the controller is assessed using a building emulator that simulates the dynamic operation of the AHU.

- House and Smith (1995) studied the optimum control of heating, ventilation and air conditioning systems in order to achieve minimization of energy costs without sacrificing comfort and functionality of the occupied zones. Their methodology utilizes a system approach to the optimum control problem where the HVAC components, the building and their associated variables in an interactive form are taken into account and an optimal control solution is sought via a cost function. A building with five zones and time-varying loads and occupancy schedules is examined. The optimum control responses obtained by the system are compared with a conventional control approach with night setback. The conventional control approach fails to take advantage of the interaction of the system variables and ultimately causes increased energy use and less comfortable solutions.

- Kolokotsa *et al* (2001b) developed a fuzzy PID, a fuzzy PD and an adaptive fuzzy PD controller for the preservation of the air quality and thermal and visual comfort for buildings' occupants while simultaneously, energy consumption reduction was achieved. The adaptive fuzzy PD controller is compared with a non-adaptive fuzzy PD controller and an On–Off controller. The comparison criteria are the energy required and the controlled variables' response. Both energy consumption and variables' responses are improved if the adaptive fuzzy PD type controller is used.

Previous European research projects have developed optimum control strategies for HVAC systems. The aim of the GENESYS project, for example, was based on multi-criteria analysis and developing tuning strategies or controllers. The targeted buildings for the implementation of such strategies were office and school buildings. Initial goals could be achieved through two main innovations:

- use fuzzy, rule-based control

- development and comparison of smart tuning techniques.

Major results obtained during this project are as follows. Simulation results showed that global cost functions were reduced by 1.5% up to 17% with fuzzy control when compared with On–Off control strategies according to test sites and seasons, while energy savings at the same time range from 1.5% to 19% under the same or improved thermal comfort and indoor air quality conditions.

- tuning techniques resulted in improvements of initial strategies from 1.6% up to 14% according to controller type and season

- experimental results performed during the summer resulted in energy savings from 12.5% up to 30% while they ranged from 2.5% to 10% only in Greece corresponding to simulation results

- simulation performed on a 6-month basis with fuzzy switching techniques showed that 8.5% energy savings could be achieved with a 5.7% overall fitness improvement.

This work outlines the high potential of fuzzy control strategies and their corresponding tuning techniques for a least-cost operation of HVAC systems. However, additional work has to be performed. The main approach to the exploitation of these results is to work on the reduction of the overall design cost of the fuzzy controller, definition of the fuzzy architecture, hardware design, tuning procedure and implementation process.

Another related European project is the BUILTECH (JOE3-CT97–0044) (BUILTECH, 2001). The technical developments of the project can be summarized as follows:

- development of an Intelligent buildings energy management system (IBEMS) which:
  - achieves indoor comfort (thermal and visual comfort and indoor air quality) by giving priority to passive techniques
  - integrates the building user's preferences in the control strategy using the evolving smart card technology
  - minimizes the energy consumption and simultaneously satisfies the user's preferences by the development of a GA optimization tool that embeds the indoor comfort variables, the building user's requirements and the energy consumption in a single cost function
  - integrates conventional automation equipment such as PLC with advanced equipment such as LON modules and nodes
  - can be applied in existing buildings which are the most energy inefficient using the LON capabilities
- installation and monitoring of the developed BEMS to five buildings throughout Europe
- more than 25% energy saving is achieved
- elaboration of a cost effectiveness study which showed that:
  - the IBEMS contributes significantly to the reduction of the greenhouse gas emissions
  - the IBEMS's payback period is 7 years after installation
  - in 10 years the total costs saving will be M€93, which corresponds to a benefit of 3%
  - development of the *Intelligent Energy Management Guidelines and Handbook.*

Hence the realization of solar buildings with BEMS equipment relies on both architectural practice and research and development actions to supply building designers with a range of components or energy systems:

- natural ventilation and energy savings
- hybrid techniques for ventilation, heating, cooling, lighting and solar electricity
- demand for local control of ventilation and indoor air quality
- solar heating floor, thermal comfort and indoor quality
- solar heating systems, optimization between solar gains and auxiliary energy.

Commissioning, which is a systematic process of ensuring that building systems perform interactively according to the design intent of the owner's operational needs, is a new dimension to the requirements of BEMS systems. In fact, BEMS offer new opportunities to automate some parts of commissioning. This may be specific to solar techniques development in buildings.

The technical systems of buildings tend to become more complex and new control strategies of solar systems are the one of fastest adaptable and the most efficient energy-saving technologies in both new and existing buildings.

Integration of controls of many energy functions into a BEMS makes it easy for the operators to reduce the number of sensors and in the future to integrate new possibilities, major factors for solar buildings.

4.6 Smart buildings and internet-based energy services

The energy management and the energy services provided in the building sector involve actors from a range of areas, each one having specific objectives. Furthermore, it is important to provide integrated energy services to the end users in a simple way, without having to be fully familiar with the variety of devices and systems involved. It is also essential that this integration should not affect the individuality, integrity and functionality of those systems (Smart Homes, 2001a).

The energy-related services in buildings require the integration of information technology, intercommunication and telecommunication. A solution to internet-based energy services is the gateway approach. According to this approach, the general structure of the system requires the combination of the following elements:

- A *Local Network* installed in the buildings. This network supports the intercommunication between the various connected devices (mainly in the meaning of sensors and/or actuators). The controlled appliances are end-point devices located on the local network. A large range of devices can be supported, ranging from simple sensors (temperature, humidity, electric energy consumption, etc.) to actuators (power switches, etc.) and more sophisticated devices for user interaction (keyboards, screens, etc.).

- A *Gateway* that is used to connect the local network with the external/access network. The gateway is an edge server that provides the access to the external network and the necessary application environment that permits the Service Provider to control the appliances on the local network and also to receive any necessary information from the building (e.g. measuring data from sensors).

- An *External/Access Network* that permits one to establish a two-way communication. The external network possibly consists of several layers according to the system design. A management system and a network operator can serve the communication between the gateway and the Service Provider, especially when the Service Provider accesses multiple blocks of buildings. However, the internet is the most convenient medium to link the building to the outside, thereby accessing the Service Provider.

● *One or More Service Providers* that provide and support various energy services. The services mainly concern the energy management of the connected buildings, individually or at the level of building blocks.

A general representation of this structure is presented in Figure 4.1. In this figure buildings or blocks of buildings are connected through internet with the Service Providers, using two-way communication.

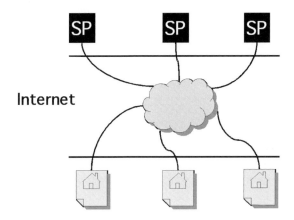

SP : Service Provider

Figure 4.1 *The general structure of the internet-based energy services system*

A more detailed representation of an internet-based energy services system is illustrated in Figure 4.2. In this figure the 'indoor' part of the system consists of the end-point devices (sensors, actuators, etc.), the local network and the gateway. According to the energy services that will be provided, a range of sensors should be installed to measure various indoor parameters (temperature, air movement, moisture, energy consumption, etc.). In addition, the desirable services determine diverse procedural aspects such as the monitoring time interval, the location of the sensors, etc. Since the end-point devices can be also be actuators to control an appliance (e.g. HVAC system, lighting system, etc.), the adopted control strategy must be also determined (On–Off, fuzzy, etc.). Finally, the installation of user interaction devices ('User Control' in Figure 4.2) is important since the user should have a level of interaction in order to define his/her preferences and at the same time to be informed about the application of the services.

Another aspect that is strongly related to the energy services is weather data acquisition, because the energy performance of buildings depends on the local climate. The data logging of the weather parameters can be accomplished at the site where the building is located or by using the measurements of a nearby meteorological station. Another convenient approach is to measure some of the required parameters *in situ* (such as outdoor temperature and relative humidity) and use the data supplied by a neighbouring meteorological station to acquire the rest of the necessary data. Another feature of the weather data acquisition concerns the communication technology applied to transfer the information to the Service Provider or to a storage system. According to Figure 4.2, the monitoring data can be transferred through the local network, the external network, or both. The adopted procedure depends on the case.

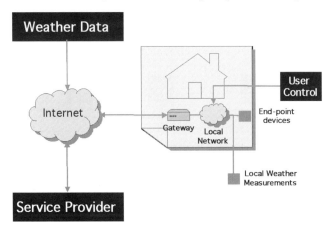

Figure 4.2 *The main elements of an internet-based energy services system*

Some of the energy services that can be provided by the Service Provider are outlined below (Smart Homes, 2001b).

4.6.1 Services of interest to occupants

● Alarms
  ● detection of gas leaks and smoke in homes or in sensitive areas (bathrooms, boiler rooms, garages or in buildings situated in the vicinity of industrial areas) or humidity and pollen (can be important, e.g. for people suffering from asthma)
  ● detection of open windows to prevent burglary and air leakage
  ● checking for appliances and lights that have not been switched off
  ● detection of water flow in the mains (emergency signal for the case when nobody is present in the apartment or house and water leakage is detected)
  ● resource targeting to alleviate fuel poverty (monitoring of temperatures/fuel consumption of local authority housing)
  ● cold alarm for the elderly to avoid hypothermia
● Statistics
  ● indoor/outdoor air quality monitoring
  ● optimizations based on statistics
  ● counting hours in-use of various appliances and automatic prompting for regular/emergency service

- evaluation of heating/cooling energy consumption (including the price of energy) for different set-points of internal dry bulb temperature versus current external dry bulb temperatures
- services and strategies related to the weather forecast (heating, night cooling, grass watering, use of rain water, etc.)
- operation of the heating (air conditioning) system matching the presence/absence of occupants
- remote On–Off switching of various appliances based on statistics (heating, ventilation, etc.)
- automatic anti-freezing regimes of heating systems enabled during long-term absence of occupants (taking into account the weather conditions)

4.6.2 Services of interest to maintenance operators/property managers

- Alarms
  - alarm signal for the failure of any devices or systems for quick identification and action
  - detection of water flow in the mains (emergency signal for the case when nobody is present in the apartment or house and some water flow is detected)
  - detection of adverse indoor climate
- Statistics
  - instantaneous demand of energy, heat, water, gas, etc.
  - consumption of heating, electrical or other energy over a period
  - measurement and control of required quantities (temperature, humidity, etc.)
  - automatic reading of delivered energy (gas, heat, electricity, water, etc.) for invoicing
  - automatic reporting of consumption statistics to authorities. These figures can be actual or normalized (e.g. compensated for weather conditions)
  - occupants' response (feedback) to control interventions of the operator (people-meters)
- Optimization
  - optimization for remote On–Off switching of various energy supply systems
  - optimization of heating/cooling system operation with respect to the weather conditions, such as weather forecasting
  - optimum operation of solar heating systems, PV cells, rain water usage, etc., based on the weather forecast
  - application of statistics in predictions of energy demand (different regimes, maximum and minimum demand, etc.)

4.6.3 Services of interest to energy management

● Statistics
  - environmental monitoring
  - planning resources and networks on the basis of energy demand monitoring
  - short text information exchange with the population via mini-terminal
  - monitoring of the occupancy in buildings
  - services related to the weather conditions
  - energy and water consumption in public buildings
  - collection of timely consumption data for communities for reporting to national authorities
  - application of statistics in predictions of demands and behaviour of energy consumers

Also, potentially interesting energy services concern the individual energy metering (for heating, cooling, lighting, appliances and domestic hot water) and the energy rating/certification of buildings according to their consumption.

The internet-based energy services are very promising especially owing to the fast development of IT technologies. At the present time, the trend is to develop open systems and the main problems concern the incompatibility between the technologies involved and the determination of the necessary communication interfaces. Therefore, during the implementation of internet-based energy services a careful selection of the technology for each entity of the previously mentioned scheme (Figure 4.2) is required.

4.7 Conclusion

Implementation of new approaches to energy in building design has been observed in recent years with links between researchers and professionals.

The main objective of control techniques is to elaborate an overall approach for the development of optimized control systems in order to improve the management of systems for heating, cooling, ventilation and lighting. Control strategies will improve energy efficiency and indoor climate in spaces through smart management of switching opportunities between passive techniques and active systems. These optimized strategies will contribute to an increasing energy efficiency and a growing use of renewables in buildings. Indoor climate will be improved (thermal and visual comfort, indoor air quality, noise), contributing to a more healthy indoor environment and better working conditions in general. Pollutant emissions will also be reduced owing to the smart control of hybrid technologies. However, many buildings have problems with BEMS and control strategies, resulting in increased consumption, the greatest challenge that faces all new hybrid techniques. In addition, the supply of internet-based energy services is another very promising approach which will enable the orchestrated energy management of individual buildings or blocks of buildings and potentially decrease building energy consumption and increase indoor comfort conditions.

Exploratory actions have to be conducted concerning on the one hand end-user interfaces adapted in particular to multiple and changing occupancy, and on the other hand measurement to ensure the quality and accuracy of BEMS inputs, both leading to potential industrial developments.

In conclusion, these smart strategies require accurate inputs to be efficient; technical solutions will be explored for the interface algorithms and occupants' satisfaction for the measurement systems of the BEMS and for coupling control systems with solar systems in new and retrofitting buildings. Hence these technologies will contribute to the development and adaptation of solar technologies to the requirements of urban buildings.

4.8 References

Aronsson, M and Tholén, D, 2000, *Which Broadband Services Do Tenants Want? – An Office Residential Survey Report in Sundby Park, Strängnäs*, Gothenburg, Department of Building Economics and Management, Chalmers University of Technology.

ASHRAE, 1985, 'Natural ventilation and infiltration', in *ASHRAE Fundamental Handbook*, Atlanta, GA, American Society of Heating, Refrigerating and Air Conditioning Engineers, Ch. 22.

ASHRAE, 1989, 'Psychological principles for comfort and health', in *ASHRAE Fundamentals*, Atlanta, GA, American Society of Heating, Refrigerating and Air Conditioning Engineers, Atlanta, Ch. 8.

ASHRAE, 1989–93, *ASHRAE Handbooks*, Atlanta, GA, American Society of Heating, Refrigerating and Air Conditioning Engineers.

ASHRAE, 1992, *Thermal Environment Conditions for Human Occupancy*, ASHRAE Standard 55, Atlanta, GA, American Society of Heating, Refrigerating and Air Conditioning Engineers.

Baker, N V, Fanchiotti A and Steemers K, 1993, *Daylighting in Architecture: A European Reference Book*, London, James & James.

Bos, J and van Leest, E, 2001, *[...Switch On–Off...] Home Automation and Energy – Future Perspectives for Saving Energy in a World of Smart and Intelligent Homes*, Project No. Novem 140.100.3302 The Hague, B&A Groep Beleidsonderzoek & -Advies.

BUILTECH, 2001, *BUILTECH, Combining Smart Card and Local Operating Network Technologies with Advanced Decision Support Techniques to Develop an Intelligent Industrial Energy Management System for Buildings*, Publishable Final Report, July 2001.

Bushby, S T, 1997, 'BACnet™: a standard communication infrastructure for intelligent buildings', in *Automation in Construction*, 6, 529–540.

CIBSE, 1994a, *CIBSE Code for Interior Lighting*, London, Chartered Institution of Building Services Engineers.

CIBSE, 1994b, *CIBSE Guide, Section A4, Air Infiltration and Natural Ventilation*, London, Chartered Institution of Building Services Engineers.

Clarke, D W, 1995, 'Sensor, actuator and loop validation', in *IEEE Control Systems*, August.

Dexter, A L and Hawkins, M E, 1993, 'The use of simulation data to design rule-based controllers for HVAC systems', in *Proceedings of 3rd International Conference, Australia*, International Building Performance Simulation Association.

Dounis, A I, Santamouris, M J and Lefas, C C, 1992, 'Implementation of artificial intelligence techniques in thermal comfort control for passive solar buildings', in *Energy Conversion Management*, 33(3), 175–182.

Dounis, A I, Lefas, C C and Argiriou, A, 1995, 'Knowledge base versus classic control for solar building design', in *Applied Energy*, 50, 281–292.

Dounis, A I, Bruant, M, *et al*, 1996a, 'Indoor air quality control by a fuzzy-reasoning machine in naturally ventilated buildings', in *Applied Energy*, 54(1), 11–28.

Dounis, A I, Bruant, M, Santamouris, M, Guaraccino, G and Michel P, 1996b, 'Comparison of conventional and fuzzy control of indoor air quality in buildings', in *Journal of Intelligent and Fuzzy Systems*, (4), 131–140.

Echelon, 1995, *LonWorks Engineering Bulletins*, January, San Jose, CA, Echelon.

Egilegor, B, Uribe, J P, Arregi, G, Pradilla, E and Susperregi, L, 1997, 'A fuzzy control adapted by a neural network to maintain a dwelling within thermal comfort', presented at the 5th International IBPSA Conference, Building Simulation '97, September 8–10, 1997.

Fanger, P O, 1970, *Thermal Comfort Analysis and Applications in Environmental Engineering*, New York, McGraw Hill.

Fanger, P O, 1972, *Thermal Comfort*, New York, McGraw-Hill.

Foster, M and Oreszczyn, T, 2001, 'Occupant control of passive systems: the use of Venetian blinds', in *Building and Environment*, 36, 149–155.

Fraisse, G, Virgone, J and Roux, J J, 1997, 'Thermal comfort of discontinuously occupied building using a classical and a fuzzy logic approach', in *Energy and Buildings*, 26, 303–316.

Fukuda, T and Shibata, T, 1994, 'Fuzzy-neuro-GA based intelligent robotics', in J M Zurada, R J Marks, II and C J Robinson (eds), 1994, *Computational Intelligence Imitating Life*, New York, IEEE Press, 352–362.

Guillemin, A and Morel N, 2001, 'An innovative lighting controller integrated in a self-adaptive building control system', in *Energy and Buildings*, 33(5), 477–487.

House, J, and Smith, T, 1995, 'A system approach to optimal control for HVAC and building systems', in *ASHRAE Trans*, SD-95–3–1, 647–660.

Kolokotsa, D, Kalaitzakis, K, Stavrakakis, G, Sutherland, G and Eftaxias, G, 2001a, 'Local Operating Networks technology aiming to improve building energy management system performance satisfying the users preferences', in *International Journal of Solar Energy*, 21(2–3), 219–242.

Kolokotsa, D, Tsiavos, D, Stavrakakis, G, Kalaitzakis, K and Antonidakis, E, 2001b, 'Energy and buildings. Advanced fuzzy logic controllers design and evaluation for buildings' occupants thermal–visual comfort and indoor air quality satisfaction', in *Energy and Buildings*, 33(6), 531–543.

Lin, C T and Lee, G S, 1996, *Neural Fuzzy Systems – A Neuro-Fuzzy Synergism To Intelligent Systems*, Englewood Cliffs, NJ, Prentice Hall.

Lowry, G, 1996, 'Survey of building and energy management systems user perceptions', in *Building Services Engineering Research and Technology*, 17, 199–202.

Miriel, J and Fermanel F, 2001, 'Classic wall gas boiler regulation and a new thermostat using fuzzy logic. Improvements achieved with a fuzzy thermostat', in *Applied Energy*, 68(3), 229–247.

Oreszczyn, T, 1993, 'The energy duality of conservatories: a survey of conservatory use', in *3rd European Conference on Architecture, May 1993*, 522–525.

Pu, S and Moore, P R, 1995, 'Component/image-based design of distributed manufacturing machine control systems', presented at ICRAM '95, Istanbul.

Smart Homes, 2001a, *Online Energy Services for Smart Homes, Work Package No. 1 Report*, Contract ENK6-CT-2000–00319.

Smart Homes, 2001b, *Online Energy Services for Smart Homes, Work Package No. 2 Report*, Contract ENK6-CT-2000–00319.

So, A T P, Chan, W L and Tse, W L, 1997, 'Self learning fuzzy air handling system controller', in *Building Services Engineering Research and Technology*, 18(2), 99–108.

Xie, C, Pu, J-S and Moore, P R, 1998, 'A case study on the development of intelligent actuator components for distributed control systems using LONWORK neuron chips', in *Mechatronics*, 8(2), 103–119.

Yener, A K, 1999, 'A method of obtaining visual comfort using fixed shading devices in rooms', in *Building and Environment*, 34, 285–291.

Zadeh, L, 1973, 'Outline of a new approach to the analysis of complex systems and decision processes', in *IEEE Transactions on Systems, Man and Cybernetics*, SMC-3, 28–44.

4.9 Bibliography

AIOLOS, *Creation of an Educational Structure on the Use of Passive Cooling Ventilation Techniques for Buildings*, Contract ALTENER 4.1030/Z/95 087.

Bruant, M, Guarracino, G, Michel, P, Santamouris, M and Voeltzel, A, 1996, 'Impact of a global control of bioclimatic buildings in terms of energy consumption and buildings' performance', presented at the 4th European Conference on Solar Architecture and Urban Planning, Berlin, March 1996.

Goulding, J, Owen Lewis, J and Steemers, T, 1992, 'Energy in architecture', in *The European Passive Solar Handbook*, Chapter 8, Control of Passive Solar Systems, Brussels, European Union.

GENESYS, *Fuzzy Controllers and Smart Tuning Techniques for Energy Efficiency and Overall Performance of HVAC Systems in Buildings*, Contract JOE-CT98–0090.

IEA, Annex 35, *HybVent, Hybrid Ventilation in New and Retrofitted Office Buildings*.

IEA, Annex 36, REDUCE, *Retrofitting of Educational Buildings – Energy Concept Advisor for Technical Retrofit Measures*.

MEDIABEMS, *Instrument Educatif Multi-média sur les Systèmes de Gestion Energétique des Bâtiments*, Contrat SAVE SA/171/97/FR.

Santamouris, M and Asimakopoulos, D N, 1994, *Passive Cooling of Buildings*, Athens, CIENE.

SIG-BIO, *Systèmes Intégrés de Gestion des Bâtiments Bioclimatiques*, Contrat ALTENER 4.1030/A/94–167.

5 IT systems for energy and environment monitoring, planning and design

Joseph A. Clarke

ESRU, Department of Mechanical Engineering, University of Strathclyde, Glasgow G1 1XJ, UK
Tel: +44 (0)141 548 3986; fax: +44 (0)141 552 5105; e-mail: joe@esru.strath.ac.uk

Throughout the EU, as elsewhere, sustained economic growth is the *raison d'être* of government. To this end, efficient energy utilization and the mitigation of environmental impact are regarded as important influencing factors. Energy policy objectives are essentially twofold: to eliminate the negative economic impact of profligacy and to develop and exploit new technologies in the energy/environment sector. Energy efficiency and clean supply technologies may therefore be expected to receive enhanced levels of support in the coming years. The challenge facing society is to direct this resource towards viable schemes. How can we improve our performance on energy efficiency or even measure progress? How can we embrace clean and low carbon technologies? How can climate change mitigation be brought about? Should the introduction of new and renewable energy (RE) technologies be market driven or derive from a step-change investment in R&D? And how can the wider environmental costs of energy be incorporated into market prices without retarding economic development? These are some of the burning questions of our time.

The energy and environment domain is inherently complex and, consequently, conflicting viewpoints abound, proffered solutions are typically polarized and consensus is impossible to attain. Indeed, the different vested interests serve only to render vacuous the relationship between sustainability and energy action. This unacceptable situation gives rise to three fundamental engineering challenges:

● how to consider energy systems in a holistic manner – in order to address the inherent complexity

● how to include environmental and social considerations in the assessment of cost-performance – in order to improve overall performance

● how to embrace inter-disciplinary working – in order to derive benefit from the innovative approaches to be found at the interface between the disciplines.

The most effective way to address these challenges is to help stakeholders to look beyond their preconceptions, to see the real state of the world and differentiate between the promising and the possible. The essential element in promoting the rational use of energy is that decision-makers at all levels (including citizens) be given access to relevant sources of information. In the present context, these include energy demand profiles, the characteristics of potential sources of supply and the outputs from modelling studies to assess the benefit and impact of alternative options. However, indications are that, at present, comprehensive information is rarely in the hands of those who require it and the use of modelling in strategy formulation is virtually unknown. This chapter describes four complementary application areas for energy and environment IT that, if taken up, have the potential to change this situation radically:

- *digital cities* – entailing the monitoring of fuel use and availability in order to identify areas of concern and assist with the identification of options for change

- *rational planning* – entailing the matching of energy demand and supply in order to assist with the deployment of new and RE systems at all scales

- *virtual design* – by which energy systems simulation may be used to conjecture and test specific designs prior to construction

- *energy services* – entailing the internet delivery of 'up-to-the-minute' information to professionals and citizens and the enactment of demand management at the aggregate scale.

The form and technical content of these four IT constructs, along with application examples, are the subject matter of Sections 5.2–5.5.

5.1 The sustainable energy systems challenge

The fossil fuels are at present abundant and relatively inexpensive, with sufficient reserves to last for approximately 50 years at current consumption rates (Lomborg, 2001). The principal objection to their continued use is their impact on climate change through the related emission of greenhouse gases (Climate Change, 2001). The decarbonization of the fossil fuels and the sequestration of this carbon are seen as prudent steps to mitigate climate impact in the short term. Two further actions are required to assist the smooth transition to a non-fossil fuel economy.

First, a greater level of energy efficiency is required in order to extend the life of the fossil fuels and re-shape demand profiles to better accommodate the introduction of new and RE technologies. The UK target, for example, is a 20% improvement by 2010 with a further 20% by 2020 (PIU, 2002). Table 5.1 identifies some of the technologies that may be harnessed to attain the sector-specific savings as indicated.

Such technologies give rise to further complexity in relation to their competitive selection, installation and intrinsic operation. For example, a cost–benefit comparison between passive solar and embedded RE options for a building is entirely non-trivial. Moreover, where the latter option is favoured, there exists a dichotomy between power exporting and local utilization, in addition to the problems related to non-standard installation and operation. By addressing such complexity, modelling

Table 5.1 *Energy efficiency technologies by sector*

Transport (25–65%)	Buildings (30–85%)	Industry (15–75%)
Journey curbing	Smart materials	Heat recovery
Efficient engines	Closer control	Efficient plant
Alternative fuels	Heat recovery	Load scheduling
Fuel cells	Passive solar	Waste reduction
Hybrids	Embedded RE	Materials recycling

tools (as described in Section 5.4) can be used to compare options in terms of their match with requirements and their performance under realistic operating assumptions.

Second, the widespread adoption of new and RE systems is required at both the distributed (network-connected) and embedded (building-integrated) scales. All renewables derive from solar energy: the total energy content of the annual solar radiation incident on the earth has been estimated at some 2,895,000 EJ (Craig *et al*, 1996) or some 7200 times more than the present annual global energy consumption. In contrast to its vastness, this solar resource is difficult to harness because of its intermittent nature and low temperature availability. It is for these reasons that the indirect, higher power density forms of solar energy are being targeted. Table 5.2, for example, gives the UK potentials of the most promising RE technologies relative to the UK total electricity demand. Although the least developed, marine power (wave and tidal stream) offers the major advantage that, like fossil-derived power, it has an ability to meet base load because of its predictable nature.

Such RE technologies, although more expensive than fossil-derived energy at present (this situation changes dramatically if the environmental and social costs of energy are included), are potentially cheaper, easier to maintain and less polluting, with low or no carbon emissions. The present level of renewable-derived energy in the EU is expected to rise rapidly (from a present low of around 0.06% of consumed energy) as the technologies become competitive from 2020 onwards. The UK target, for example, is to generate 20% of electricity from RE sources (primarily wind power) by 2020. This translates to 30% in Scotland, where the resource is greater or approximately 4000 wind turbines each of 10 MW capacity! Clearly, the identification of locations that are both technically feasible and policy unconstrained is highly problematic. The IT system described in Section 5.2 can assist the development control process by providing developers and planners with information on resource location and the policy-related barriers to exploitation.

RE systems have typically been pursued at the strategic level, with distributed hydro stations, bio-gas plants and wind farms being connected to the electricity networks at

Table 5.2 *RE potential*

Technology	Potential (%)
Hydro	5
On-shore wind	10
Off-shore wind	25
Solar PV	50
Marine	200

the transmission or distribution levels. To avoid problems with fault clearance, network balancing and power quality, it has been estimated that the deployment of RE systems with limited control possibilities should be restricted to around 25% of the total installed capacity (EA, 1999). This limitation is due to the intermittent nature of RE sources, requiring controllable, fast-responding reserve capacity to compensate for fluctuations in output and energy storage to compensate for non-availability. To achieve a greater penetration level, new and RE systems can be embedded within the built environment where they serve as a demand reduction device. Figure 5.1 summarizes the approach.

Embedded generation requires the matching of local supply potentials to optimized demands arrived at by the application of demand reduction measures. For example, passive solar, smart material, heat recovery and/or close control may be used to reduce energy requirements and μCHP and/or RE systems used to meet a significant portion of the residual demand. Any energy deficit is then met from the public electricity supply operating in co-operative mode. The important point is that, for the embedded approach to be successful, the energy efficiency measures must be deployed alongside the new and RE systems. This requires modelling systems whereby appropriate technology matches may be identified and specific schemes designed: Section 5.3 describes such a system. The approach also requires a means to assess the detailed performance of proposed schemes in terms of a range of relevant criteria: air quality, human comfort, energy use, environmental impact and cost. This may best be achieved by the use of integrated modelling systems as described in Section 5.4.

Finally, there is an opportunity to involve society in the decision-making process. This is required in order to ensure that adopted schemes represent a value proposition for citizens. What good are clean μCHP and RE systems if running costs rise dramatically owing to increased maintenance needs. Such an involvement may be brought about by making current information on energy use and impact widely available and offering new commercial services based on this information. Sections 5.2 and 5.5 describe technologies for information processing that may be used to address this issue.

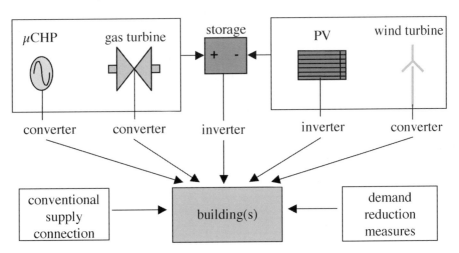

Figure 5.1 *The embedded generation approach*

5.2 Digital cities

Figure 5.2 summarizes the digital city concept. Acting in partnership, utilities, local authorities and others feed information to a shared database covering some geographical area of interest. To accommodate the temporal and scope mismatches between its component parts, the database is distributed, with internet-resident control agents acting to recover suitable integrations when enquiries at the aggregate scale are submitted (e.g. regional fuel use and gaseous emissions).

These data may then be analysed in order to supply relevant and 'up-to-the-minute' information to a range of possible recipients, from policy makers, through planners and designers, to citizens. To assist with interpretation, a Geographical Information System (GIS) (Clarke and Grant, 1996) may be employed to overlay the energy and environment information on conventional types of information such as street layouts or power cable routings. To assist with policy formulation, an energy model is included to enable an appraisal of options for change. Where an option proves beneficial, its predicted fuel use may be returned to the database to be held alongside the present fuel use data. This enables the side-by-side display of information relating to the present and future cases in support of extensive inter-comparisons before deployment decisions are taken.

EnTrak (Clarke *et al*, 1998; Evans, 2000) is an example of an existing system that seeks to deliver this functionality. The system offers constant monitoring and integration of fuel data relating to properties and RE schemes, consumption/supply classification, trend analysis and targeting and the assessment of cost-effectiveness. It is foreseen that the extent to which the system can provide comprehensive planning and energy management support is limited only by the availability of high quality data of

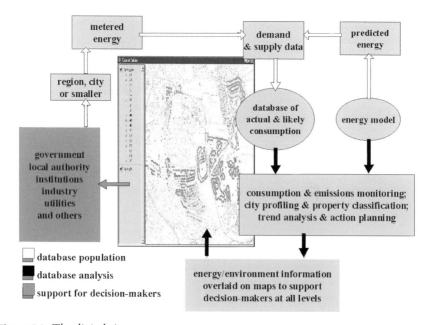

Figure 5.2 *The digital city concept*

adequate resolution – or the ability to generate this by simulation at the time of need. The capacity exists within *EnTrak* to record time-based output figures from RE conversion systems of any kind. Such systems are, of course, still few in number. To investigate future scenarios, in which development is more intensive, two approaches are possible:

- where a system already exists, which may be regarded as prototypical, it can be 'duplicated' in a new location, or

- the output of hypothetical systems may be modelled as a function of climate and other variables, using simulation techniques as elaborated in Section 5.3.

The ability to access temporal distributions, and later to correlate them with corresponding distributions of demand, is seen as a major advance on traditional methodologies as implicit within regional surveys (e.g. ScottishPower *et al*, 1993).

EnTrak is built upon a distributed, SQL-compliant database architecture using JDBC technology (Sun, 2002) to achieve database connectivity. Web-enabled analysis modules operate on this database to produce information tailored to the requirements of the various users. For example, Figure 5.2 depicts the fuel use and related gaseous emissions for a portion of a city. Such information can support a range of activities, from energy action planning, to the wider participation of citizens (see Section 5.5). By modelling proposed measures prior to their deployment, alternative options can be compared in terms of relevant criteria, including the impact on the energy supply system and the mitigation of greenhouse gas emissions. Furthermore, the impact of previous actions is implicit within the monitoring process so that schemes with a poor return can be quickly discarded and those with a high return retained.

Many rural areas are of great natural beauty and/or ecological concern and are important for tourism and leisure pursuits. Environmental issues will therefore affect the development of RE projects and must be given full consideration. Table 5.3, for example, lists some of the environmental sensitivity factors that might need to be evaluated for a proposed RE project. In most countries, such developments must obtain planning permission prior to construction and local authorities are empowered to examine applications. Any such examination requires a large number of issues to be assessed. While the technical issues are well known and are set out in National Planning Guidelines and Planning Advice Notes, the non-technical issues are usually difficult to assess. At the present time environmental assessment methods for RE schemes are not highly developed and regional authorities have substantial freedom of action. In response to policy directives on sustainability, planners are seeking to introduce a structure into their assessment procedures.

Table 5.3 *Environmental sensitivity factors*

Environmental feature:	Community and rural economy:
Landscape quality	Noise
Archaeology	Potential forestry
Nature conservation	Agriculture

To assess the overall viability of proposed schemes, the influencing factors are split within *EnTrak* into three categories: those which affect the technical feasibility of the proposal, those which are influenced by local or national environmental policy, and those which relate to socio-economic issues. The factors are then classified on a three-point scale. An assessment may then be made by computing a total 'score' for a given proposal; alternatively, a poor rating in one or more key categories might be deemed to make the proposal unacceptable.

Figure 5.3 presents an example for the case of wind farm development control in Caithness, Scotland (Bamborough *et al*, 1996). Here, the two GIS maps present policy (environmental only) and technical information to a 1 km² resolution using the following scoring criteria:

Technical:

● 275, 132 and 33 kV electricity grid line road and vehicle tracks (for access purposes)
● land cover (MLURI land classification) to identify where turbine location would be physically inappropriate
● proximity to settlements or houses (as defined by public roads) for community turbines.

Environmental:

● key bird population distribution
● landscape assessment and character type
● landscape designations, e.g. Areas of Great Landscape Value (AGLV)

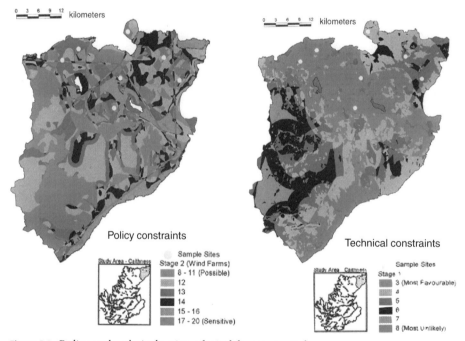

Figure 5.3 *Policy and technical rating of wind farm potentials*

● nature conservation designations, e.g. Sites of Special Scientific Interest (SSSI)

● areas of archaeological importance

● caution areas because of airports and masts

● telecommunications microwave link corridors

● proximity to public roads (and therefore housing)

● proximity to railway lines.

The technical parameters dictate whether a wind farm proposal is technically 'Unlikely', 'Likely' or 'Favourable' according to various physical factors. As shown in Table 5.4, these can be scored 3, 2 and 1 respectively, for each of the subjects under consideration.

Table 5.4 *Technical classifications*

Unlikely (3)	Likely (2)	Favourable (1)
More than 15 km from a grid line	Between 5 and 15 km from a grid line	Less than 5 km from a grid line
Within MLURI 'Woodland', 'Wetland', 'Montane' and 'Built-Up'	Within MLURI 'Peatland'	Within MLURI 'Rough Grazings' and 'Agricultural'
More than 6 km from any road or vehicle track	Between 3 and 6 km from any road or vehicle track	Less than 3 km from any road or vehicle track

Caithness will then be covered by areas that score between a minimum of 3 ('most favourable') and a maximum of 9 ('most unlikely') on technical grounds. By this mechanism *EnTrak* can produce an 'opportunity' map (Figure 5.3, right).

Likewise, the environmental factors can be defined as 'Sensitive', 'Intermediate' or 'Possible' and given a score of 3, 2 or 1, respectively, for each of the subjects as summarized in Table 5.5. All the various overlapping areas in Caithness will then have a score, ranging from a possible maximum of 25 to a possible minimum of 9. Figure 5.3 (left) shows the resulting map where a score of 11 or less is classed as being 'Possible' and 17 or more as 'Sensitive'.

Table 5.5 *Wind farm, environmental policy issues*

Sensitive (3)	Intermediate (2)	Possible (1)
All bird areas	Not assigned	All non-bird areas
Landscape types 3, 5 and 7	Landscape types 2, 4 and 8	Landscape types 1, 1b and 6
AGLVs	Not assigned	The rest
SSSIs	Not assigned	The rest
Areas of exceptional archaeological interest	Areas of above-average archaeological interest	The rest
Not assigned	Caution areas for airports and masts	The rest
Within 200 m of telecommunications link	Not assigned	The rest
Within 1 km of a dwelling	Between 1 and 2 km from a dwelling	More than 2 km from a dwelling
Not assigned	Within 2 km of a railway line	The rest

It should be noted, however, that this is simplistic because a low score may still contain a 'Sensitive' factor and so in reality any development would be problematic. Therefore, the alternative approach, by which an area is classified 'Sensitive' overall if any one issue is rated 'Sensitive', is probably preferable. In this case the zones of opportunity are classified as 'Some Sensitive', 'Intermediate' and 'Possible Only'. A comparison of the two maps in Figure 5.3 shows that environmental rather than technical issues are likely to be the constraint on wind farm development within the district.

The central and crucial requirements of systems such as *EnTrak* are database construction and maintenance. In the former case, two data collection methods are extant: electronic data interchange (EDI) and direct meter reading via the internet. EDI entails the regular exchange of data via computer files adhering to a pre-agreed format. It is a typical interaction mode between large organizations such as local authorities and utilities. Direct meter reading requires the embedding of sensors throughout the monitored estate and the connection of these sensors to a local electronic gateway device giving access to the internet. This approach, which is elaborated in Section 5.5, is suitable for application at all scales – from a home to a power station.

5.3 Rational planning

Future cities are likely to be characterized by a greater level of new and RE systems deployment. Maximum impact will be achieved when such systems are used to offset local energy demands, in contrast to current philosophy dictating the grid connection of large schemes (i.e. distributed generation). To assist with the integration of such systems at the local level, it is important to utilize energy efficiency techniques to reduce energy demands to magnitudes that present a favourable load for the new and RE systems being targeted. The technologies to be employed therefore fall into two categories:

● *demand reduction systems* – mainly passive in nature and used to reduce peak demands and reshape the demand profile, e.g. advanced glazing systems to maximize daylight capture and distribution, smart control to eliminate waste and solar thermal collectors to offset heating capacity

● *power supply systems* – mainly active technologies, which convert captured energy into electrical power and heat for use to meet the building's reduced demand.

Several modelling systems exist that may be used to identify suitable demand reduction and supply technologies and ensure the effective operation of these technologies when deployed together (Smith, 2002). To support the range of possible technology combinations, such systems will possess several key features:

● in-built databases containing demand profiles for various sectors and against variable time resolutions

● the ability to import site-specific data (as metered or predicted)

- a simulation engine to predict the impact of possible demand reduction measures

- models of the different possible supply technologies

- a mechanism to automatically match heterogeneous supplies to demand.

The *Merit* system (Born, 2001), for example, is built upon the interacting components shown in Figure 5.4.

In use, the first task is to specify the climate context of the appraisal. This is achieved by selecting from a database of standard climates or by importing site-specific weather data. The second task is to establish a set of demand profiles for the problem in hand. This set can be established to represent a problem at any scale: appliance, building, city district or national region. Large-scale sets may be produced by combining specific profile types after manipulation to reflect the scale. For example, a multiplying factor can be applied to the heating or power demand profile for a single house to obtain the corresponding profile for a community. Alternatively, a reduction factor can be applied to reflect the application of some energy efficiency measure. Where a monitoring programme has produced appropriate demand data for a specific site, this can be imported (e.g. from a monitoring system as described in Section 5.2).

The next task is to select a range of possible supply technologies to meet the demands in whole or part. This specification is undertaken in two steps. First, energy systems (renewable or otherwise) are selected from a model library or, where performance data exist for a specific technology, this can be imported. Each technology can be held individually or combined with other types to establish a combination supply. Second, an auxiliary supply system may be selected, comprising battery storage, a connection to the local electricity supply network or a back-up generator. Where a local network connection is specified, a tariff is defined.

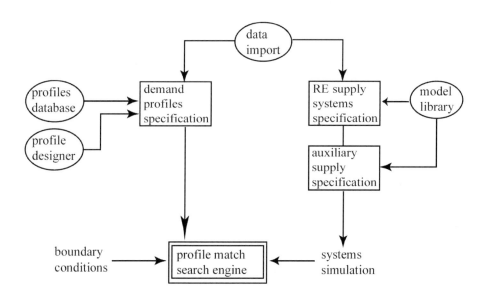

Figure 5.4 *Components of the* Merit *system*

Merit is now ready to conduct an automated search in order to identify those combinations that best match specified search criteria. Figure 5.5 illustrates a possible outcome. The first graph shows the demand superimposed on the supply to illustrate the temporal match. The second graph shows the associated energy residual, the portion above the *x*-axis representing a deficit. The third graph is active when an auxiliary system is selected and details its performance and duty cycle. The tabulated statistics include an inequality metric (to indicate the quantitative fit) and a correlation coefficient (to indicate the dynamic fit). The energy surplus or deficit is also displayed.

In this way, a user can call for the identification of the best supply match per individual demand or best supply match overall. This search performance benchmarks each match before initiating a search ordering process, which presents possible matches in order from best to worst. The benchmark uses Spearman's rank correlation coefficient (Scheaffer and McClave, 1982) to establish the phase matching between the demand and supply streams and an inequality coefficient described by Williamson (1994) to ascertain the magnitude of the match.

Systems such as *Merit* allow energy managers, planners and designers to appraise the potential for new and RE systems deployment at an early stage in the design process. This allows site-specific technologies to be identified and their required capacities to be established. The stage is then set for a detailed, integrated performance appraisal of viable schemes. This is the subject of the next section.

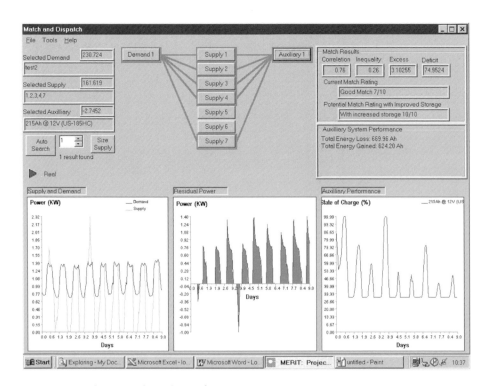

Figure 5.5 *Matching supply to demand using* Merit

5.4 Virtual design

Because the built environment consumes the greater portion of total delivered energy and is responsible for most of the avoidable CO_2 emissions, many initiatives are focused on this sector. However, buildings are complex and in the absence of a means to predict the performance benefit of proposed measures, such initiatives will probably fail. Modelling methods, when embedded within the building design process, allow the industry to pursue new designs and refurbishments that

● conform to legislative requirements

● provide the requisite levels of thermal, acoustic and lighting comfort

● attain high indoor air quality standards

● embody high levels of new and RE technologies

● incorporate innovative solutions

● lessen environmental impact.

It is widely accepted that integrated modelling defines a new best practice approach (CIBSE, 1998) to energy systems design because it allows designers to address important new challenges such as the linking of energy, the environment and health. In use, the approach requires the gradual evolution of a problem's description, with performance outputs becoming available at discrete stages as summarized in Table 5.6. The design team is then free to terminate model building when the objectives have been achieved.

Consider the scenario implied by Figure 5.6, which highlights the integrated appraisal approach and, by implication, indicates one possible future design practice [this scenario is based on the ESP-r system (Clarke, 2001) when its data model is cumulatively refined as described in Table 5.6].

Table 5.6 *Mapping problem description to performance results*

Cumulative model description	Typical behaviour enabled
Pre-existing databases	Simple performance indicators (e.g. U value)
+ Geometry	Visualization, photomontage, shading
+ Constructional attribution	Material quantities, embodied energy
+ Operational attribution	Casual gains, electricity demands
+ Boundary conditions	Illuminance distribution, no-systems comfort
+ Special materials	Photovoltaic components, switchable glazings
+ Control system	Daylight utilization, energy use, response time
+ Flow network	Ventilation, heat recovery evaluation
+ HVAC network	Psychrometric analysis, component sizing
+ CFD domain	Indoor air quality, thermal comfort
+ Electrical power network	Renewable energy integration, load control
+ Enhanced resolution	Thermal bridging
+ Moisture network	Local condensation, mould growth, health

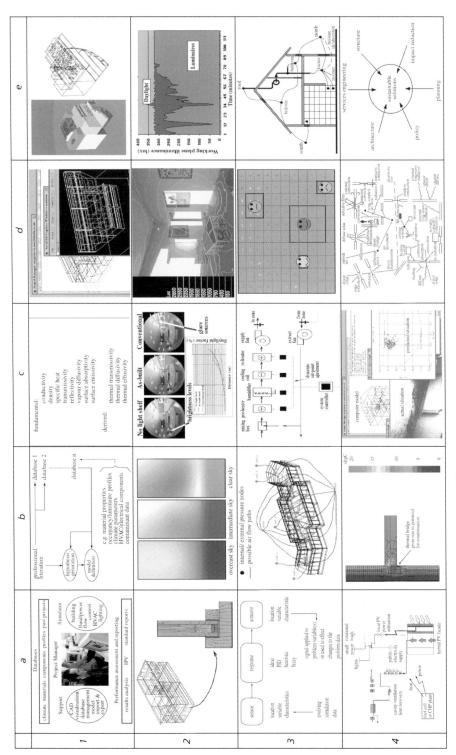

Figure 5.6 *Progressive aspects of the integrated building modelling approach*

a1   A Project Manager (Hand, 1998) gives access to support databases, a simulation engine, performance assessment tools and third-party applications for CAD, visualization, report synthesis, etc. The manager's function is to co-ordinate problem definition and pass the data model between the supporting applications. Importantly, it supports an incremental evolution of the problem description process and gives access to the simulation engine's corresponding functionality at each stage.

b1   Projects commence by making ready the system databases. These include hygro-thermal, embodied energy and optical properties for constructions, typical occupancy profiles, pressure coefficient sets for use with air flow modelling, plant components for use in HVAC modelling, mould species data for use with predicted surface conditions to assess mould growth risk and climate collections representing different locations and weather severity.

c1   Embedded within such databases is knowledge that supports the design conceptualization process. For example, the construction elements database contains sets of hygro-thermal and optical properties for a range of construction materials and derived properties from which behaviour may be deduced (e.g. thermal diffusivity to characterize a construction's rate of response or thermal transmittance to characterize its rate of heat loss).

d1   Although the procedure for problem definition is a matter of personal preference, it is common to commence with the specification of a building's geometry using an external CAD tool or in-built equivalent. ESP-r can inter-operate with dxf compatible programs (e.g. MicroGDS; Morbitzer, 2002) that can be used to create models of arbitrary complexity for import to Project Manager where the attribution process is enabled.

e1   Simple wire-line or false coloured images can be generated as an aid to the communication of design intent or the study of solar/daylight access. The Project Manager provides wire-line photomontages (Parkins, 1977) and coloured, textured images via the *Radiance* system (Larson and Shakespeare, 1998), automatically generating the required input models, driving *Radiance* and receiving back its outputs.

a2   Constructional and operational attribution is achieved by selecting products (e.g. wall constructions) and entities (e.g. occupancy profiles) from the support databases and associating these with the problem geometry. It is at this stage that the simulation novice will appreciate the importance of a well-conceived problem abstraction that achieves adequate resolution while minimizing the number of entities requiring attribution, simulation processing and performance appraisal.

b2   Temperature, wind, radiation and luminance boundary conditions, of the required severity, are now associated with the model. This permits an appraisal of environmental performance (e.g. thermal and visual comfort levels) in order to gain an insight into the extent of any required remedial action. As appropriate, the boundary conditions can be modified to represent extreme weather events or local climate phenomena.

c2   As required, geometric, constructional or operational changes can be applied to the model in order to determine the impact on performance. For example, alternative constructional systems might be investigated, different occupancy levels imposed or different approaches to daylight utilization assessed along with the extent and location of glare as shown here for the case of an office with added light shelf. The possibilities are limited only by the designer's imagination.

d2   Special facade systems might be considered: photovoltaic (PV) components to transform part of the solar power spectrum into electricity (and heat); transparent insulation to passively capture solar energy; or electro-, photo- or thermochromic glazings to control glare and/or solar gain. In each case, the contribution to improved performance and reduced energy use can be determined. It is even possible to study ways to eliminate conflict as in the case of a PV facade generating electricity (and heat) but reducing daylight penetration to the interior spaces and so increasing the electricity required for lighting.

e2   To access the energy displacement potential of daylight, a luminaire control system might be introduced, comprising photocells linked to a circuit switch or dimming device. Simulations can then be undertaken to optimize the parameters of this control system in order to minimize the use of electricity for lighting purposes. In this way, conflicts between the beneficial aspects of daylight capture and the detrimental effect on heating load (from the reduced heat gain) can be avoided.

a3   The issue of integrated environmental control can now be explored by establishing a control system conceived as a collection of open or closed loops. Some of these loops will dictate the availability of heating, cooling, ventilation, lighting, etc., while others serve to resolve conflict between these delivery systems. Previous aspects of the model may now be revisited in order to change the building's dynamic response to accommodate the intended control action.

b3   To study the feasibility of building ventilation, a flow network can be associated with the building model so that the dynamic interactions are explicitly represented. The control definition may then be extended to apply to the components of this network, e.g. to emulate window opening or flow damper control. Such a model can be used to examine the impact of alternative ventilation approaches as an aid to the design of robust natural or mixed-mode schemes.

c3   Where mechanical intervention is necessary, a component network can be defined to represent the HVAC system for association with both the building model and any active flow network. The control definition previously established may be further extended to provide internal component control and link the room states to the supply condition. Such a model can be used to determine the capacity of individual plant components and study the operational characteristics of the overall system.

d3   To examine indoor air quality, one or more spaces within the building model can be further discretized to allow the application of computational fluid dynamics (CFD) in order to evaluate the intra-space air movement and the distribution of temperature, humidity and contaminants such as CO. These data may then be combined to determine the comfort levels and air quality at different points within the space.

e3   Although the components of a model, the building, flow and HVAC networks and the CFD domain, may be processed independently, it is usual to subject them to an integrated assessment whereby the dynamic interactions are included. In the example shown here, a house model has been assigned a flow network to represent natural ventilation, an HVAC network to represent a ventilation heat recovery system, a CFD domain to enable the detailed analysis of air quality and a moisture flow model to allow an assessment of humidity distribution.

a4   A further network might now be added to represent the building's electrical power circuits. This can be used in conjunction with the previously established models for facade-integrated PV, luminaire control, HVAC and flow networks to study scenarios for the local utilization of the outputs from building-integrated RE components, the co-operative switching with the public electricity supply and the shedding of load as an energy efficiency measure. Other technologies, such as µCHP and fuel cells, can also be assessed.

b4   For specialist applications, the resolution of parts of the model can be enhanced to allow the detailed study of particular issues. For example, a portion of a multi-layered wall might be finely discretized to allow the identification of possible thermal bridges. A moisture flow network might then be added to support an assessment of the potential for interstitial or surface condensation.

c4   By associating the time series pairs of near-surface temperature and relative humidity (to emerge from the integrated building, CFD and network air/moisture flow models) with the growth limit data as held in the mould species database, it is possible to determine the risk of mould growth. Remedial actions may then be explored, from the elimination of moisture at source, to modifying the wall composition or arrangement in order to prevent optimum growth conditions from occurring.

d4   The core message is that any problem, from a single space with simple control and prescribed ventilation, to an entire building with systems, distributed control and enhanced resolutions, can be passed to the Simulator where its multivariate performance is assessed and made available to inform the process of design evolution. By integrating the different technical domains, the approach supports the identification of trade-offs. This, in turn, nurtures innovative approaches to building design and operation.

e4   Integrated modelling supports team working because it provides a mechanism whereby the different professional viewpoints can come together and contribute equally to the eventual outcome. Moreover, given the electronic form of the underlying model and the possibility of updating this model as the design hypothesis evolves, team members may operate from different locations and within different time zones. Such an inter-disciplinary approach is likely to give rise to more innovative and sustainable solutions.

To further support inter-disciplinary working, it is possible to collate the different aspects of performance and to present these in the form of an Integrated Performance View (IPV). As shown in Figure 5.7, an IPV might typically cover issues such as seasonal fuel use, gaseous emissions, thermal/visual comfort, daylight utilization, RE contribution, etc. Citherlet (2001) has extended the integrated performance modelling approach by adding a life cycle impact assessment (LCIA) procedure. This supports the assessment of the energy use and environmental emissions corresponding to the manufacture, transport, assembly, maintenance and disposal of construction materials, in addition to those associated with building environmental control. Four environmental impact indicators are used to quantify the overall impact: global warming potential, acidification potential, ozone generation potential and the use of non-renewable energy. Such impacts may be directly estimated from the predicted energy demand given that suitable conversion factors are available.

At the present time a significant number of modelling systems exist that may be used to address, in whole or part, the performance issues presented above. Details on these systems are available elsewhere (DOE, 2002).

5.5 Energy services

The internet is now attaining a level of resilience and capacity that will enable it to support a wide range of beneficial information services. The challenge is to develop products that represent a value proposition to citizens and to establish new service

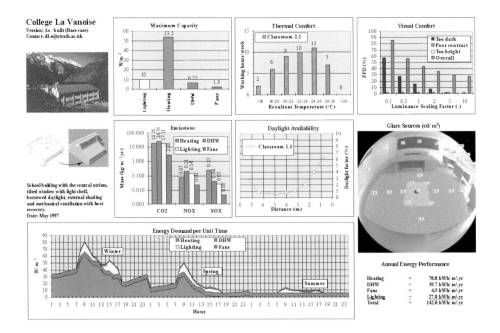

Figure 5.7 *Multivariate performance summaries support team working*

providers to deliver these products. Insofar as these challenges can be met, services can be tailored to assist the process of good governance by providing real-time data to decision-makers on issues relating to sustainability. Examples include:

● fuel use by time, type and sector in support of energy efficiency and RE systems deployments

● emissions monitoring in support of air quality and climate change targets attainment

● city performance profiling in support of energy/environment action planning.

Complementary services may also be established to provide direct links to citizens and to support their greater participation in sustainability issues. Examples include:

● home conditions monitoring (e.g. CO and temperature) in support of responsive care provision for vulnerable members of society

● large-scale, synchronized home appliance control in support of electricity base load management

● the provision of personalized energy use data in order to encourage desirable changes in usage patterns.

In addition to the benefits to the service recipients, it is likely that new employment opportunities will arise, in terms of both the jobs associated with service provision and the establishment of new market opportunities for the telecommunications industry. Furthermore, the approach provides an efficient mechanism to implement (low-cost) energy systems monitoring in order to track the effectiveness of actions taken in response to future legislation (such as the new European Directive on Building Energy Performance). An internet service reaches many residences and organizations simultaneously so that decisions relate to the large, aggregate scale. While impacts at the home scale will be of interest to the occupant, the impacts at the large scale will be of interest to local authorities and utilities. There are many stakeholders involved in the chain of service delivery including home owners/occupiers and related organizations, property owners/managers/operators, energy suppliers/distributors, local/national authorities, service providers and telecommunications operators.

The EC-funded *SmartHomes* Project (Clarke *et al*, 2002) set out to develop and test, by real-scale field trial, a range of new energy/environment services. The aim was to demonstrate that homes could be adapted to acquire and transfer high frequency fuel, power, appliance operation and space temperature data in support of new services of benefit to home owners/occupiers, utilities and local authorities. Examples include:

● environmental monitoring, e.g. detection of gas, smoke, temperature and humidity

● smart metering, e.g. of gas, electricity and water consumption

● appliance control, e.g. for heating, lighting and small power

● weather related services, e.g. heating control, night cooling, use of rain water, etc.

● performance evaluation, e.g. of city energy consumption by fuel type

- remote switching of appliances, e.g. for load manipulation and HVAC control
- renewable energy trading, e.g. as a function of electricity prices and demand.

The expectation was that substantial energy savings could be achieved by increasing the energy awareness of home owners/occupiers by providing them with statistics on their energy use in relation to that of others in similar circumstances.

The project utilized Ericsson's home gateway, or 'e-box', technology (Figure 5.8) to capture relevant data to support the new on-line services. It was envisaged that this would enable energy sector organizations to contribute technical, social and economic benefits through running cost reductions, management of demand in real-time, provision of added value services to customers, optimized operation of supply systems and better management of service quality according to customer requirements. Such services require the deployment of data acquisition and remote actuation devices and protocols that offer service value at appropriate cost.

The *SmartHomes* system is summarized in Figure 5.9. Sets of related sensors and actuators exist to support the needs of particular energy services. While these devices are typically wireless and based on radio frequency (RF) technology, they may also correspond to conventional wire-based installations. Although RF sensors exist at present, they are focused on home security applications, not energy and environment.

Figure 5.8 *Ericsson e-box*

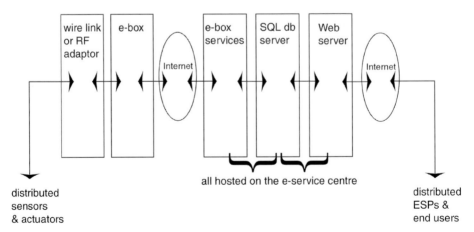

Figure 5.9 SmartHomes *system architecture*

The e-box exists to receive/send information from/to the sensors/actuators and send/receive data to/from an e-service centre located elsewhere on the internet. It is a low-cost device utilizing the Linux operating system (Linux, 2002) within a solid-state hardware architecture. The data obtained for a given site is transferred, by wireless or cable technology, to an e-service centre placed at some arbitrary location on the internet. There, the data are conflated with the private data arriving concurrently from the other sites within a given serviced region. That is, the e-service centre holds the software necessary to receive and organize the returns from registered e-boxes and energy service providers (ESP). All data are held within an SQL server database (such as that supported by the *EnTrak* system described in Section 5.2). Software agents closely associated with this database then act to extract the aspect data set corresponding to the particular energy services being supported at any time. Such a data set is either aggregate e-box data, for onward transmission to an ESP (via a service-specific web site) or actuation requests from an ESP for transmission back to homes (via the e-boxes and actuation devices).

Typically, an ESP will add value by interpreting the data and providing the actual energy/environment service (e.g. by raising an alarm, instigating a home control action or by updating a secondary web site). For example, information comprising home temperatures and CO levels would permit an ESP to provide a progressive care for the elderly service. Alternatively, information comprising fuel and power usage data would support two ESPs, one concerned with local action planning and the other with the routine dissemination of personalized consumption information to citizens. Where the outcome from a service requires the imposition of on-site control, an ESP transaction request is transmitted back to the site(s) via the e-service centre. This ensures that such actuations are authentic (i.e. that it is a valid component of the service selected by the customer).

Figure 5.10 shows an example of a web site corresponding to the delivery of personalized fuel use, environmental conditions and cost information to home owners/occupiers.

To test the market potential of the new energy services, four national field trials were initiated:

- *Czech Republic* – Individual metering of energy use and thermal comfort in multi-family buildings with remote actuation of set-point temperatures of heating systems for entire housing blocks. The data are reported to occupants, the energy supplier and authorities.

- *Greece* – Cooling load predictions based on real time data input to neural networks and information to occupants on how to reduce space-cooling demand effectively.

- *Scotland* – The services target the public housing sector and comprise cold condition alarms, CO-level monitoring, and fuel use metering with reporting to energy suppliers, health care agencies and local authorities.

- *Sweden* – Individual metering of space and domestic water heating and electricity, plus electricity use in multi-family buildings. The data are reported to the occupants, the energy supplier and the local authorities.

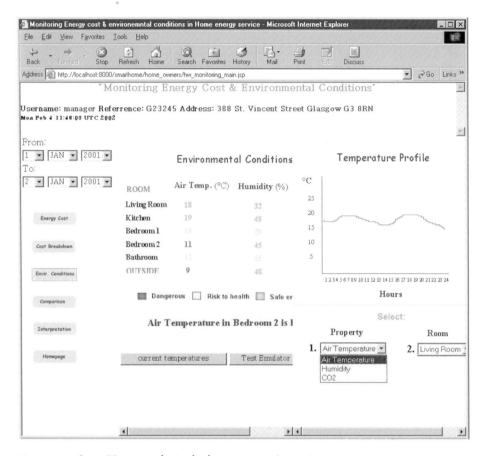

Figure 5.10 SmartHomes *web site for home owners/occupiers*

The coupling of metered values to a simulation programme allows the imposition of related considerations such as the estimate of the heat exchange between neighbouring apartments as an input to energy consumption debiting models.

5.6 Case study

To illustrate the IT approach to energy and environment, consider the embedding of RE systems within the refurbished Lighthouse Building in Glasgow, shown in Figure 5.11 (Clarke *et al*, 2000).

Network connection is often the preferred configuration for building-integrated new and RE systems. The generated electricity is exported to the local distribution network, while the building's electricity demands are separately imported. The additional capital and operating costs that such isolated schemes place on network operators in terms of maintaining acceptable network performance are significant. The short-term acceptability of this approach is assured owing to the small number of

Figure 5.11 *Lighthouse Building in Glasgow*

currently connected schemes and the existence of government subsidies. In the longer term, an increase in the number of intermittent, single-phase supply systems using the public electricity supply (PES) network as a buffer device will introduce network imbalance and power quality problems (EA, 1999). The increasing costs associated with correcting these problems will not be absorbed by the network operators but passed on to the generators. In many cases, this additional cost will compromise the viability of small-scale new and RE schemes and thus prove a hurdle to the attainment of national targets for such systems.

Building-embedded (i.e. non-exporting) systems have the potential to make a significant contribution towards the attainment of targets for reduced gaseous emissions. For this to happen, new approaches to system configuration, component sizing and power utilization are required to maximize the efficiency of energy use while not adversely affecting the quality of power available from the PES or local building network. At the macro scale, RE-generated power is a small fraction of the total power in the network and therefore can be absorbed without creating problems. Diversity ensures that there is always a demand that is matched to the power available from the RE systems. At the micro scale, the power ratings of the RE systems are a greater fraction of the demand so that the degree of matching is more crucial.

The first task in the Lighthouse project was to employ *EnTrak* to establish a demand scenario for the building: typical demand profiles from similar monitored buildings were scaled to equate to the design in hand. The embedded systems of interest were then specified to *Merit* and a demand/supply matching search carried out to locate suitable schemes. These were then passed to ESP-r where they were subjected to an integrated heat, light, air, moisture and power flow simulation in support of detailed design (e.g. component sizing and the elimination of conflict).

Based on the *EnTrak* and *Merit* analyses, four supply technologies were identified for deployment, but only after aggressive demand reduction measures had been put in place to reduce the total demand and reshape the demand profiles to provide a better match. The technologies included:

- an array of ducted wind turbines (DWT) to meet a portion of the power demands during the winter and transitional seasons

- a PV array to meet a portion of the power demand during the transitional and summer seasons (this array was subsequently incorporated within the spoiler of the DWT)

- a PV facade to meet a portion of the power and heat demands during the transitional and summer seasons

- a battery storage system to meet the temporal mismatch between demand and supply.

The ESP-r system was then used to identify suitable demand reduction measures:

- advanced glazings to minimize heat loss without significantly reducing daylight penetration

- a facade with transparent insulation and integral blind to translate solar energy over time to offset heating requirements

- dynamic temperature and illuminance set-point adjustment.

Figure 5.12 shows the cumulative impacts of the demand reduction measures: a 68% reduction in annual energy demand (corresponding to a 58% reduction in heating and an 80% reduction in lighting). Significantly, the final demand profiles are better matched to the output from the locally deployed RE systems.

As shown in Figure 5.13, the hybrid PV component was subsequently incorporated within the South-facing facade, whereas the DWTs were mounted on the South- and West-facing edges of the roof. Also shown are the predicted power outputs from the two RE technologies superimposed on the most favourable demand profile. Because of the temporal mismatch, the RE supply could be used to meet approximately 65% of

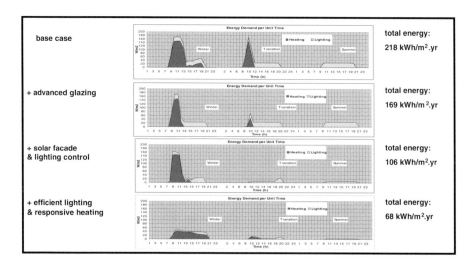

Figure 5.12 *Impact of demand reduction measures*

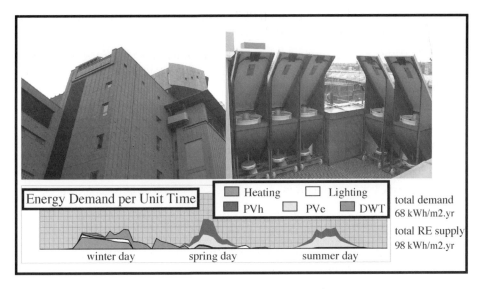

Figure 5.13 *Embedded RE systems, Lighthouse Building in Glasgow*

the total demand. This figure would fall to approximately 20% for the case where the energy efficiency measures were not first applied.

To determine the accuracy of the approach, the building was monitored over a heating season. From the outcome it was concluded that the predictions of Figure 5.13 were an adequate representation of the systems as deployed.

To complete the loop, the system could be monitored using a system such as *SmartHomes* and the performance data made available to decision-makers at all levels.

5.7 Technology transfer

While accepting the potential benefits of the above IT methods, most businesses still perceive barriers to uptake: not least in relation to the cost/complexity of software, the required changes to work practices and the degree of preparedness of employees. For this reason, innovative approaches to technology transfer are required whereby program application is supported within live projects.

The Scottish Energy Systems Group (or IBPSA Scotland, http://sesg.strath.ac.uk) has initiated such an approach whereby companies are able to obtain in-house support from application specialists seconded to the design team. By allowing design teams to gain risk-free access to modelling and simulation in the context of live projects and normal work practices, the industry is better able to identify the financial and human resource barriers to routine tool deployment. Further, by placing specialists within the design team, a two-way flow of information is supported: simulation know-how is passed directly to practitioners and specialists are exposed to real design issues.

Such an approach to technology transfer gives rise to several benefits. Companies are able to appraise the impact of the technology on their current work practice and so develop an appreciation of the required organizational development path. They are able to refine their design process by providing rapid and accurate assessments of a variety of design options, hitherto impossible within the time-scales available to designers. Further, by becoming equipped to address the complex dynamic interactions inherent in energy systems, companies are able to enhance the quality of their process and product. Several distinct messages have emerged from work to date:

- contemporary modelling systems can be cost-effectively deployed where appropriate support is available

- the largest portion of the cost relates to staff training, not to the acquisition of hardware and software

- a change in work practice is needed if the profession is to move to a new best practice based on a computational model of design

- many companies have reported that they anticipate no impact on their professional indemnity insurance due to the uptake of simulation

- project fees are likely to remain the same despite the added service value (because access to modelling engenders the confidence to implement innovative solutions which would not be possible using conventional methods).

To guide IT applications in the future, quality assurance procedures are required that relate to the spectrum of modelling issues. These include identification of objectives, mapping of objectives to simulation tasks, identifying uncertainties and risks, commissioning simulations, maintaining an audit trail, translating simulation outcomes to design evolution, client reporting and model archiving. Also, to guide results analysis, benchmark data are required to provide a means to judge the integrated performance of a building against others in the same class (DETR, 1994).

In the longer term, the creation of a progressive, IT-oriented construction industry will consolidate and strengthen the market position and growth potential of companies owing to the increased depth of service that they can provide. It will also give rise to a better balance between energy supply and demand, reflecting the fact that demand-side measures impact on supply-side decision-making and that opportunities exist for embedding new and RE generation within society at all levels. Finally, such IT deployments will assist the process of design process decentralization by enabling co-operative working between disparate partners. While the benefits are palpable, so too are the barriers derived from the industry's vested interest in maintaining the status quo.

5.8 References

Bamborough, K, Brown, A, Clarke, J A, Evans, M, Grant, A D, Lindsay, M, Morgan, J, *et al*, 1996, *Integration of Renewable Energies in European Regions, Final Report for Project RENA-CT94–0064*, Brussels, European Commission – DG XII.

Born, F J, 2001, 'Aiding renewable energy integration through complimentary demand–supply matching', *PhD Thesis*, University of Strathclyde, http: //www.esru.strath.ac.uk/.

CIBSE, 1998, *Applications Manual AM11: Building Energy and Environmental Modelling*, London, Chartered Institute of Building Services Engineers.

Citherlet, S, 2001, 'Towards the holistic assessment of building performance based on an integrated simulation approach', *PhD Thesis*, Swiss Federal Institute of Technology, Lausanne.

Clarke, J A, 2001, *Energy Simulation in Building Design*, Oxford, Butterworth-Heinemann.

Clarke, J A and Grant, A D, 1996, 'GIS and planning decision-support tools for renewable energy integration at the regional level', in *Proceedings of the European Conference on Renewable Energies in Regions and Cities, Ulm*, EuroSolar, Bonn 27–32.

Clarke, J A, Evans, M, Grant, A D, Karatolios, A and Mumaw, G, 1998, 'The role of information technology in urban energy policy formation, in *Proceedings of REBUILD, Florence*, EuroSolar, Bonn.

Clarke, J A, Johnstone, C M, Macdonald, I A, French, P, Gillan, S, Glover, C, Patton, D, Devlin, J and Mann, R, 2000, 'The deployment of photovoltaic components within the Lighthouse Building in Glasgow', in *Proceedings of the 16th European Photovoltaic Solar Energy Conference*, Glasgow. James & James, London.

Clarke, J A, Johnstone, C M, Kim, J and Strachan, P A, 2002, 'On-line energy services for smart homes', in G. Guarracino (ed), *Proceedings of EPIC '02*, Ecole Nationale des Travaux Publics de l'Etat, Lyon.

Climate Change 2001 *The UK Climate Change Programme 2001*, London, Dept. of Environment, Transport and the Regions.

Craig J R, Vaughan D J and Skinner B J, 1996, *Resources of the Earth: Origin, Use and Environmental Impact*, Prentice Hall.

DETR, 1994, *Best Practice Programme – Introduction to Energy Efficiency in Buildings*, UK Department of the Environment, Transport and the Regions.

DOE, 2002, http: //www.eren.doe.gov/buildings/tools_directory/.

EA, 1999, *Proceedings of Workshop on Connection of Photovoltaic Systems*, Capenhurst, EA Technologies.

Evans, M S, 2000, 'Energy management in diverse estates', *PhD Thesis*, University of Strathclyde, ESRU.

Hand, J W, 1998, 'Removing barriers to the use of simulation in the building design professions', *PhD Thesis*, University of Strathclyde, http: //www.esru.strath.ac.uk/.

Larson, G W and Shakespeare, R, 1998, *Rendering with Radiance – the Art and Science of Lighting Visualization*, San Francisco, Morgan Kaufmann.

Linux, 2002, http: //www.linuxhq.com.

Lomborg, B, 2001, *The Skeptical Environmentalist*, Cambridge, Cambridge University Press.

Morbitzer, C, 2002, 'Towards the integration of dynamic simulation into the building design process', *PhD Thesis*, University of Strathclyde, http: //www.esru.strath.ac.uk/.

Parkins, R P, 1977, *VIEWER Users Manual*, Glasgow, University of Strathclyde, Department of Architecture.

PIU, 2002, *The Energy Review*, London, UK Cabinet Office: Performance and Innovation Unit.

Scheaffer, R L, and McClave, J T, 1982, *Statistics for Engineers*, Boston, PWS Publishers.

ScottishPower, Hydro-Electric, Department of Trade and Industry, Scottish Office, Scottish Enterprise, Highlands and Islands Enterprise and the Convention of Scottish Local Authorities, 1993, *An Assessment of the Potential Renewable Energy Resource in Scotland*.

Smith, N, 2002, 'Decision support for new and renewable energy systems deployment', *PhD Thesis*, University of Strathclyde, http: //www.esru.strath.ac.uk.

Sun, 2002, *JDBC*, http: //java.sun.com/products/jdbc/.

Williamson, T J, 1994, *A Confirmation Technique for Thermal Performance Simulation Models, Technical Report*, Adelaide, University of Adelaide, Department of Architecture.

6 Natural ventilation in an urban context

Cristian Ghiaus and Francis Allard

LEPTAB, Universite de la Rochelle, Av. M. Crépeau, 17000 La Rochelle, France
Tel: +33 5 464 57259; fax: +33 5 464 58241; e-mail: cristian.ghiaus@univ-lr.fr,
francis.allard@univ-lr.fr

James Axley

School of Architecture, Yale University, New Haven, CT 06520, USA
Tel: +44 (0) 1203 432 2283; fax: +44 (0) 1203 432 7175; e-mail: james.axley@yale.edu

6.1 Introduction

Buildings-related services account for approximately one third of total energy consumption in the European Union. Residential and tertiary buildings have been identified as the largest energy end users, mainly for heating, lighting, appliances and equipment. Numerous studies and practical experience show that there is a large potential for energy savings here, probably larger than in any other sector. With initiatives in this area, significant energy savings can be achieved, thus helping to attain objectives on climate change and security of supply. Modifications in technologies and behaviour have already resulted in up to 50% reduction in energy use in some Nordic countries.

Traditional architecture shows how people carefully designed passive cooling systems that did not make use of any mechanical energy to operate (e.g. ground cooling, wind towers, fountains and whitewash). A major change occurred at the turn of the twentieth century, when W. H. Carrier invented the refrigeration chiller, which was developed on a large scale after Second World War. Air-conditioning technology and the availability of cheap energy allowed architects and engineers to keep buildings at a comfortable temperature whatever their orientation, insulation level, shading and thermal mass. Thus, in many parts of the world, passive cooling design and techniques were abandoned until they gained renewed interest in the last couple of decades encouraged by energy and environment concerns. In recent years, European scientists, engineers and architects designed successful innovative buildings that use passive cooling techniques, such as natural ventilation.

This chapter presents the main physical concepts and basic techniques for natural ventilation and gives orders of magnitude that allow us to compare them. Creative combinations of these techniques are possible and, in fact, have been fruitfully applied. However, careful design, detailed computation, attentive execution and automatic control of operation are needed to achieve a successful solution.

6.2 Role of natural ventilation

6.2.1 Purposes

The role of the ventilation in buildings is to maintain acceptable levels of oxygen in air and to remove odours, moisture and internal pollutants. It may also remove excess heat by direct cooling or by using the building's thermal mass.

6.2.2 Performance criteria

Performance criteria are related to the objectives of ventilation: air quality control and thermal comfort. Criteria for air quality control are defined in terms of minimum ventilation rates or by restricting the contaminant concentration to acceptable levels [e.g. ASHRAE Standard 62 (ASHRAE, 1999)]. Whereas designing for a minimum ventilation rate is straightforward, designing to restrict air contaminant concentrations is far more difficult. Consequently, most often the minimum ventilation rate is the approach taken in the design of natural and mechanical ventilation systems, although the minimum recommended ventilation rates have been amended many times (Figure 6.1a).

Criteria for thermal comfort in naturally ventilated buildings and air-conditioned buildings seem to be different. Growing evidence shows that individuals are more likely to adapt to seasonal variations when they are given the opportunity to control solar shading and air velocity, thus allowing larger variation range for indoor air temperature when natural ventilation is used (Figure 6.1b). This range is augmented

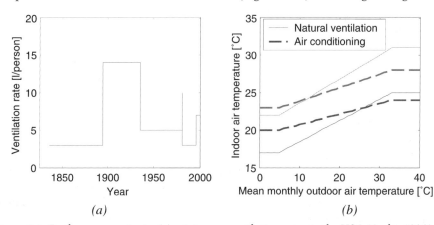

Figure 6.1 *Performance criteria: (a) minimum ventilation rates in the USA (Awbi, 1998); (b) thermal comfort in natural ventilation (Brager and de Dear, 1998) and air conditioning (ASHRAE, 1993)*

when natural or hybrid ventilation is used for night cooling of building thermal mass since the mean radiant temperature of wall surfaces will fall below indoor air temperature. The benefits of air velocity and radiant temperature may be estimated using a thermal comfort index equal to the weighted average of the mean radiant temperature in the room, T_{mr} and the room air temperature, T_a (CIBSE):

$$T_c = \frac{T_{mr} + T_a \sqrt{10u}}{1 + \sqrt{10u}} \qquad (6.1)$$

where T_c (°C) is the comfort temperature, T_{mr} (°C) is the mean radiant temperature, T_a (°C) is the room air temperature and u (m/s) is the air velocity.

For low air velocities, of the order of $u \approx 0.1$ m/s, the resultant temperature approximates the simple average of the mean radiant temperature and room air temperature, $T_c = (0.5T_{mr} + 0.5T_a)$. At relatively high air velocities, $u \approx 2$ m/s, close to the upper acceptable limit in office buildings, the weighted average tends to be dominated by the room air temperature, $T_c \approx (0.2T_{mr} + 0.8T_a)$, reducing the impact of radiant exchange. When night cooling strategies are applied, daytime natural ventilation should normally be limited to the minimum rate needed for air quality control to avoid advective overheating of the building, and, by reducing the air velocity, radiant impact will be maximized, as desired.

When natural ventilation is used for cooling, the upper limit of the thermal comfort zone may be exceeded from time to time owing to the stochastic variations of the natural driving forces. Thus, besides a well-defined and appropriate thermal comfort zone, a limiting criterion for overheating is needed. The BRE Environmental Design Manual (Petherbridge *et al*, 1988) places limits on the mean and standard deviation of summer and indoor air temperatures of 23 ± 2°C for 'formal offices' and 25 ± 2°C for 'informal offices'. In the Netherlands, dry resultant temperatures should not exceed 25°C for more than 5% of working hours and 28°C for more than 1% of working hours. However, these and similar absolute values do not quantify the degree of overheating. A standard that does is used in Zurich, Switzerland (Irving and Uys, 1997). It accounts both for adaptive behaviour (by employing an upper limit of thermal comfort that varies with outdoor air temperature) and for the stochastic variations (by considering the integrated degree-hour estimate of overheating calculated as the difference between indoor air temperature and comfort upper limit).

6.3 Physics of natural ventilation

The air flow is described mathematically by a set of differential equations for mass, momentum and energy conservation. Solving such a complex set of differential equations is indeed a formidable problem. No general integral of these equations has yet been found and numerical solution for an arbitrary three-dimensional unsteady motion requires the use of a supercomputer.

6.3.1 Eddy, turbulent and mean description of flow

Turbulent flow is one of the unsolved problems of classical physics. Despite more than 100 years of research, we still lack a complete understanding of turbulent flow.

Nevertheless, the principle physical features of turbulent flows, especially in their engineering applications, are by now well determined.

Turbulent flow distorts in patterns of great complexity, containing both coarse and fine features. The flow is said to contain *eddies*, regions of swirling flow that, for a time, retain their identities as they drift with the flow but which ultimately break up into smaller eddies. The velocity field of a turbulent flow can be regarded as the superposition of a large number of eddies of various sizes, the largest being limited by the transverse dimension of the flow and the smallest being those that are rapidly damped out by viscous forces. Mathematical analyses of steady laminar viscous flows show that infinitesimal disturbances to the flow can grow exponentially with time whenever the Reynolds number is sufficiently large. Under these conditions, the flow is unstable and cannot remain steady under practical circumstances because there are always some flow disturbances that may then grow spontaneously. The most rapidly growing disturbances are those whose size is comparable to the transverse dimension of the flow. These disturbances grow to form the largest eddies. Their velocity amplitude is generally about 10% of the average flow speed. These large eddies are themselves unstable, breaking down into smaller eddies and being replaced by new large eddies that are being generated continually.

The generation and break-up of eddies provides a mechanism for converting the energy of the mean flow into the random energy of molecules by viscous dissipation in the smallest eddies. Compared with a laminar flow of the same Reynolds number, a turbulent flow is like a short circuit in the flow field; it increases the rate at which energy is lost. As a consequence, a turbulent flow produces higher drag forces and pressure losses than would a laminar flow under the same flow conditions.

When the unsteadiness of the flow is not an overwhelming feature but more nearly a small disturbance of the average flow, the velocity field can be expressed as the sum of a mean value, obtained by averaging the velocity in time and a variable component. The variable component has the characteristics of a random noise signal of zero-mean. The turbulent kinetic energy, which is a measure of how much kinetic energy has been invested in the random turbulent motion of the flow, amounts, in general, to only a few percent of the kinetic energy of the time-averaged flow. Even so, the random velocity field produces shear stresses in the flow that are much larger than those that would exist if the flow were laminar. The largest eddies contribute most to the turbulent energy while the smallest eddies contribute most to the energy dissipation.

6.3.2 Mean flow through openings

The air flow through an opening is derived from the Navier–Stokes equation. By assuming steady, fully developed flow, the pressure drop for a flow between infinite parallel plates or for a flow impinging on a hole, nozzle or orifice in a thin plate is

$$\Delta p = 0.5 \rho Q^2 / (C_d A)^2 \tag{6.2}$$

where Δp is the pressure difference across the opening (Pa), ρ is the air density (kg/m^3), Q is the mean air flow rate (m^3/s), C_d is the discharge coefficient, a dimensionless number that depends on the opening geometry and Reynolds number, and A is the cross-sectional area of the opening (m²).

The openings in a building are much less uniform in geometry and, generally, the flow is not fully developed. The flow may be described by Equation (6.2), where A is an equivalent area and C_p depends on opening geometry and the pressure difference. Alternatively, an empirical power law equation is used:

$$\Delta p = (Q/c)^{1/n} \qquad (6.3)$$

where the flow coefficient c [m³/(s·Pa^n)] and the dimensionless flow exponent n are determined from experiments and do not have a physical meaning. For laminar flow, $n = 1$, for turbulent flow $n = 0.5$ and for transitional flow n is between 0.6 and 0.7. An empirical power law may be used also to model self-regulating vents. These self-regulating vents are pressure controlled inlets that provide relatively constant air flow rates over the pressure range. The low dependence of flow with pressure may be modelled with a small value of the exponent n, for example $n = 0.1$. A normal opening in a building that would provide the same air flow rate at a design pressure of 12 Pa would have a different behaviour, modelled by the exponent $n = 0.5$ (Figure 6.2).

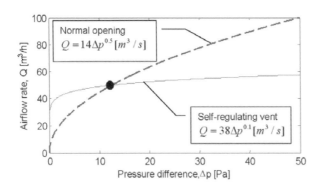

Figure 6.2 *Power law for a normal opening and for a self-regulating vent that provide the same air flow rate at 12 Pa*

6.3.3 Wind pressure

The time-mean pressure due to wind flow on to or away from a surface is given by

$$p_w = C_p \rho v^2 / 2 \qquad (6.4)$$

where C_p is the static pressure coefficient and v (m/s) the time-mean wind speed at a given level, commonly at the height of the building or opening.

Pressure coefficients, C_p, are usually measured in wind tunnels or calculated using computational fluid dynamics (CFD) methods. They can have positive or negative values that depend on building shape and location. According to Walker and Wilson (1994), for an isolated, parallelepipedal building, this variation is:

$$C_p(\phi) = \frac{1}{2}\left[\begin{array}{l}\left(C_p(0°) + C_p(180°)\right)\left(\cos^2\phi\right)^{1/4} + \left(C_p(0°) - C_p(180°)\right)\cos\phi\left|\cos\phi\right|^{1/4} \\ +\left(C_p(90°) + C_p(270°)\right)\sin^2\phi + \left(C_p(90°) - C_p(270°)\right)\sin\phi\end{array}\right] \tag{6.5}$$

where $C_p(0°)$, $C_p(90°)$, $C_p(180°)$ and $C_p(270°)$ are pressure coefficients for four walls making an angle of 0, 90, 180 and 270°, respectively, with the wind. Their values are given in Table 6.1 as a function of wind direction, ϕ.

Table 1 *Example of spatial variation of wind pressure coefficients for a rectangular building (Orme et al, 1998)*

Level	Wind pressure coefficients			
	$C_p(0°)$	$C_p(90°)$	$C_p(180°)$	$C_p(270°)$
6	0.70	−0.58	−0.36	−0.58
5	0.70	−0.58	−0.36	−0.58
4	0.72	−0.55	−0.35	−0.55
3	0.58	−0.48	−0.34	−0.48
2	0.41	−0.38	−0.29	−0.38
1	0.44	−0.17	−0.28	−0.17

The wind direction and velocity vary with time as a result of wind turbulence and effects of obstacles making the pressure coefficients difficult to estimate in urban environment and for complex-shaped buildings.

6.3.4 Buoyancy pressure

The static pressure difference between two points separated on vertical direction by distance $z = z_2 - z_1$ is:

$$p_2 - p_1 = \rho_2 g z_2 - \rho_1 g z_1 \tag{6.6}$$

The air density depends on temperature. From the gas law, $p = \rho RT$, we have:

$$\rho = \frac{\rho_0 T_0}{p_0} \cdot \frac{p}{T} \tag{6.7}$$

where the subscript 0 designates standard conditions for dry air (ρ_0 = 1.2929 kg/m³, T_0 = 273.15K, p_0 = 101325 Pa). Since the pressure differences in ventilation systems is of three to four order of magnitude lower than p_0, the density variation with temperature may be written as:

$$\rho = \frac{\rho_0 T_0}{T} = \frac{1.299\left[\text{kg/m}^3\right] \times 273.15\,[\text{K}]}{T\,[\text{K}]} = \frac{352.6\left[\text{kg·K/m}\right]}{T\,[\text{K}]} \tag{6.8}$$

For an increase in temperature with height, there will be a corresponding decrease in pressure. The pressure difference between two points vertically separated by a distance Δz, also called stack pressure, p_s, is:

$$p_s \equiv p_2 - p_1 = (\rho_2 - \rho_1)\,g\Delta z = \rho_0 T_0[1/T_2 - 1/T_1]g\Delta z \tag{6.9}$$

where T_0 is the temperature at a reference point.

6.3.5 Urban environment

In an urban environment, although the eddies and the turbulence are important, the mean velocity of wind is reduced significantly, by about an order of magnitude. As a result, wind-induced pressure on a building surface is also reduced. In order to have an approximate idea of the amount of this reduction, let us consider the case of a building having a height of 20 m and a much larger length, exposed to a perpendicular wind having a reference velocity of 4 m/s at 10 m over the building. The pressure difference between two opposite facades is then about 10–15 Pa in the case of an isolated or exposed building and about zero for a building located in a dense urban environment (Figure 6.3).

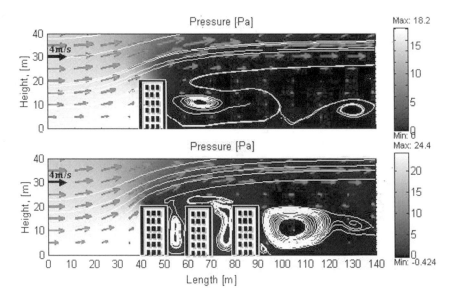

Figure 6.3 *Wind velocity and wind-induced pressure are reduced in urban environment*

6.4 Component sizing based on mean behaviour – pressure loop method

The performance criteria for ventilation may be formulated in terms of ventilation rates, air quality or thermal comfort. Most often, ventilation rates are used in the practice of ventilation design. For this case, Axley proposed a method based on the pressure drops along loops that follow a ventilation flow path from inlet to exhaust and back to the inlet (Axley, 1998, 2000). The *loop design method* allows for direct sizing of air flow components, accounts for both buoyancy and wind-induced air flow and their combination, and can be applied to buildings modelled by multi-zone ideal-izations. This approach may use statistical representations of environmental conditions to account better for local climatic conditions.

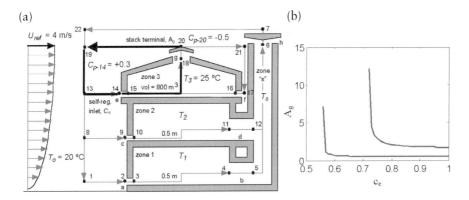

Figure 6.4 *(a) Building geometry and pressure loops for a design example based on the Inland Revenue Building, England (Braham, 2000); (b) minimum feasible sizes for self-regulating inlet and stack terminal*

The loop design method is a systematic procedure. The procedure steps are shown for an example inspired by the Inland Revenue Building (Figure 6.4).

1. Lay out the ventilation flow loops to be considered (i.e. flow component types and connectivity) typically on a building sectional drawing (see Figure 6.4).

2. For each flow loop, identify an ambient pressure node and pressure nodes at entries and exits of each flow component (see Figure 6.4).

3. Establish design conditions: envelope node wind pressure coefficients, design outdoor temperature, wind speed and direction, desired interior temperature conditions and evaluate ambient and interior air densities. For the purposes of this example, the design conditions will be representative conditions for a summer day – an approach wind velocity of $v_{ref} = 4$ m/s, an outdoor air temperature of $T_0 = 20°C$ and desired indoor air temperature of $T_3 = 25°C$. Applying Equation (6.8), the corresponding air densities are $\rho_0 = 1.2028$ kg/m^3 and $\rho_3 = 1.1826$ kg/m^3.

4. Establish the design ventilation rate for each inlet by applying continuity. For the purposes of this example, the design objective will be to provide a room ventilation rate of 5 ACH (e.g. based on a thermal analysis to maintain indoor air temperatures at the desired $T_3 = 25°C$). For the given room volume of 800 m^3, we would then need a room ventilation rate of 5×800 m^3/h or 1.10 m^3/s. To maintain a uniform distribution of this supply air, it would be reasonable to admit half this flow rate through the leftmost inlets and half through the right. Consequently, the volumetric flow rate through the self-regulating inlet e would have to be $Q_e = 0.55$ m^3/s while that through the stack exhaust g would have to be $Q_g = 1.10$ m^3/s.

5. For each loop selected in the first step above, form the pressure loop equations by accounting for all pressure changes along the loop. Pressure changes due to component resistances will be expressed in terms of the component design

parameter (i.e. the component size). It is useful to keep the stack and wind pressure contributions separate so that *with-wind* and *without-wind* cases can be more easily evaluated:

$$\Delta p_e + \Delta p_g = \Delta p_s + \Delta p_w \tag{6.10}$$

For the present example:

$$\Delta p_s = \left(\rho_o - \rho_i\right)g\Delta z = \left(1.2028 - 1.826 \ \frac{\text{kg}}{\text{m}^3}\right)\left(9.8 \ \frac{\text{m}}{\text{s}^2}\right)(3.5 \text{ m}) = 0.69 \text{ Pa}$$

$$\Delta p_s = (C_{p-14} - C_{p-20})\frac{\rho v_{ref}}{2} = (0.3 + 0.5)\frac{1.2028[\text{kg} / \text{m}^3] \times 4 \text{ [m} / \text{s]}}{2} = 7.70 \text{ Pa}$$

Here we will consider the inlet as being a self-regulating vent, modelled with Equation (6.3), with $n = 0.10$:

$$\Delta p_e = \frac{Q_e^{1/n}}{c_e^{1/n}} = \frac{(0.55 \ m^3 / s)}{c_e^{1/0.1}} = \frac{0.002533}{c_e^{10}}$$

and the stack terminal with the classic orifice Equation (6.2):

$$\Delta p_g = \frac{\rho Q_g^2}{2C_d^2 A_g^2} = \frac{(1.1826 \text{ kg/m}^3)(1.10 \text{ m}^3/\text{s})^2}{2 \times 0.6^2 \times A_g^2} = \frac{1.9874}{A_g^2}$$

Substituting these results into Equation (6.10) yields the loop equation that defines feasible combinations of the component design parameters c_e and A_g:

$$\left(\frac{0.02533}{c_e^{10}} + \frac{1.9874}{A_g^2}\right) = \begin{cases} 0.69 \text{ Pa without wind} \\ 0.69 + 7.70 \text{ Pa with wind} \end{cases}$$

6. Determine the minimum feasible size for each of the flow components by evaluating the asymptotic limits of each component design parameter for the loop equation (Figure 6.4b):

$$\lim_{A_g^2 \to \infty} \left(\frac{0.02533}{c_e^{10}} + \frac{1.9874}{A_g^2}\right) = \frac{0.02533}{c_e^{10}} \leq \begin{cases} 0.69 \text{ Pa} & \text{without wind} \\ 0.69 + 7.70 \text{ Pa} & \text{with wind} \end{cases}$$

or

$$c_e \geq \begin{cases} 0.72 & \text{without wind} \\ 0.56 & \text{with wind} \end{cases}$$

and

$$\lim_{c_e^{10} \to \infty} \left(\frac{0.02533}{c_e^{10}} + \frac{1.9874}{A_g^2}\right) = \frac{1.9874}{A_g^2} \leq \begin{cases} 0.69 \text{ Pa} & \text{without wind} \\ 0.69 + 7.70 \text{ Pa} & \text{with wind} \end{cases}$$

or

$$A_g \geq \begin{cases} 1.70 \text{ m}^2 & \text{without wind} \\ 0.49 \text{ m}^2 & \text{with wind} \end{cases}$$

Thus, the designer may conclude that the exhaust opening must be larger than 1.70 m^2 for the without-wind case and 0.49 m^2 for the with-wind case (Figure 6.4b).

7. Develop and apply a sufficient number of technical or non-technical design rules or constraints to transform the *under-determined* design problem defined by each loop equation into a *determined* problem. For example, let us assume an operable exhaust terminal is available with a maximum opening of 0.50 m^2. Four of these terminals could be used to provide a maximum total opening of $A_g = 2.00$ m$^2 \geq 1.70$ m^2 for the without-wind case. Substituting this *design constraint* into the governing loop equation, we determine the inlet vent size for the without-wind case:

$$\left(\frac{0.02533}{c_e^{10}} + \frac{1.9874}{A_g^2} \right) = \left(\frac{0.02533}{c_e^{10}} + \frac{1.9874}{2^2} \right) = 0.69 \text{ Pa}$$

or

$$c_e = 0.82 \text{ m}^3/(\text{s} \cdot \text{Pa}^{0.1})$$

The self-regulating vent size parameter may be determined from vent manufactures' literature and, thereby, an appropriate vent (or set of vents) may be selected.

8. Develop an appropriate operational strategy to satisfy the ventilation rates for variations in design conditions (e.g. for the *with-wind* and *without-wind* cases). In this case it is reasonable to reduce the exhaust opening for the with-wind case while maintaining the same self-regulating inlet vent conditions. This operational strategy is actually used in the Inland Revenue Building where exhaust openings are adjusted daily for prevailing wind conditions. To determine the with-wind exhaust opening, we again simply substitute into the loop equation, now using $c_e = 0.82$ m$^3/(\text{s} \cdot \text{Pa}^{0.1})$:

$$\left(\frac{0.02533}{c_e^{10}} + \frac{1.9874}{A_g^2} \right) = \left(\frac{0.02533}{0.82^{10}} + \frac{1.9874}{A_g^2} \right) = (0.69 + 7.70) \text{ Pa}$$

obtaining

$$A_g = 0.49 \text{ m}^2$$

Thus, one feasible final design 'solution' would be realized if the total stack opening were designed to be adjustable from 0.49 to 2.0 m^2 for a self-regulating inlet vent with a characteristic size of $c_e = 0.82$ m$^3/(\text{s} \cdot \text{Pa}^{0.1})$. At this point, the designer may then turn to the task of sizing components for the rightmost loop at the third level (i.e. remembering to use the stack opening size just determined as the stack is shared by both third-level loops) and the lower two loops (Axley, 1999).

6.5 Natural ventilation strategies

The driving forces for natural ventilation may be used for different ventilation strategies: wind variation-induced single-sided ventilation, wind pressure-driven cross ventilation and buoyancy pressure-driven stack ventilation. When ventilation is needed for individual rooms, single-sided ventilation, the most localized of all natural ventilation strategies, may be the only choice available. Cross ventilation systems provide ventilation to a floor of a building and depend on building form and urban environment. Stack ventilation systems provide ventilation to the building as a whole and depend on building form and internal layout. Combinations of all these strategies exploit their individual advantages.

6.5.1 Wind variation-induced single-sided ventilation

For the uninitiated, natural ventilation means opening a window to let air flow into a room which is otherwise airtight (Figure 6.5a). The air flow through the opening is due to wind and buoyancy. The wind has a mean and a fluctuating component which may vary over the opening and produce a 'pumping effect.' When the indoor temperature is higher than outdoor, the buoyancy makes the cold air enter at the lower part and the hot air exit at the upper part of the opening. An empirical model of this complex phenomena is as follows (de Gidds and Phaff, 1982):

$$v_{eff} = (c_1 v_r^2 + c_2 H \cdot \Delta T + c_3)^{1/2} \tag{6.11}$$

where c_1 ($c_1 \approx 0.001$) is a dimensionless coefficient depending on window opening, c_2 and c_3 ($c_2 \approx 0.0035$, $c_3 = 0.01$) are buoyancy and wind constants, respectively, v_r (m/s) is the mean wind speed for the site, H (m) is the height of the opening and T (K) is the mean temperature difference between inside and outside.

The flow rate through the opening is:

$$Q = 0.5 A_w v_{eff} \tag{6.12}$$

where A_w is the effective area of the open window.

Recommendations for single-sided ventilation are a window area of 1/20th of the floor area, a height of about 1.5 m and a maximum room depth of 2.5 times the ceiling height (BRE, 1994).

Let us consider a typical office room with height b = 2.75 m, window height H = 1.5 m and window area = 1/20th of the floor area, A_w = A/20. The volume of this room would be $V = whl = 2.5b$. The flow rate through the opening would be $Q = 0.5Av_{eff}$. Expressing this flow in air changes per hour, $Q = ACH/3600V$, we obtain:

$$ACH = \frac{3600}{V} \cdot 0.5 A_w v_{eff} = \frac{3600}{2.5b} \cdot \frac{0.5}{20} \cdot v_{eff}$$

The dependence of ACH as a function of v_{eff} and ΔT is shown in Figure 6.5b. When the difference between indoor and outdoor temperature is low or when the wind velocity is low, the air flow rate is low. Single-sided ventilation is a solution that is not very effective for cooling by ventilation during warm weather periods.

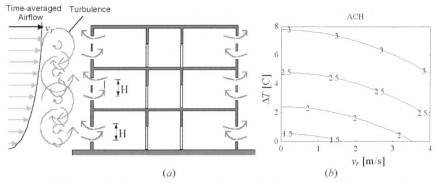

Figure 6.5 *(a) Single-sided wind-driven ventilation; (b) air changes per hour calculated for a room of 2.7 m height with windows of 1.5 m height and a window area of 1/20th of the floor area*

6.5.2 Wind-driven cross ventilation

Wind air flow over a building tends to induce positive (inward-acting) pressures on windward surfaces and negative (outward-acting) pressures on leeward surfaces, thereby creating a net pressure difference across the section of the building that drives cross ventilation air flows. Two-sided or cross ventilation takes place when air enters the building on one side, sweeps the indoor space and leaves the building on another side (Figure 6.6a).

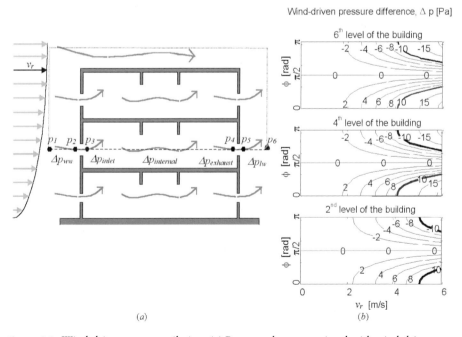

Figure 6.6 *Wind-driven cross ventilation. (a) Pressure drops associated with wind-driven cross ventilation; (b) wind-pressure differences for a rectangular, isolated building*

The positive windward pressure Δp_{ww} and the negative leeward pressure Δp_{lw} are, in fact, pressure differences from the ambient air pressure of the free-field air flow. While these pressure differences often vary rapidly with time (owing to turbulence in the wind air flow) and position (owing to the aerodynamic effects of building form), on average, they may be related to a reference time-averaged approach-wind velocity v_r:

$$p_{ww} = C_{p-ww}\left(\frac{\rho v_r^2}{2}\right); \quad p_{wl} = C_{p-lw}\left(\frac{\rho v_r^2}{2}\right)$$

where ρ is the density of the air, $\rho v_r^2/2$ is the kinetic energy per unit volume of the reference wind velocity and $C_{p-ww} > 0$, $C_{p-lw} < 0$ are the so-called wind pressure coefficients of the windward and leeward surface locations under consideration. The reference wind velocity is most commonly (but not always) taken as the time-averaged wind velocity at 10 m above the building height. The wind pressure difference between the facades is:

$$\Delta p_w = p_{ww} - p_{wl} = \left(C_{p-ww} - C_{p-lw}\right)\frac{\rho v_r^2}{2}$$

Considering, for example, the pressure changes along a given cross-ventilation air flow path in Figure 6.6a:

$$\Delta p_w = \Delta p_{inlet} + \Delta p_{interval} + \Delta p_{exhaust}$$

For typical design conditions, the reference wind velocity is around 4 m/s, windward wind pressure coefficients are typically around +0.5, leeward wind pressure coefficients –0.5 and the density of air approximately 1.2 kg/m³. Therefore, we may expect the driving wind pressure for cross-ventilation to be approximately 10 Pa:

$$\Delta p_w = \left(C_{p-ww} - C_{p-lw}\right)\frac{\rho U_{ref}^2}{2} \approx \left((+0.5)-(-0.5)\right)\frac{1.2\ \text{kg/m}^3\left(4\ \text{m/s}\right)^2}{2} = 9.6\ \text{Pa}$$

A 10 Pa driving pressure is small relative to typical fan-driven pressure differences that are of one or two orders of magnitude larger. Hence, to achieve similar ventilation rates, the resistance offered by the natural ventilation system will have to be small relative to ducted mechanical ventilation systems.

This simple natural ventilation scheme suffers from a critical shortcoming: it depends on wind direction and intensity. As wind directions change, so do the wind pressure coefficients. Consequently, the driving wind pressure may drop to low values even when windy conditions prevail, making the natural ventilation air flow rates drop. When wind speeds drop to low values, again the driving wind pressure will diminish and ventilation air flow will subside regardless of wind direction. For example, Figure 6.6b shows the wind pressure difference calculated for a six-storey building by using Equation (6.5). We can see that the estimated value for the pressure difference, $\Delta p \approx 10$ Pa, occurs for a restricted range of wind direction. The variability of wind-induced pressure demands special measures such as self-regulating vents for pressure reduction, wind catchers or a design that makes the building insensitive to wind variations (e.g. double facades). The variability of wind-induced pressure puts forward the 'zero-wind' design condition as a critical case, although some limited studies indicate 'zero-wind' conditions are not only unlikely at many locations but they may well be short-lived (Skaret *et al*, 1997; Deaves and Lines, 1999; Axley, 2000).

In spite of these shortcomings, wind-driven cross ventilation has been employed in some recently built non-residential buildings, although its use is uncommon. Examples include the machine shop wing of the Queen's Building of De Montfort University, Leicester, England, designed by Short Fort Associates architects and Max Fordham Associates environmental engineers, and a number of skyscrapers designed by architect Ken Yeang of TR Hamzah & Yeang Sdn Bhd, Malaysia.

Even within the time-averaged modelling assumptions, there are significant sources of uncertainty that should be kept in mind. Wind pressure coefficients, C_p, are seldom known with certainty – they vary from position to position over the building envelope, being sensitive to small details of form, they are altered significantly by the shelter offered by other buildings, they vary with wind direction and are affected by building porosity. Wind characteristics are generally known with certainty only for regional airports where detailed records are maintained. Consequently, evaluation of the reference wind speed and direction for a given site is always problematic and subject to error. Finally, empirical coefficients associated with flow resistance models introduce another source of uncertainty, although perhaps not as significant as that due to wind uncertainties.

6.5.3 Buoyancy-driven stack ventilation

Warm air within a building will tend to move up and flow out of upper level exhausts while cooler outdoor air will tend to flow in through lower inlets to replace it. For example, the pressure loop shown in Figure 6.7a is:

$$\rho_0 g \cdot \Delta z - \Delta p_{\text{inlet}} - \Delta p_{\text{internal}} - \rho_0 g \cdot \Delta z - \Delta p_{\text{exhaust}} = 0$$

The stack pressure, $p_s = (\rho_0 - \rho_i)g \cdot \Delta z$, equals the pressure losses:

$$\Delta p_s = \Delta p_{\text{inlet}} + \Delta p_{\text{internal}} + \Delta p_{\text{exhaust}}$$

The driving pressure stack varies with building height, h, and the temperature difference between indoor and outdoor:

$$\Delta p_s = (\rho_o - \rho_i)g \cdot \Delta z = \left(\frac{352.6}{T_o} - \frac{352.6}{T_i} \right) g \cdot \Delta z. \qquad (6.13)$$

During warm periods, as outdoor temperatures approach indoor air temperatures, the stack pressure differences for all but very tall multi-storey buildings may be expected to be small relative to typical wind-driven pressure differences. Figure 6.7b shows the dependence of stack pressure as a function of temperature difference and height given by Equation (6.13). For a three-storey building about 10 m high, the difference between indoor and outdoor temperatures should be about 23°C in order to obtain a pressure difference of approximately 10 Pa, typical for wind-driven pressure. For an eight-storey building, this temperature difference should be 10°C (Figure 6.7a). Furthermore, for higher floors, the stack pressure difference available to drive natural air flow will be proportionately smaller. For wintertime air quality control, when large

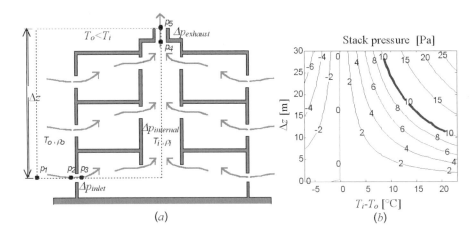

Figure 6.7 *Stack-pressure driven natural ventilation: (a) pressure drops associated with buoyancy-driven stack ventilation; (b) pressure stack variation as a function of temperature difference and building height*

indoor–outdoor temperature differences may be expected, buoyancy-driven stack ventilation may be expected to be effective although differences of air distribution with storey level must be accounted for by proper sizing of inlet vents. However, buoyancy-driven stack ventilation alone cannot be expected to be a very effective strategy for cooling. In practice, stack configurations have often achieved acceptable ventilation rates but the wind forces that also drive flow in stack ventilation systems complicate the system behaviour. Given that low wind conditions may be unlikely and short-lived at most locations, simple buoyancy-driven stack flow is not likely to occur often in practice. Therefore, combined wind- plus buoyancy-driven stack ventilation should be considered instead.

6.5.4 Combined wind- and buoyancy-driven ventilation

When properly designed, stack ventilation systems use both wind- and buoyancy-driven pressure differences. For example, let us consider a stack ventilation system under the combined influence of wind and buoyancy differences (Figure 6.8a). This system is similar to that illustrated in Figure 6.7a but with a stack terminal device added that can respond to the prevailing wind direction to maximise the negative pressure induced by the wind (e.g. operable louvers, rotating cowls).

A representative pressure loop, e.g. loop $p_1 - p_2 - p_3 - p_4 - p_5 - p_6 - p_1$, will now include both buoyancy-driven and wind-driven pressure differences that appear as a simple sum:

$$\Delta p_s + \Delta p_w = \Delta p_{inlet} + \Delta p_{internal} + \Delta p_{exhaust}$$

where

$$p_s = (\rho_o - \rho_i)g \cdot \Delta z$$

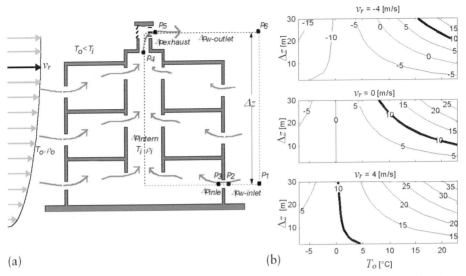

(a)   (b)

Figure 6.8 *Combined wind and buoyancy driven ventilation: (a) pressure drops; (b) total pressure as a function of wind velocity, temperature difference and building height*

and

$$\Delta p_w = \left(C_{p-inlet} - C_{p-exhaust}\right)\frac{\rho v_r^2}{2}$$

Pressure loop equations for each of the additional five ventilation loops of Figure 6.8a will assume the same general form, although the values of the various parameters will change. For the pressure loop shown in Figure 6.8a, both the inlet wind pressure coefficient $C_{p-inlet}$ and the exhaust wind pressure coefficient $C_{p-exhaust}$ are likely to be negative as both are on the leeward side of the building. Consequently, the wind-driven pressure difference will act to cause flow in the direction indicated only if the absolute value of the exhaust is greater than that of the inlet. For this reason, driving wind pressure differences for the leeward rooms of stack ventilation systems tend to be smaller than those of the windward rooms. As a result, unless inlet vents are designed accordingly, ventilation rates may be expected to be lower in these rooms and may actually reverse under certain conditions. Figure 6.8b shows the pressure difference obtained by superposing the wind-induced pressure from Figure 6.6b and stack pressure from Figure 6.7b. We can see that when stack ventilation is assisted by wind, the pressure difference may be easily achieved. Self-regulating vents can serve to maintain design-level ventilation rates and thereby mitigate this problem but can not inhibit flow reversals or provide flow when the net driving pressure $\Delta p_s + \Delta p_w$ drops to zero or becomes negative. The stack pressure contribution Δp_s will act to compensate for low or reverse wind pressures but again this contribution must be expected to be smaller for the upper floors of the building. Consequently, upper leeward rooms tend to experience the lowest driving pressures and thus lower ventilation rates (Figure 6.8b).

Ventilation stacks that extend above nearby roofs, especially when equipped with properly designed stack terminal devices, tend to create negative (suction) pressures that are relatively independent of wind direction. Thus, stack systems serve to overcome the major limitation of simple cross-ventilation systems identified above while providing similar air flows in individual rooms of the building. As a result of these advantages, stack ventilation systems – perhaps most often using a central *slot* atrium as a shared stack – have become the most popular natural ventilation system used in commercial buildings in recent years and a number of manufacturers have developed specialized components to serve these systems.

6.5.5 Combinations of fundamental strategies

Most often, the three basic strategies (single-sided, cross and buoyancy-driven ventilation) are used concurrently in single buildings to handle a variety of ventilation needs, as illustrated in Figure 6.9. The most notable example of such an approach is found in the Queen's Building of De Montfort University in Leicester, England (Figure 6.10), a building that has proven to be the most influential of the first generation of the newer naturally ventilated buildings.

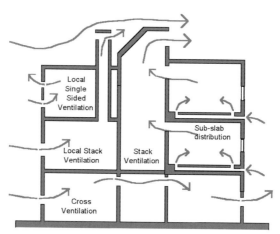

Figure 6.9 *Mixed natural ventilation strategies in a single building to satisfy local and global ventilation needs*

In other instances, the elaboration resides in the details of inlet, exhaust and distribution. One common approach involves the use of in-slab or access-floor distribution of fresh air to provide greater control of air distribution across the building section and to temper incoming air to prevent cold drafts (Figure 6.9). This type of fresh air distribution is similar to displacement ventilation, most commonly implemented mechanically and offers similar benefits, i.e. use of thermal plumes generated by equipment and occupants to assist the air flow and improved air quality in the occupied zone of rooms.

Figure 6.10 *The Queen's Building of De Montfort University, Leicester, England*

6.5.6 Solar-assisted ventilation

There is usually little difficulty in providing the required air flow rate to a building when wind assists the stack effect (Figure 6.8b). However, since wind speed is reduced in an urban environment, natural ventilation systems in urban areas are usually designed based on buoyancy-driven flow. When buoyancy pressure resulting from the difference between the internal and the external temperatures is not sufficient, then solar-induced ventilation can be an alternative. The principle is to increase the stack pressure by heating the air in the ventilation stack resulting in a greater temperature difference than in conventional systems.

The pressure losses for a solar collector are:

$$\Delta p_s = \Delta p_i + \Delta p_d + \Delta p_e \qquad (6.14)$$

where Δp_i, Δp_d and Δp_e are the inlet, distributed and exit pressure losses, respectively. Depending on the position of the control damper, Δp_i and Δp_e include the control damper pressure losses. The stack pressure is:

$$\Delta p_s = \rho_0 T_0 [1/T_e - 1/T_i] g \Delta z \qquad (6.15)$$

where T_i is the inlet air temperature of the collector, usually equal to the indoor temperature, and T_e is the exit temperature of the collector (Awbi, 1998):

$$T_e = A/B + (T_i - A/B) \exp[-BwH / (\rho_e c_p Q)] \qquad (6.16)$$

with $A = h_1 T_{w1} + h_2 T_{w2}$ and $B = h_1 + h_2$, where h_1 and h_2 (W/m² K) are surface heat transfer coefficients for internal surfaces of the collector, T_{w1} and T_{w2} (°C) are surface temperatures of internal surfaces of the collector, w (m) is the collector width, H (m) is the height between inlet and outlet openings, ρ_e (kg/m³) is the air density at exit, c_p [J/(kg K)] is the specific heat of air and Q (m³/s) is the volumetric air flow rate.

The principle of the solar collector may be used for different types of devices: Trombe walls, double facades, solar chimneys or solar roofs. A Trombe wall is a wall of moderate thickness covered by a pane of glass separated by the wall by a gap of 50–100 mm. It may be used for ventilation or for heating (Figure 6.11). A solar chimney is a chimney with a gap of about 200 mm placed on the South or South-west facade of the building. Solar roofs are used when the solar altitude is large. In this case, a roof has a larger surface area for collecting the solar radiation than a vertical wall or chimney.

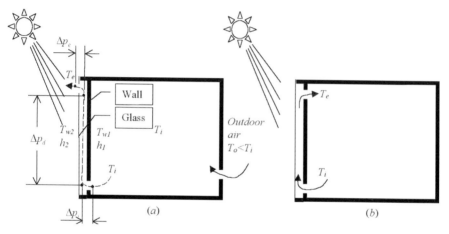

Figure 6.11 *Solar collector used as (a) ventilator and (b) heater*

6.6 Natural ventilation strategies for urban environment

The use of natural ventilation in urban environment should take into account the lower wind velocity but also the noise and pollution. The ventilation systems cannot rely on low-level inlets since outdoor air at street levels may be contaminated and inlets will be shielded from winds.

6.6.1 Balanced stack ventilation

A number of ancient Middle Eastern strategies using both roof level inlets and exhausts – including the traditional Iranian wind towers or *bagdir* and the Arabian and Eastern Asian wind catchers or *malkaf* – are being reconsidered for broader application and technical refinement.

In these *balanced* stack ventilation schemes, air is supplied in a cold stack (i.e. with air temperatures maintained close to outdoor conditions through proper insulation of the stack) and exhausted through a warm stack (Figure 6.12).

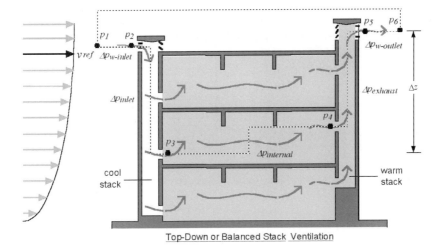

Top-Down or Balanced Stack Ventilation

Figure 6.12 *Top-down or balanced stack natural ventilation systems use high-level supply inlets to access less contaminated air and to place both inlet and outlets in higher wind velocity exposures*

Let us consider, for example, the loop through the second level of Figure 6.12. The equation for this pressure loop will be similar in form to the case of combined wind- and buoyancy-driven ventilation:

$$\Delta p_s + \Delta p_w = \Delta p_{inlet} + \Delta p_{internal} + \Delta p_{exhaust}$$

The stack pressure is determined by the indoor–outdoor air density difference and the height difference from the stack exhaust and the floor level inlet locations $\Delta p_s = (\rho_o - \rho_i)g\Delta z$, if air temperatures within the cold stack can be maintained close to outdoor levels. The air flow through each floor level will, therefore, be identical with that expected in the simpler single stack scheme if the air flow resistance of the supply stack (and its inlet and outlet devices) is similar to that provided by the air inlet devices of Figure 6.8. The driving wind pressure is determined by the difference between inlet and exhaust wind pressure coefficients and the kinetic energy content of the approach wind velocity, $\Delta p_w = (C_{p-inlet} - C_{p-exhaust})\, \rho v_{ref}^2 / 2$. However, in this case, the high location of the inlet ensures a higher inlet wind pressure and insensitivity to wind direction. This, combined with the potential of a wind direction-insensitive exhaust stack, makes this scheme particularly attractive for urban environments. Balanced stack systems have been commercially available in the UK for, apparently, over a century (Axley, 2001), although these commercially available systems have, until recently, been designed to serve single rooms rather than whole buildings. The *Windcatcher* natural ventilation systems distributed by Monodraught Limited in the UK (Figure 6.13) offer air change rates as high as five air changes per hour under relatively low wind conditions (3 m/s) measured 10 m above the building (Monodraught, 1997, 2002). These systems may also be supplied with co-axial fans to provide mechanical assistance during extreme weather conditions.

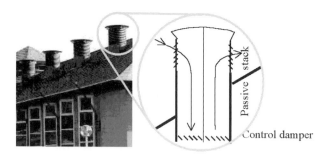

Passive stack

Control damper

Figure 6.13 Windcatcher *for natural ventilation systems (Monodraught Limited, reproduced with approval)*

In cold conditions, it is possible to achieve ventilation air heat recovery with *top-down* schemes by using co-axial supply.

6.6.2 Passive evaporative cooling

An improvement to the *balanced stack* ventilation system, also based on ancient Middle Eastern and Eastern Asian solutions, consists in adding evaporative cooling to the supply stack. Traditionally, evaporative cooling was achieved through water-filled porous pots within the supply air stream or the use of a pool of water at the base of the supply stack (Santamouris and Asimakopoulos, 1996; Allard, 1998). In more recent developments, water sprayed high into the supply air stream cools the air stream and increases the supply air density, thereby augmenting the buoyancy-induced pressure differences that drive air flow (Bowman *et al*, 2000).

The loop analysis of this so-called *passive downdraught evaporative cooling* scheme is similar to that of the *balanced stack* scheme but now the buoyancy effects of the increased moisture content must be accounted for. Consider the representative diagram of such a system shown in Figure 6.14. Two height differences must now be distinguished: z_a, the height above the room inlet location of the moist air column in the supply stack, and z_b, the height of the exhaust above this moist column.

The air density in the moist air supply column, ρ_s, will approach the saturation density corresponding to the outdoor air wet bulb temperature – more specifically, experiments indicate that these supply air conditions will be within 2°C of the wet bulb temperature. Hence the loop equation describing the (time-averaged) ventilation air flow in this system becomes:

$$(\Delta p_{inlet} + \Delta p_{internal} + \Delta p_{exhaust}) = \Delta p_s + \Delta p_t$$

where

$$\Delta p_s = \left[\rho_o z_b + \rho_s z_a - \rho_i(z_a + z_b)\right]g$$

and

$$\Delta p_w = \left(C_{p-inlet} - C_{p-exhaust}\right)\frac{\rho v_r^2}{2}$$

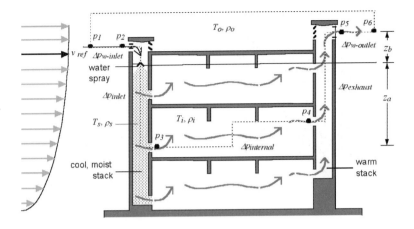

Figure 6.14 *Passive downdraught evaporative cooling stack ventilation*

For a quantitative measure of the impact of this strategy, let us consider a case similar to that discussed above for wind- and buoyancy-induced natural ventilation, but with a cool moist column height that equals the stack height of 10 m (i.e. $z_a \approx 0$ m and $z_b \approx 10$ m). If the outdoor air having a temperature of 25°C and a relative humidity (RH) of 20% (i.e. with a density of approximately 1.18 kg/m^3) is evaporatively cooled to within 2°C of its wet bulb temperature (12.5°C), its dry bulb temperature will drop to 14.5°C and its density will increase to approximately 1.21 kg/m^3 and RH to 77%. If the internal conditions are kept just within the thermal comfort zone for these outdoor conditions (i.e. 28°C and 60% RH), using an appropriate ventilation flow rate given internal gains, then the internal air density will be approximately 1.15 kg/m^3. Consequently, the buoyancy pressure difference that will result will be:

$$\Delta p_s = \left(1.18 \frac{\text{kg}}{\text{m}^3}(0\text{ m}) + 1.21 \frac{\text{kg}}{\text{m}^3}(10\text{ m}) - 1.15 \frac{\text{kg}}{\text{m}^3}(0 + 10\text{ m})\right)9.8 \frac{\text{m}}{\text{s}^2} = 6.4 \text{ Pa}$$

Without the evaporative cooling (i.e. with $\Delta z_a \approx 10$ m and $\Delta z_b \approx 0$ m):

$$\Delta p_s = \left(1.18 \frac{\text{kg}}{\text{m}^3}(10\text{ m}) + 1.21 \frac{\text{kg}}{\text{m}^3}(0\text{ m}) - 1.15 \frac{\text{kg}}{\text{m}^3}(10 + 0\text{ m})\right)9.8 \frac{\text{m}}{\text{s}^2} = 2.9 \text{ Pa}$$

Hence, in this representative example, evaporative cooling more than doubles the buoyancy pressure difference while at the same time providing adiabatic cooling.

6.6.3 Double-skin facade

A double-skin facade construction consists of a normal concrete or glass wall combined with a glass structure outside the actual wall. Double-skin facades offer several advantages. They can act as buffer zones between internal and external conditions, reducing heat loss in winter and heat gain in summer. In combination with ventilation of the space between the two facades, the passive thermal effects can be used to best advantage. Natural ventilation can be drawn from the buffer zone into the building by opening windows in the inner facade. The stack effect of thermal air currents in tall buildings offers advantages over lower buildings. This eliminates potential security and safety problems caused by having opening windows and also wind pressure differentials around the building. Double facades can be used for solar-assisted stack ventilation or balanced stack ventilation.

6.7 Conclusion

Recent advances in natural ventilation techniques contribute to the development of new ecological buildings. The building envelope is considered now as an active element that contributes to achieving thermal comfort by taking advantage of local climate. Since the building envelope interacts with the indoor environment, both should be controlled by the same building energy management system. The symbiosis of building envelope and building equipment (heating, ventilating, air conditioning, lighting and security) forms the basis for intelligent buildings.

6.8 References

Allard, F (ed.), 1998, *Natural Ventilation in Buildings. A Design Handbook*, London, James & James.

ASHRAE, 1993, *ASHRAE Handbook, Fundamentals*, SI Edition, Atlanta, GA, ASHRAE.

ASHRAE, 1999, *Ventilation for Acceptable Indoor Air Quality*, ASHRAE Standard 62–99, Atlanta, GA, ASHRAE.

Awbi, H, 1998, 'Ventilation', in *Renewable and Sustainable Energy Reviews*, 2, 157–188.

Axley, J W, 1999, 'Natural ventilation design using loop equations', in *Indoor Air 99*, Edinburgh, ISIAQ and AIVC, CRC Ltd, London, UK.

Axley, J W, 2000, *AIVC TechNote 54: Residential Passive Ventilation Systems: Evaluation and Design*, Coventry, AIVC.

Axley, J W, 2001, *Application of Natural Ventilation for US Commercial Buildings*, Report GCR-01–820, Washington, DC, NIST.

Bowman, N T, Eppel, H, Lomas, K J, Robinson, D and Cook, M J, 2000, 'Passive downdraught evaporative cooling', in *Indoor + Built Environment*, 9(5), 284–290.

Brager, G and de Dear, R, 1998, 'Thermal adaptation in the built environment: a literature review', in *Energy and Buildings*, 27, 83–96.

Braham, G D, 2000, 'Comparative performance of U.K. fabric energy storage systems', in *ASHRAE Transactions*, 106(Part 1), 811–818.

BRE, 1994, *Natural Ventilation in Non-domestic Buildings*, BRE Digest 399, Garston, Building Research Establishment.

de Gidds, W and Phaff, H, 1982, 'Ventilation rates and energy consumption due to open windows – a brief overview of research in the Netherlands', in *Air Infiltration Review*, 4, 4–5.

Deaves, D M and Lines, I G, 1999, 'On persistence of low speed conditions', in *Air Infiltration Review*, 20(1), 6–8.

Irving, S and Uys, E, 1997, *CIBSE Applications Manual: Natural Ventilation in Non-domestic Buildings*, London, CIBSE.

Monodraught, 1997, 'Monodraught Windcatcher – passive stack ventilation systems', The Builder Group plc, in *Building Services Journal*, OPUS '98, 144–145.

Monodraught, 2002, *Natural Ventilation Systems*, http: //www.monodraught.co.uk.

Orme, M, Liddament, M W and Wilson, A, 1998, *Numerical Data for Air Infiltration and Natural Ventilation Calculations*, Coventry, AIVC.

Petherbridge, P, Millbank, N O and Harrington-Lynn, J, 1988, *Environmental Design Manual: Summer Conditions in Naturally Ventilated Offices*, Garston, Building Research Establishment.

Santamouris, M and Asimakopoulos, D (eds), 1996, *Passive Cooling of Buildings*, London, James & James.

Skaret, E, Blom, P and Brunsell, J T, 1997, 'Energy recovery possibilities in natural ventilation of office buildings', in *18th AIVC Conference – Ventilation and Cooling, Athens, Greece*, AIVC, 311–321.

Walker, I S and Wilson, D J, 1994, 'Practical methods for improving estimates of natural ventilation rates', in *15th AIVC Conference – The Role of Ventilation, Buxton, UK, 27–30 September*, vol. 2, 517–526.

7 Cooling by natural sinks

Servando Álvarez and José L. Molina

Department of Thermal Energy Engineering, AICIA – University of Seville, Seville, Spain
Tel: +34 9544 87252; fax: + 34 9544 63153; e-mail: SAD@tmt.us.es; JLMolina@tmt.us.es

7.1 Introduction

Natural cooling is the dissipation of heat from buildings to a lower temperature environmental sink such as the air, water, sky or ground, using systems that require negligible electric or fossil fuel energy. These are the traditional cooling systems that dominated architectural design in hot climates prior to the availability of low-cost electricity.

Natural cooling is termed *passive* whenever the processes used do not require the expenditure of any non-renewable energy and *hybrid* when motor-driven fans or pumps are used.

The classification of natural cooling techniques (NCT) can be made according to different criteria: nature of the sink, heat and mass transfer phenomena involved, storage period or material, type of application, etc. We shall distinguish between

- direct systems when the heat sink promotes a direct cooling action on the building structure and/or the interior air

- indirect systems when the system first cools a working fluid (air or water), which is then discharged (with or without intermediate storage to the building).

This chapter concentrates on hybrid indirect cooling systems: to be precise, ground cooling using buried pipes, direct and indirect evaporative systems (including an application of a passive downdraft evaporative cooling (PDEC) system to a building) and radiative cooling through lightweight radiators. It discusses the concepts, the physical principles, the applicability in different climates, the more relevant technologies and the ways to improve its efficiency. It also includes direct cooling systems such as earth sheltering (ground cooling) and roof solutions (combination of evaporative and radiative cooling).

7.2 Conventional cooling and cooling based on environmental sinks

The common feature among the indirect NCT is the availability of a medium at a temperature below the air temperature that should be maintained in the building.

As is explained later, the accessibility to the heat sinks is very variable for the different techniques, and also the ability of the sinks to evacuate the heat transferred from the working fluid. These two effects are characterized in terms of a fictitious temperature called the effective environmental temperature (Álvarez *et al*, 1997), defined as the actual temperature to which the heat is transferred.

The performance of a certain application depends on the following:

1. The climate, which provides the availability of the heat sink in terms of its thermal level and its variability throughout the year and on a daily basis.

2. The cooling requirements of the building (absolute values and load profiles). The combination of 1 and 2 gives the extent to which the requirements can be covered by the cooling technique.

3. The efficiency of the technology used to transfer heat from the working fluid to the environmental sink.

The conceptual difference between conventional cooling and cooling based on environmental sinks is as follows: in conventional systems the air is usually cooled by exchanging energy with cool water (produced in the chiller). The heat goes to a refrigerant and is finally transferred to the environment thanks to a compressor (Figure 7.1). The environmental sink promotes a cooling effect over the intermediate working fluid (generally air or water), which is then used (with or without storage) to cool the interior air of the building (Figure 7.2).

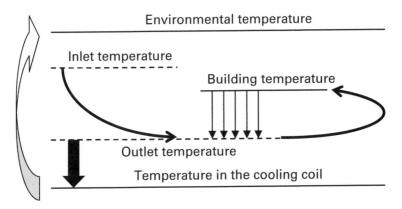

Figure 7.1 *Conventional cooling*

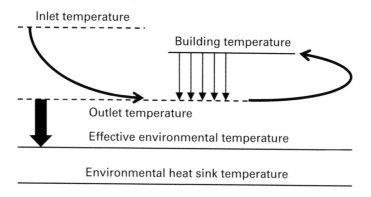

Figure 7.2 *Cooling based on environmental sink*

The techniques considered in detail are as follows (Table 7.1):

● ground cooling by means of ground to air heat exchangers (buried pipes)

● evaporative cooling by using evaporative coolers of different types

● radiative cooling by means of lightweight night sky radiators + storage.

Systems using combinations in series or in parallel of the cooling media are possible and in some cases are recommended.

Table 7.1 *Elements of environmentally driven cooling processes*

	Cool medium (sink)	Effective environmental	Dissipator	Working fluid	Hot medium
Ground cooling	Deep ground temperature	Ground temperature at a certain depth	Pipe temperature	Ambient air	Building Temperature
Radiative cooling	Sky temperature	Stagnation temperature	Radiator temperature	Intermediate fluid	Storage temperature
Evaporative Direct cooling	Wet bulb temperature	Wet bulb temperature	Wet bulb temperature	Ambient air	Building Temperature
Indirect	Wet bulb temperature	Wet bulb temperature	Plate heat-exchanger	Ambient air	Building Temperature
Regenerative	Dew-point temperature	Dew-point temperature	Plate heat-exchanger	Ambient air	Building Temperature

The electricity consumption (in fans and/or pumps) linked to the use of NCT is very low compared with that required for conventional cooling systems (in compressor, fans and/or pumps).

A significant difference between conventional cooling and the use of NCT, from the practical point of view, is that the temperature of the water in the cooling coil is considerably lower than the effective environmental temperature. This can have three serious drawbacks for the NCT:

1. A lower temperature drop is achieved in the working fluid. To cover the same cooling requirements, the NCT must circulate higher mass flow rates and use larger heat exchangers.

2. In some periods (the hottest days), the cooling produced will not be sufficient to cover 100% of the cooling requirements. Therefore, an auxiliary system has to be operated to provide the complement.

3. Even worse, it can happen that at or near the peak cooling period, the NCT cannot be operated at all, because the outlet temperature of the working fluid is above the indoor temperature. During these periods, the cooling requirements have to be covered totally by the auxiliary equipment. This fact implies that the size of the auxiliary conventional system will be the same as without using the NCT.

Case 3 can be avoided in radiative cooling applications if a careful control strategy is applied. For ground and evaporative cooling, situation 3 can limit their application considerably. Having the same (or higher) initial costs as the conventional system, only a significant reduction in the running costs will make clear the feasibility of the use of the NCT from a cost–benefit point of view. Higher running costs are linked to non-residential buildings, so that for residential buildings the NCT will be feasible if no auxiliary cooling is required.

7.3 Ground cooling

7.3.1 The cool medium

The undisturbed underground earth temperature at a depth of several metres is almost constant and close to the average annual air temperature. Therefore, in summer, it is always below the daytime air temperature. The patterns of soil temperature variations with depth and time can be determined from the solution of the thermal field in a semi-infinite solid under periodic boundary conditions at the surface. This kind of analysis reveals that the soil temperature swings are damped and the dates of maximum and minimum temperatures are delayed with increasing depth below the surface.

Figure 7.3 shows an example of the variation of the thermal field with depth during six typical days in January, March, May, July, September and November. The amplitude damping can be clearly seen, and also how, for instance, the daily fluctuations are damped out at a depth of 1 m while the annual wave will penetrate up to 14 m.

This constant temperature for a given location and for a reference ground cover type will hereafter be referred to as deep ground temperature and provides the temperature of the cool medium for ground cooling applications.

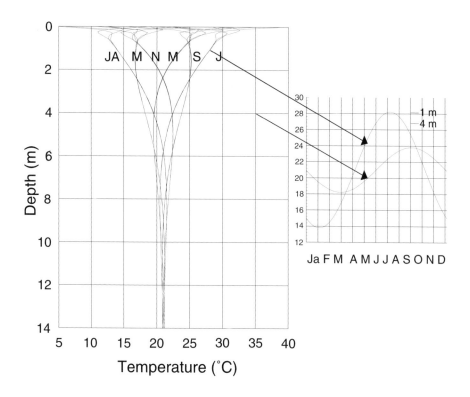

Figure 7.3 *Temperature field in the ground*

7.3.2 Effective environmental temperature

The effective environmental temperature will differ from the deep ground temperature if pipes are placed at a different depth (which is the normal situation) and/or if the ground surface is treated (which is highly recommendable, as we shall see later).

The close-up in Figure 7.3 shows the temperature wave at two different depths, 1 and 4 m. The phase shift moves from several days at 1 m depth to more than 2 months at 4 m depth. For the locality in this study (Seville, Spain), this figure reveals that the layer of soil at 4 m depth is a medium which provides in summer a suitable temperature drop between ambient temperatures in the central hours (typically above 34°C) and the ground temperatures (ranging from 20 to 22°C).

One of the most compelling aspects of ground cooling is the opportunity for manipulating ground temperature. The ground temperature can be reduced by modifying the terms of the heat balance at the surface with actions such as shading, increasing reflectivity or dissipation of surface heat by evaporation (Cook, 1989).

A practical implication of the surface treatments is that they allow us to obtain the same soil temperature at a lower depth. It must be pointed out that the efficiency of a surface treatment depends not only on the intensity of such treatment but also on the size of the area to be treated (Álvarez, 1993). The influence of the local treatment is only significant in the first few metres. Hence, when an intensive surface treatment must be limited in size, the pipes should be installed near the surface.

7.3.3 System description and performance

The concept of a ground to air heat exchanger involves the use of a metallic, PVC or concrete ducts buried at a certain depth. Outdoor warm air blown by a fan passes through the underground ducts and is delivered into the building. In this way, the system provides air which is cooler and in humid regions also dryer than the ambient air. If 100% fresh air is not required, the ducts can use also indoor air. The length of the ducts varies typically between 10 and 40 m, and the diameters are between 10 and 30 cm (Mihalakaku *et al*, 1992). To ensure the required air flow rate, arrays of ducts can be placed in parallel at the same or different depths. Either air can be circulated using the same fan for all ducts or each duct or group of ducts is equipped with a separate fan which operates under a certain control strategy.

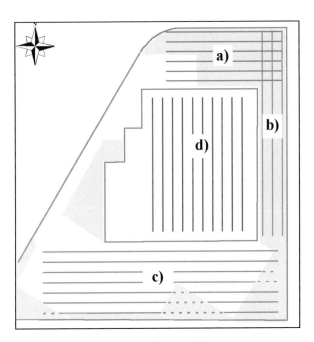

Figure 7.4 *Four different scenarios for a buried duct installation (Maldonado and Coronel, 1996). Option (d) could also be considered if the building was planned to work with buried ducts from the beginning*

Case	No. of ducts	Length (m)	Overall efficiency
(a)	6	12	0.24
(b)	3	20	0.25
(c)	7	25	0.32
(d)	10	15	0.38

For the evaluation of the heat exchange process that takes place in buried pipes, the effect of thermal saturation of the ground surrounding the pipe must be carefully considered. This effect occurs owing to the low conductivity of the soil (due basically to the air occluded), which makes impossible the continuous dissipation of the heat transferred from the pipe. Consequently, the ground surrounding the pipe becomes hotter after a short period of continuous operation and the efficiency decreases.

One of the ways to counteract this effect is to increase the conductivity of the soil by increasing its water content. To increase the performance, the soil around the ducts should be kept as moist as is practical, if necessary by watering it with perforated water pipes around the air ducts.

The building was simulated with an installed buried duct system plus an auxiliary conventional cooling system, for different overall efficiencies of the buried ducts. The energy savings obtained with the natural cooling technique with an overall efficiency of 0.32 cover almost 72% of the cooling needs of the building.

7.3.4 Innovative design options

Taking into account the two strategies previously mentioned, Figure 7.5a and b show some cost-effective and energy-efficient designs which have been proposed and implemented in practice (Álvarez *et al*, 1992). Both are based in the placement of the ducts

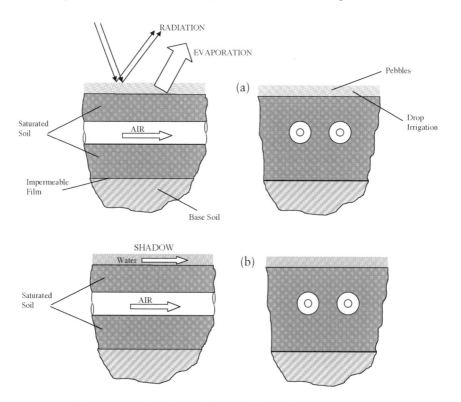

Figure 7.5 *Different practical and cost-effective solutions for ground cooling*

near an intensively locally treated surface. In the solution of Figure 7.5a, the phenomenon responsible for the low temperature is the evaporation cooling at the irrigated surface underneath the pebbles. In the solution of Figure 7.5b the water (preferably shaded) removes the heat from the soil.

7.4 Evaporative cooling

7.4.1 The cold medium

When water is brought into contact with non-saturated hot air, a simultaneous heat and mass transfer process takes place. On the one hand, the temperature difference between the air and the water gives rise to a net heat transfer between them. On the other hand, the concentration gradient of water vapour between the water surface and the non-saturated air induces the evaporation of the water, which requires a certain energy for the phase change. In relation to the thermal level of the water, these two phenomena have opposing effects: the heat transfer tends to increase the water temperature whereas the latent energy absorbed by the evaporated water cools the water. The result is an equilibrium temperature called wet bulb temperature.

Once the water has reached the wet bulb temperature, the latent heat of evaporation must come from the air and consequently its temperature decreases.

In summary, in evaporative cooling processes we first cool the water and then the water cools the air. The cold medium is the water at the wet bulb temperature and the driven force is the temperature difference between the air and the water. For a given pressure, the wet bulb temperature depends on the air temperature and the humidity content of the air. As an example, for typical summer conditions in Seville (38°C, 30% relative humidity), the wet bulb temperature is 23.5°C.

7.4.2 System description and performance

The simplest evaporative cooling system consists of an air supply duct incorporating a water spray system or a wetted porous pad. In such a system, the adiabatic process described below takes place, resulting in cool air with about 80% relative humidity that is blown through the rooms to be cooled at velocities that create indoor circulating rates well above the rates caused by a conventional refrigerated supply air. This system is called a *direct evaporative system* and its use is recommended in very low-humidity areas.

The standard evaporative cooler is made from cellulose. Its thickness varies typically between 5 and 10 cm. The cell size varies between 1 and 2 cm.

In applications where an increase in the humidity ratio of the air is not acceptable, *indirect evaporative systems* can be employed (see Figure 7.6). In these systems a stream of outdoor air (primary air) is cooled without gaining humidity by transferring heat to an evaporative cooled stream (secondary air). Most modern indirect coolers use plate-type heat exchangers. The primary air is drawn through narrow parallel spaces inside multiple thin plates that are externally wet and subjected to the secondary air flow. Plastics are ideal materials as far as cost, weight and corrosion resistance are concerned.

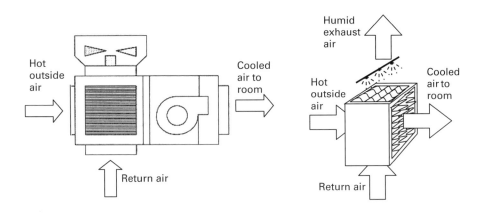

Figure 7.6 *Indirect evaporative system*

The efficiency of exchange can be improved by using, for instance, parallel plates with protrusions and adequate ratios of the air flow rates.

The psychrometric chart in Figure 7.7 shows the conditions of the ambient air (E0), the outlet conditions of air which is cooled by the direct evaporative cooling system (E1) and the outlet conditions of air which cooled by the indirect evaporative cooling system (E2).

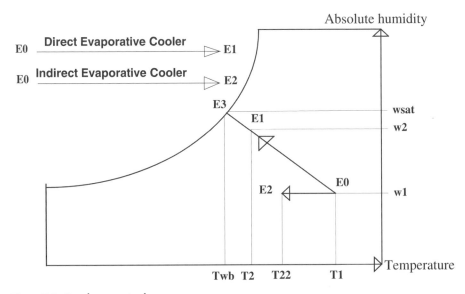

Figure 7.7 *Psychrometric chart*

7.4.3 Innovative design options

The applicability of evaporative systems in regions other than arid is closely linked to the use of these systems in combination with other techniques or strategies. An innovation consists of replacing the wetted pads with rows of atomizers (nozzles which produce an artificial fog by injecting water at high pressure through minute orifices). This possibility produces much better regulation of the system, a significant reduction of the pressure losses and a smaller size of the equipment. The location of the micronizers in a tower gives rise to a natural downdraught effect that eliminates the fan and updates the old Middle East tradition of cooling towers as cited, for instance, by Bahadori (1978). An application of such system called PDEC is presented in Figure 7.8.

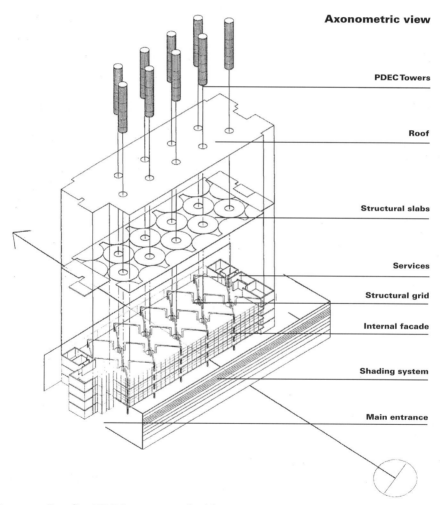

Figure 7.8 *Coupling PDEC towers to a building*

The tower is composed of the 'body', which crosses all the floors, and the 'head', which rises above the floor.

The head acts as the air inlet for PDEC and as a light catcher and diffuser. It contains a ring of micronizers and the evaporative zone (4.2 m high). The air opening is designed in order to control the wind effect and avoid turbulence inside the tower.

The body distributes air and light to the offices. It is a glazed cylinder of 3 m diameter with circular openings (air inlets) close to the ceiling at each floor.

The optimization of the tower design involved various connected issues:

● height of the head

● shape, size and position of the body–building connections (inlets)

● shape, size and position of the building–outdoor connections (outlets)

● layout of the towers in the building plan.

The office building is designed for an industrial owner occupier and the building, situated in Catania (Sicily), has a floor area is of 5600 m².

The core of the building is formed by three floors (each 60 × 27 m) where the evaporative cooling is applied. The role of the towers is central so the geometry of the building is generated by these elements.

The PDEC tower creates a modular unit providing structure, lighting, ventilation and cooling.

An open-plan distribution is used, with the permanent working desks along the facade and the more flexible ones on the central axis. The pillars are situated around the tower and leave the plan completely free from any vertical support. (Figure 7.9).

The facade consists of a double layer. The internal one is a glazed facade with aluminium mullions with openings for the PDEC outlet. The external layer is composed of a series of light stone bricks, that provide shading to the internal layer. The bricks are juxtaposed on horizontal lines, creating a texture with variable density, more dense on the top floors and less dense on the lower floor, to equilibrate the natural lighting provided by the towers.

The water droplets in the tower evaporate, taking energy from the surrounding air, which in turn becomes cooler. The air in the tower is then heavier than the indoor air of the offices. This creates the downdraught effect. Different inlets and outlets are required in order to equalize the air flow rate of the three floors (Figure 7.10).

The towers were sized so as to meet a building cooling requirement of 31 W/m² (about 65% of the peak cooling load), which occurs with an outdoor air temperature of about 29.5°C (see Table 7.2).

Table 7.2 *Indoor conditions in the three floors when the outdoor temperature is 29.5°C and the load is 31 W/m²*

	1st floor	2nd floor	3rd floor
Horizontal temperature difference (°C)	2.00	1.50	1.00
Vertical temperature gradient (°C)	0.16	0.35	0.42
Maximum air velocity (m/s)	0.21	0.11	0.04
Average temperature (°C)	26.10	26.40	26.60

Figure 7.9 *Interior view of the building with PDEC towers*

The indoor conditions achieved in terms of average temperature, temperature gradients and air velocity are totally comparable to those prescribed for conventional HVAC systems.

When the outdoor temperature is higher than the design, the tower is not, in general, able to cover the cooling requirements of the building. A conventional system provides the extra cooling required to maintain the building at the prescribed indoor temperature.

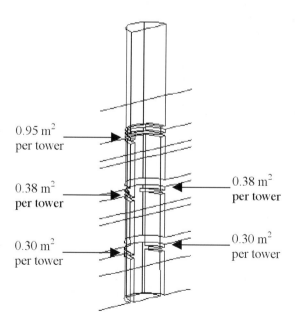

0.95 m^2 per tower

0.38 m^2 per tower

0.38 m^2 per tower

0.30 m^2 per tower

0.30 m^2 per tower

Figure 7.10 *Opening areas per floor*

The PDEC system only operates when the supply air temperature is at least 2°C below the indoor temperature. In such cases, when the supply relative humidity is larger than a prescribed value, the control modulates the number of micronizers so that this maximum is achieved.

A second modulation of the number of micronizers in operation appears when the outdoor air temperatures (and consequently the load) are lower than the design value.

Even if the load is zero, the PDEC system operates so as to provide the ventilation needs of the building and an eventual night cooling effect.

The seasonal results, assuming that the maximum supply relative humidity is of 75%, are as follows:

energy saving: 50%
working hours (PDEC only):   42%
working hours (auxiliary only):   29%
working hours (both):   31%.

The PDEC system covers in all cases 100% of the ventilation needs during the cooling period. The water consumption required for the evaporative cooling is less than 10 litres/day per occupant. The percentage of the cooling requirements covered by the PDEC system would obviously be greater for a dryer location, taking into account the severe humidity restrictions imposed.

The architectural design of the towers and the building was performed by M. Cucinella of MCA in the frame of the EU DGXII JOR3CT950078 PDEC project.

Figure 7.11 shows a bird's eye view of velocity contours on first floor. The first floor is the worst situation, with higher velocities, and there it can be seen which zones are

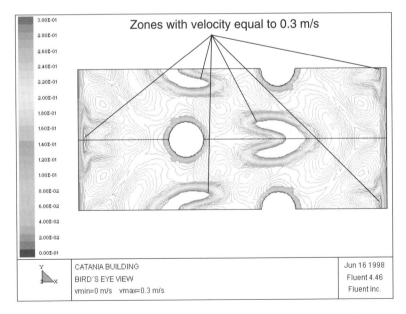

Figure 7.11 *A bird's eye view of velocity contours on first floor*

going to be 'uncomfortable' in the sense of velocities close to 0.4 m/s. The diagram indicates zones with velocity equal to 0.3 m/s. Inside these zones the velocity is higher than this value and they should be kept free in order not to receive the cold jet directly.

If no control is provided, the effect of the towers on the building performance shows a significant reduction of the indoor air temperature compared with the outdoor air temperature (Figure 7.12).

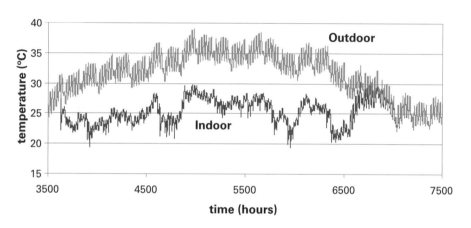

Figure 7.12 *Indoor and outdoor temperatures where there is no humidity control*

7.5 Radiative cooling

7.5.1 The cold medium

The cold upper atmosphere and outer space represent the ultimate cool medium for radiative cooling and the origin of all the other heat sinks. However, the elements at the ground surface do not exchange radiant energy directly with space because of the existence of the atmosphere, which acts as a barrier for that exchange. The effect of the barrier is due to the presence of certain substances in the atmosphere, mainly water vapour, CO_2 and aerosols, which absorb and emit long-wavelength radiation.

The net outgoing radiative flux from a terrestrial object is equal to the emitted flux minus the incident flux that it absorbs from the above-mentioned participative components of the atmosphere. The incident flux depends basically on the concentrations of participative gases and aerosols, on the wavelength and on the temperature of the atmosphere at different levels. The emission is a minimum at a certain region of the spectrum from 8 to 14 mm. In other words, this region is partially transparent (recall than transmissivity is equal to 1 minus emissivity) and for that reason it is called the atmospheric window.

In order to characterize in a simple way the radiation emitted from the sky, the concept of sky temperature is introduced. This is defined as the temperature of a blackbody emitting the same amount of radiative power as the sky. Hereafter we shall consider the sky temperature as the thermal level of the cool medium. The gross driven force of the radiative cooling will then be the temperature difference between the radiator and the sky.

It should be considered, however, that the dominance of the solar radiation during daytime makes the balance between the sky and any terrestrial object effective only during the night for cooling purposes. Obviously, this effectivity will be higher under a clear sky and low humidity conditions.

7.5.2 Effective environmental temperature

In this case, as for ground cooling, the effective environmental temperature differs from the sky temperature. This is because the radiator exchanges heat not only with the sky (by radiation), but also convectively with the ambient air. The ambient air starts to heat the radiator when its temperature drops below the ambient temperature. Therefore, the final temperature of the radiator is not the sky temperature, but a higher one called stagnation or threshold temperature. This is the effective environmental temperature. The effective environmental temperature can be improved by reducing the convective heat gains of the radiator. This can be achieved by covering the surface of the radiator with a special polymer film, called a wind screen. Obviously this film has to be transparent within the range of the atmospheric window. This film protects the radiator surface from the wind and therefore the stagnation temperature of the radiator plate decreases even more.

The effective environmental temperature depends on two types of parameters:

● meteorological parameters such as the sky temperature (or in other words the air temperature, relative humidity and cloud cover) and the wind velocity

● radiator characteristics such as the total emissivity in the long-wavelength region and the presence or not of a wind screen.

7.5.3 System description and performance

A flat-plate radiative cooler looks like a flat-plate solar collector; the main difference is that there is no glazing, since ordinary glazing absorbs long-wavelength radiation. In some cases the cooler is covered with a polymer film, transparent to the long-wavelength radiation, to improve the efficiency of the system.

There are two types of flat plate radiators:

● air radiators, when the heat transfer fluid used is air

● liquid radiators, when the heat transfer fluid used is water or another liquid (in the case of closed-loop systems).

The main component of the radiator is the radiating plate. This is commonly a metal plate, usually painted or covered with a special coating. Various radiator materials have been tested and reported in the literature. Among these we distinguish the following (Pytlinsky *et al*, 1986):

- corrugated galvanized steel

- corrugated galvanized steel with corrugated clear fibreglass cover

- corrugated clear fibreglass cover

- black-painted galvanized steel

- white-painted galvanized steel

- electroplated anodized aluminium sheet with a blue plastic protective cover

- anodized aluminium sheet with white finish

- anodized aluminium sheet with clear finish.

Studies have been performed also to test the thermal performance of selective radiators. These are radiators provided with coatings that show high absorptivity (and therefore high emissivity) in the 8–13 m range of the electromagnetic spectrum and high reflectivity (and therefore low absorptivity) above and below this range. Givoni (1982) compared the various studies and concluded that selective surfaces do not provide any specific advantage over ordinary surfaces regarding the radiant cooling potential. The higher cost of selective surfaces must also be taken into account.

In the previous section, it was discussed how the wind screen affects the effective environmental temperature. The wind screen must have good mechanical properties to resist the effects of the ambient conditions. It also has to be transparent to the long-wavelength radiation within the range of the atmospheric window. Because of this requirement, wind screens are usually thin polyethylene films, without ultraviolet inhibitors. This is a low-cost, common material and about 70% transparent to the long-wavelength region.

Typical air radiators consist of a 10 m long (direction parallel to the flow) to 1 m wide radiator plate. This plate is the upper surface of a 0.02 m thick rectangular duct. Air circulates though this duct by means of electrical fans and is cooled because of the direct contact between the air and the radiator plate.

A typical liquid radiator has the same radiator plate as air radiators. Under this plate are fixed the tubes inside which circulates water or any other liquid. The diameter of these tubes is 0.03 m. There are about 15 tubes per metre of width of the radiator plate.

These modules can be connected between them, in series or in parallel, to cover the cooling load required in each particular application. As in the case of solar collectors, attention must be paid during this connection to balance the pressure drop through the network. Therefore, a Tickelman network is suggested.

The ideal placement of flat plate radiators is in the horizontal position, since in this case the radiative losses towards the sky are maximized. In order to avoid additional heat exchange with the surrounding objects, it is better to place the radiators in positions as high as possible (e.g. roofs).

7.6 Climatic qualification

A first estimate of the applicability of the NCT in a certain location can be obtained from the climatic data. There are many variables that can be used as indexes to characterize the cooling potential (Álvarez *et al*, 1997).

The cooling energy that can be transferred from the building to the working fluid over a certain period of time is given by

$$Q = \int_t \dot{m}(t)\,c_p\,(T_{\text{indoor}}(t) - T_{\text{outlet}}(t))\,dt$$

If the mass flow rate and the indoor air temperature can be assumed to be constant during the period, the corresponding specific cooling energy in degree-hours (DH) can be written as

$$\frac{Q}{\dot{m}c_p} = \int_t (T_{\text{indoor}} - T_{\text{outlet}}(t))\,dt$$

Obviously, the minimum value of the outlet temperature would be (in a theoretical optimum situation) equal to the temperature of the environmental sink. Consequently, an upper bound of the specific cooling energy would be

$$\left(\frac{Q}{mc_p}\right)_{\text{max}} = \int_t (T_{\text{indoor}} - T_{\text{sink}}(t))\,dt$$

The map in Figure 7.13 shows the values of the maximum specific cooling energy obtained from July to September, assuming an indoor temperature of 25°C. The integral is extended to the operation period (from 8 a.m. to 6 p.m.) of an office building used as reference.

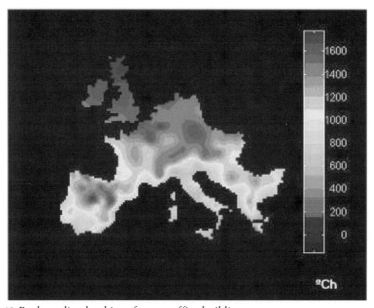

Figure 7.13 *Peak cooling load in reference office building*

7.7 Earth sheltering

Underground buildings give good thermal behaviour during the summer period. By being in contact with the ground, their indoor environment is protected from the extreme variations of the outdoor conditions, while conductive heat losses are increased and the thermal inertia of the building increases.

Labs (1989) classified earth-sheltered buildings in various categories, Two main categories, 'berm' and 'subgrade' buildings, have been defined. Then, for each category, four types are found: 'windowless chamber', 'atrium or courtyard', 'elevational: wall exposed' and 'penetrational: wall openings'.

Carmody *et al* (1985) summarized the main advantages and disadvantages of earth-sheltered buildings. The main advantages reported are as follows:

- low visual impact – aesthetics (good integration into the landscape)

- preservation of surface open spaces

- noise and vibration control: the heavy mass of the buildings absorbs ambient noise and vibration

- low maintenance: the major part of their envelope is sheltered and therefore not degraded by the weather

- other benefits: fire protection, protection against earthquakes, suitability for civil defence, protection against storms and tornadoes and higher security against outside intrusions.

The major limitations of earth-contact buildings are the following:

- structural and economic limitations: earth-contact buildings require more expensive structures since the roofs must bear the great weight of the soil

- daylight aspects: earth-contact buildings may experience poor daylight conditions

- condensation – indoor air quality: condensation might occur on the internal surfaces of the building, if their temperature drops below the dew point temperature; low infiltration and ventilation rates may create major air quality problems.

Various examples of buried or semi-buried buildings can be found (Santamouris and Asimakopoulos, 1996). On the island of Santorini, in the Aegean sea in Greece, there are many semi-buried dwellings built during various historical periods.

Figure 7.14 shows an example of the surrounding temperature field and the heat flows for the underground walls and floor of a earth-shelter building. The indoor air temperature to be maintained is 25°C in the cooling period and 19°C during the heating period. The heat flows in the example are the heat transferred to the indoor air from the underground walls and floor and referred to as kWh/m^2 of floor area.

As can be seen, they are positive in winter and negative in summer. Their order of magnitude is analogous to the seasonal heating or cooling requirements of residential buildings (Álvarez and Téllez, 1996), which implies that, thanks to the ground, the basement will be self-conditioned and will have spontaneous indoor air temperatures even more comfortable than those in the example.

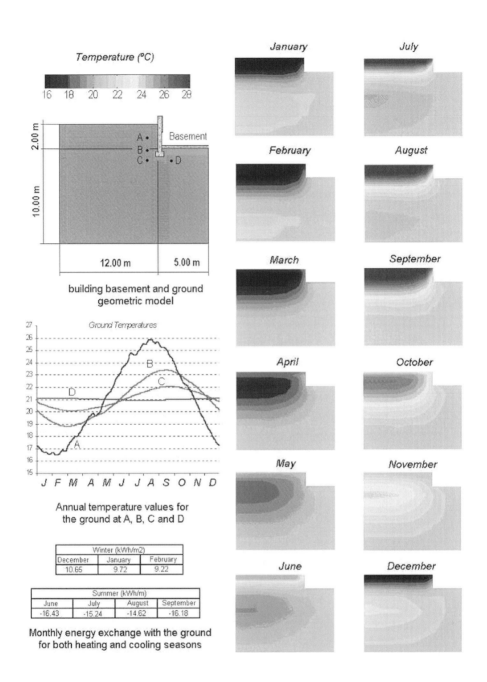

Figure 7.14 *Earth-sheltering performance example*

7.8 Roof solutions

This material, including figures, is extracted from the draft version of *Roof Solutions for Natural Cooling, Design Handbook*, produced in the context of the EC JOULE III Programme ROOFSOL Project in 1998 (Yannas, 1998).

7.8.1 Roof pond

The roof pond concept (Figure 7.15) combines the traditional functions of a roof with a means of natural heating and cooling. The key elements of the concept are as follows:

- use of water for heat storage and as interim heat sink
- thermal coupling of the water with the occupied spaces
- exposure of the water pond to sunshine for heating
- exposure of the water pond to the night sky for cooling.

The principal constituents of a roof pond system are the container for the water, the supporting structure and the thermal insulation with which the thermal coupling and decoupling of the water are achieved. With these elements a roof pond can contribute to thermal comfort in all seasons. The water is commonly contained in watertight plastic bags laid on an uninsulated metallic ceiling deck.

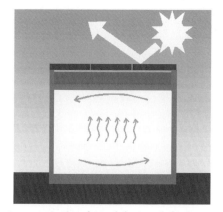 

Figure 7.15 *Roof pond during (left) day operation and (right) night operation*

7.8.2 Planted roofs

Planted roofs (Figure 7.16) have a layer of vegetation growing on a specially designed substrate over a usually flat roof structure. A planted roof may serve a number of different functions:

- replace the area of green removed by the insertion of a building on a site; on an urban site this can be particularly welcome as a form of microclimatic improvement

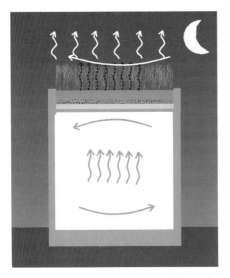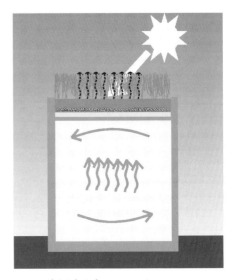

Figure 7.16 *Planted roof during (left) night operation and (right) day operation*

- provide a private roof garden (when accessible)
- act as a form of solar control on the roof
- act as thermal and acoustic insulation for the building below
- contribute to stable indoor temperatures.

Two distinct applications have evolved: intensive planted roofs (also known as 'roof gardens') and extensive planted roofs (also known as 'ecological green roofs').

7.8.3 Radiator roofs

Conventional metallic roofs (Figure 7.17) can be employed to dissipate heat by long-wavelength radiation to the night sky. The main design considerations are as follows:

- metallic roofs have very low thermal resistance and heat storage capacity; these characteristics allow instant heat transfer between their upper surface from where radiant loss takes place and the lower surface where cooling is needed.
- metallic roofs have a high emissivity.
- air or water are the heat transfer fluid between the metallic roof [heat dissipator] and the occupied space or temporary heat storage
- metallic roofs should be placed horizontally or slightly pitched to maximize radiant heat loss.

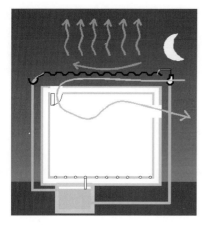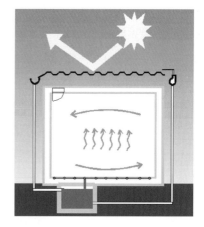

Figure 7.17 *Radiative roof during (left) night operation and (right) day operation*

7.9 Future priorities

7.9.1 Basic research on the coupling of NCT to different types of buildings

- modelling of new systems and their combinations
- adapted control strategies.

Some further basic research activities cannot yet be implemented as many of the possibilities have not yet been studied and the infinite number of possible combinations requires a strategy for simulating the behaviour when coupled to a building.

7.9.2 Incorporation in building design tools

Existing tools for calculation the energy performance of buildings do not pay attention to these types of systems.

7.9.3 Systematic study of potential applicability of NCT

- Ongoing projects (ALTENER Cluster 9).
- Optimum economic combination of NCT for different type of buildings:
  - Residential: up to 100% can be covered by solar passive design and NCT
  - Offices and other: optimum combination of NCT + conventional systems.
- Application to refurbishment in existing building stock.
- Impact on European Union energy savings.

This group is a systematic exploitation of the tools developed in the two previous items.

7.9.4 Design guidelines (for NCT, different types of buildings, climates)

Architects, and in general designers in the building sector, are not yet experts in the field; for them to appreciate the possibilities of NCT the preparation of this basic information is necessary.

7.9.5 Introduction of standards for NCT calculation

Obviously, if we have not yet completed the calculation procedures at the level of basic research, it is impossible to produce standards to be used by designers when rating the energy performance of NCT.

7.9.6 Demonstration projects for dissemination

Several carefully selected and monitored buildings, preferably coming from refurbishment work in an existing building, would help by comparing the results actually obtained with those predicted by the tools prepared.

7.9.7 NCT in the European Directive for Energy Efficiency in Buildings

The directive of the European Parliament and of the Council on the energy performance of buildings states clearly the requirement for considering NCT in building design, especially in southern European countries. In its 17th item of the preamble the official English version of the text says:

> Recent years have seen a rise in the number of air-conditioning systems in southern European countries. This creates considerable problems at peak load times, increasing the cost of electricity and disrupting the energy balance in those countries. Priority should be given to strategies which enhance the thermal performance of buildings during the summer period. To this end there should be further development of passive cooling techniques, primarily those that improve indoor climatic conditions and the microclimate around buildings.

7.10 References

Álvarez, S, 1993, 'Natural cooling techniques', in *Solar Energy and Buildings Symposium*, Athens, Academy of Athens, 10–1, 10–15

Álvarez, S and Téllez, F, 1996, *Natural Cooling Technology Assessment. Atlas for Southern Europe Countries*, Final Report of the EU-XVII/4.1030/A/94–88, Altener-SINK project. Available from the authors on request.

Álvarez, S, *et al.*, 1992, *Climatic Control of Outdoor Spaces. The EXPO'92 Project*. Publicaciones CIEMAT Madrid.

Álvarez, S, Maestre, I R and Velázquez, R, 1997, 'Design methodology and cooling potential of environmental heat sinks', in *International Journal of Solar Energy*, 19, 179–197.

Bahadori, M N, 1978, 'Passive cooling in Iranian architecture', in *Scientific American*, Vol. 238, No. 2, 144–154.

Carmody, J C, Meixel, G D, Labs, K B and Shen, L S, 1985, 'Earth contact buildings: applications, thermal analysis and energy benefits', in K W Boer and J Duffie (eds), *Advances in Solar Energy*, Vol. 2, New York, Plenum Press 297–344.

Cook, J, 1989, 'The state of the art of passive cooling research', in J Cook (ed), *Passive Cooling*, Cambridge, MA, MIT Press, Chapter 7.

Givoni, B, 1982, 'Cooling by longwave radiation', in *Passive Solar Journal*, 1(3), 131–150.

Labs, K, 1989, 'Earth coupling', in J Cook (ed), *Passive Cooling*, Cambridge, MA, MIT Press, 197–346.

Maldonado, E and Coronel, J F (eds), 1996, *Case Studies*, Final Report of the EU-XVII/4.1030/A/94–88, Altener-SINK project. Available from the authors on request.

Mihalakaku, G, Santamouris, M and Asimakopoulos, D, 1992, 'On the cooling potential of earth to air heat exchangers'. Private communication.

Pytlinsky, J T, Conrad, G R and Connel, H L, 1986, 'Radiative cooling and solar heating potential of various roofing materials', in N Veziroglu (ed), *Proceedings of International Conference on Renewable Energy Sources*, Ed. CSIC Madrid, Vol. EE, 1164–1209.

Santamouris, M and Asimakopoulos, D (eds), 1996, *Passive Cooling of Buildings*, London, James & James (Science Publishers) Ltd.

Yannas, S (ed), 1998, *Roof Solutions for Natural Cooling, Design Handbook*, EC JOULE III Programme ROOFSOL Project. Available from the authors on request.

8 Thermal comfort

Fergus Nicol

Low Energy Architecture Research Unit (LEARN), London Metropolitan University, 40 Holloway Road, London N7 8JL, UK
Tel: +44 20 7753 7006; fax: +44 20 7753 5780; e-mail: f.nicol@londonmet.ac.uk

8.1 Prologue

There was no such thing as a 'thermal index' or a 'comfort temperature' when some of the most beautiful buildings in the world were erected: buildings where the interplay of air and stone brings fresh delight at every turn – in the heat of the summer a playful breeze skirting round a corner, a cool subterranean passage or an airy courtyard complete with a refreshing fountain, in winter a sunlit room providing respite from the cold outside. Builders used the experience of centuries passed from generation to generation to ensure that their masterpieces performed the most important task of any building: to modify a hostile outdoor environment and create delight indoors.

However, in the 21st century we can decide with the flick of a switch what the indoor temperature will be. It is easier, after all, to use a little fossil fuel to run the air conditioners than to bother with the complexities of harnessing the fickle wind and the burning sun! This is where the need for thermal standards comes in: if it is in your power to decide the indoor climate of a building, then you have to know exactly what it should be. So environmental scientists set about deciding what the temperature, humidity and air movement should be and the science of thermal comfort was born.

8.2 Background

8.2.1 The need for a new approach

Following the Kyoto agreement, there is an international imperative to reduce energy consumption and its associated anthropogenic emissions which contribute to pollution and global climate change. New European energy directives will soon be enforced. In EU countries primary energy consumption by buildings represents about 40% of total energy consumption (Santamouris and Wouters, 1994). Up to 50% of this energy is used in the provision of indoor climate control. Naturally ventilated (NV) buildings typically use less than half as much energy as those with air conditioning (Kolokotroni *et al*, 1996). Yet there is no accepted way to predict the energy use of occupied NV buildings or to ensure that their occupants will find the indoor climate they produce satisfactory. In buildings where the occupants to a greater or lesser extent control the indoor climate, occupant behaviour will greatly affect energy use.

8.2.2 Why is thermal comfort important in energy conservation?

First, the energy consumption of any building is critically dependent on the indoor temperatures which the building and its services must deliver, because the heat lost from the building either through its surfaces or by ventilation depends essentially on the difference between indoor and outdoor temperature. The sensitivity of occupants to the indoor climate also has implications for how closely we need to control the environment; here again, this has energy implications.

Second, the 'success' of the building depends on whether a comfortable indoor environment is achieved. This is important for the occupants. Thermal comfort is generally listed by occupants as one of the most important requirements for any building. In addition, there is evidence that the thermal comfort of occupants is closely linked to their perception of indoor air quality (Humphreys *et al*, 2002) and productivity (McCartney and Humphreys, 2002). Comfort is also important because the occupants will react to any discomfort by taking actions to restore their comfort. These actions may themselves have an energy cost – opening a window when the heating is on, for instance, can be a costly way to cool an overheated building.

8.3 State of the art

8.3.1 The underlying processes

The thermal interaction between humans and the environment is highly complex and has been the subject of a great deal of study. The internal processes by which we produce and respond to heat have been studied by physiologists, our conscious feelings about the environment by psychologists and the processes of heat transfer between humans and the environment by physicists. In addition, there are social factors which determine the way in which we react to the environment and environmental engineers decide how our needs can be satisfied in buildings. The study of thermal comfort therefore has to take all these considerations into account.

We are not concerned here with a detailed investigation into the phenomena underlying thermal comfort, which have been adequately described elsewhere (McIntyre, 1980; Parsons, 2002a), but it is useful to touch briefly on the main points.

8.3.1.1 Physiology

We produce energy by metabolizing food and most of this energy takes the form of heat. The body produces this 'metabolic heat' all the time, although more is produced when we are active and the more active we are the more heat is produced. For the proper functioning of the organs of the body and particularly that of the brain, the temperature of the internal organs (the 'deep-body' or 'core' temperature) must be constant. The controlling mechanism is in the brain. If our brain temperature falls outside very close limits, the body will react physiologically to restore heat balance.

The unconscious thermoregulatory actions controlled from the brain are augmented by the thermal sense in the skin. This warns of conditions which might pose a danger. Our impression of the warmth or cold of our environment from the skin sensors is integrated with the core temperature so that the overall sensation may be pleasing or displeasing depending on whether the overall effect is towards or away from the restoration of deep body equilibrium.

8.3.1.2 Psychophysics

Psychophysics is the study of the relation between our sensations and the stimulus we receive from the physical world (Stevens, 1975). For a good introduction to the thinking of psychophysics applied to the built environment and particularly to lighting, see Hopkinson (1963). The thinking behind studies of thermal comfort has been that of psychophysics: relating the overall thermal sensation to the stimuli of the thermal environment.

In experiments and surveys studying thermal comfort, the feelings of a subject can be separated between those of 'hotness' and those of 'comfort'. Generally, the feelings of hotness are measured on the ASHRAE scale, a seven-point scale between Hot and Cold (Table 8.1). The number of distinct sensations that we can reliably distinguish is limited (Miller, 1956) and the seven-point ASHRAE scale is typical. Comfort is generally gauged on a scale of preference (for a warmer or cooler environment or no change); the most widely accepted is the three-point scale of McIntyre (1980), but five- and seven-point scales have been used which distinguish the extent of the desired change. In a number of experiments the seven-point Bedford scale (Bedford, 1936) has been used, which combines the notions of comfort and hotness (Table 8.1).

Table 8.1 *Seven-point ASHRAE and Bedford scales of thermal sensation. The −3 to +3 scale is generally used for mathematical evaluation of comfort (see section on PMV below); the 1 to 7 scale is used in survey work, to avoid confusion*

ASHRAE descriptive scale	Numerical equivalent		Bedford descriptive scale
Hot	+3	7	Much too warm
Warm	+2	6	Too warm
Slightly warm	+1	5	Comfortably warm
Neutral	0	4	Comfortable neither warm nor cool
Slightly cool	−1	3	Comfortable and cool
Cool	−2	2	Too cool
Cold	−3	1	Much too cool

To say how we feel does not imply a one-to-one relationship with the physical conditions – a particular stimulus gives rise to a range of sensations. We cannot say that a particular set of conditions will give rise to a particular sensation, only that there is a probability that it will.

8.3.1.3 Physics

To the physicist, the human being is a heated body with variable surface characteristics, losing heat to the environment through three principal pathways: convection, radiation and evaporation. In certain circumstances, significant amounts of heat are also lost by conduction to surrounding surfaces, but this is normally a secondary path of heat loss.

The basic equation for thermal balance is

$$H = W + S + K + C + R + E + E_{res} + C_{res} \tag{8.1}$$

where H is the metabolic heat production, W is the work done and S is heat stored in the body (assumed zero over time). K, C and R are the heat losses (or gains) from the clothing or skin by conduction, convection and radiation. E is the heat loss from the skin by evaporation. E_{res} and C_{res} are the evaporative and convective heat exchanges through respiration. Equations can be derived for all of these individual contributions to the heat balance equation if the metabolic rate, the clothing insulation and the environmental parameters are known (McIntyre, 1980; Parsons, 2002a). In all these terms except H a negative value will constitute a heat gain to the body. Note that the heat balance is essentially steady-state.

8.3.1.4 Behaviour

Behaviour plays an important role in our interaction with the thermal environment. Many approaches assume in effect that we are acted upon by the environment and react to it passively. In fact there is an interaction between humans and the environment. Thermal interactions take a number of forms and time plays a part in them. To describe people's thermal experience fully we need to take account of all these changes. The picture should be consistent with the findings drawn from physics and physiology, but it will change with climate, place and time in a dynamic and interactive way. Section 8.3.3 presents a more complete consideration of behaviour and its role in thermal comfort.

8.3.2 Developing an index of thermal comfort

For the building designer or engineer, it is necessary to define the conditions within a building which will provide a comfortable indoor climate (the 'comfort conditions' or 'comfort temperature'). Because a number of factors influence the heat balance of the human body, the specification of an 'index' of indoor conditions may include humidity and air movement in addition to the radiant and air temperatures. The 'personal' variables – metabolic rate and clothing insulation – also need to be taken into account.

8.3.2.1 Field studies

One way to approach the setting of an index for thermal standards is to conduct field studies of thermal comfort. In these studies subjects are asked for their comfort vote on the ASHRAE or similar scale and simultaneous measurements are taken of the thermal environment in the vicinity of the subject. Statistical analysis can then be used to predict the combination of thermal variables which best describes the comfort vote of the subjects. Most comfort surveys are conducted so as leave the choice of clothing and activity to the subjects, relying on the natural variability of the environment to provide the necessary variance for the statistical analysis.

By using statistical methods such as multiple linear regression, the results of field studies can be used to develop an index to predict the combination of variables which will best relate to the comfort vote. The well-known early work of Bedford (1936) and the Tropical Summer Index of Sharma and Ali (1986) are examples of this approach. The aim is to find the temperature or index of thermal variables which subjects consider 'neutral' or 'comfortable'. This analysis is then used to predict comfortable conditions in similar circumstances elsewhere.

There are problems with using a field study in this way. The environmental conditions are inherently variable and difficult to measure accurately and errors in the input data can give rise to errors in the relationships predicted by the statistical analysis (Humphreys and Nicol, 2000b). It is difficult to generalize from the statistical analysis – the results from one survey often do not apply to the data from another even in similar circumstances because the statistical analysis tends to describe the particular database rather than producing a useful predictive tool. However, a meta-analysis of the results from a number of surveys can be used to draw overall conclusions about the form and magnitude of the relationship between the subjective responses and the objective conditions. More detail of such results is given in Section 8.3.3.

8.3.2.2 'Rational' models of thermal comfort

There have been a number of attempts to present an 'index' based on heat exchange theory which will specify the likely response to any given set of conditions and much research has been directed towards this goal. The scientific study of human thermal comfort has centred chiefly on evaluating under laboratory conditions the heat exchanges that occur between a person and the thermal environment and the physiological conditions that are needed for human comfort. Usually the index is based on steady-state heat flow theory; the estimation of heat balance in these indices is based upon and underpinned by measurements in which the subjects typically remain in any one particular condition for three hours.

From this research, indices have been developed. These include the revised Effective Temperature (ET*) and its extended version, Standard Effective Temperature (SET) (Nevins and Gagge, 1972), which have been the basis of standards for the USA (ASHRAE, 1992). The most widely accepted index of comfort is the Fanger's Predicted Mean Vote (PMV) (Fanger, 1970). This index predicts the mean comfort vote of a group of people on the ASHRAE scale (Table 8.1). With the associated PPD index (see below), PMV forms the basis of standard EN/ISO 7730 (CEN/ISO, 1994), which includes a computer program for calculating it. PMV will also form the basis for the new ISO standard 7730 (Olesen and Parsons, 2002) and ASHRAE/ANSI standard 55, both in preparation at the time of writing.

8.3.2.3 Predicted mean vote (PMV) and predicted percentage dissatisfied (PPD)

Fanger's basic premise is that a balance between the heat produced by the body and the heat lost from it is a necessary, but not a sufficient, condition for thermal comfort. It is not sufficient because one can imagine situations in which a theoretical balance would occur, but which would not be considered comfortable. Hence the determination of comfort conditions is in two stages: first find the conditions for thermal balance and then determine which of the conditions so defined are consistent with comfort.

Fanger proposed that the condition for thermal comfort for a given person is that his or her skin temperature and sweat secretion must lie within narrow limits. Fanger obtained data from climate chamber experiments, in which sweat rate and skin temperature were measured on people who considered themselves comfortable at various metabolic rates. Fanger proposed that the regression line of skin temperature and sweat rate on metabolic rate from data in these experiments expressed optimum conditions for thermal comfort. In this way an expression for optimal thermal comfort can be deduced from the metabolic rate, clothing insulation and environmental conditions.

The final equation for optimal thermal comfort is fairly complex and need not concern us here. Fanger solved the equations by computer and presented the results in the form of diagrams from which optimum comfort conditions can be read, given a knowledge of metabolic rate and clothing insulation.

Fanger extended the usefulness of his work by proposing a method by which the actual thermal sensation could be predicted. His assumption for this was that the sensation experienced by a person was a function of the physiological strain imposed by the environment. This he defined as 'the difference between the internal heat production and the heat loss to the actual environment for a man kept at the comfort values for skin temperature and sweat production at the actual activity level' (Fanger, 1970). He calculated this extra load for people involved in climate chamber experiments and plotted their comfort vote against it to predict what comfort vote would arise from a given set of environmental conditions for a given clothing insulation and metabolic rate. Tables of PMV are available for different environments for given clothing and metabolic rates. Such tables form the basis of ISO standard 7730 (CEN/ISO, 1994).

Fanger realized that the vote predicted was only the mean value to be expected from a group of people and he extended the PMV to predict the proportion of any population who will be dissatisfied with the environment. A person's dissatisfaction was defined in terms of their comfort vote. Those who vote outside the central three scaling points on the ASHRAE scale (Table 8.1) were counted as dissatisfied. PPD is defined in terms of the PMV and does not add information about the interaction between people and their environment to that already available in PMV. The distribution of PPD is based on observations from climate chamber experiments and not from field measurements.

8.3.2.4 Problems with PMV/PPD

The rational indices are based on the responses of subjects measured in stable conditions in climate chambers, but it has been assumed that such an index will express the response of people in the variable conditions of daily life. The results from field surveys should therefore be predicted by the index. In recent years, the PMV/PPD model has been the subject of increasing criticism as a means of predicting people's response to the thermal conditions.

PMV does not perform well in predicting the actual votes cast on the ASHRAE scale in field surveys, overestimating discomfort by an unacceptable margin especially in variable conditions (Humphreys and Nicol, 2002). Humphreys (1976) showed that the range of temperatures that subjects found comfortable was much wider than could be predicted by PMV or Effective Temperature. deDear (1998) collected field survey results from subjects in both centrally conditioned and NV buildings all over the world to form what has become known as the 'ASHRAE database of field studies'. He calculated comfort temperature predicted by the PMV equation from the measured variables and then plotted this predicted comfort temperature against the comfort temperature obtained from the field studies. He found that the PMV prediction was reasonably accurate for air-conditioned buildings, but that for NV buildings PMV did not predict the mean comfort temperature well (Figure 8.1).

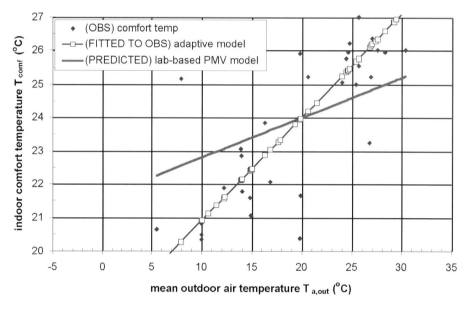

Figure 8.1 *Errors in the prediction of indoor comfort using PMV in naturally ventilated buildings (from deDear and Brager, 2002)*

The reason for this error in PMV is not entirely clear but there is evidence (Humphreys and Nicol, 2002) that the effect is partly due to errors in the PMV equation which result in an error in the calculated value of PMV. These errors may be related to another problem with PMV: the PMV equation calculates conditions for thermal neutrality using a steady-state model. The predicated vote is then related to a calculated thermal *imbalance* between the body and environment. There is clearly a contradiction between the steady-state assumption for the comfort calculation and the imbalance assumed if the body is not comfortable (Humphreys and Nicol, 1996; Parsons *et al*, 1997) – a body with a thermal imbalance will inevitably warm up or cool down and no longer fulfil the steady-state assumption.

Another problem is that calculation of PMV requires knowledge of metabolic heat production and clothing insulation. These 'personal' variables are notoriously difficult to determine (Havenith *et al*, 2002). The most accurate method to measure metabolic heat production, the 'Douglas Bag', is difficult to use in a field context because it is so cumbersome. The method commonly used, which assumes a rate for a particular activity, is inaccurate. Clothing insulation is also difficult to estimate, being fraught with possible inaccuracies such as the different ways in which clothes can be worn, the effect of the wearers' movements and accounting for the permeability of the clothing to water vapour.

ISO 7730 (CEN/ISO, 1994) gives little guidance on how to predict metabolic rate and clothing insulation in any real situation, despite the importance of these variables in the calculation of PMV. The user of PMV is therefore forced to make assumptions about people's future clothing and activity based on very little information. This results in static design indoor temperatures because a single activity and clothing level has to be assumed. Static indoor temperatures preclude most passive, energy-conscious buildings where temperatures inevitably vary.

8.3.3 Adaptive thermal comfort

Much has been made in recent years of the so-called 'adaptive' approach to thermal comfort. This refers to an empirical model of thermal comfort which has been developed based on the results of thermal comfort studies in the field.

8.3.3.1 Comfort temperature and indoor temperature

Figure 8.2 shows the mean comfort vote of subjects from a number of field surveys plotted against the mean temperature recorded. The rate of change of mean comfort

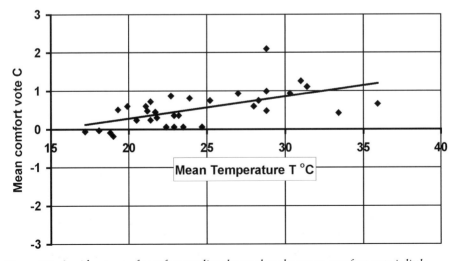

Figure 8.2 *A wide range of comfort studies shows that the mean comfort vote is little affected by the mean indoor temperature. Each point represents the mean from a complete study (from Nicol and Humphreys, 2002)*

vote with mean temperature from one survey to another is much lower than the change of comfort vote with temperature in any particular survey.

The reasons for this observation from field surveys have been the subject of considerable speculation and research, most of which has concentrated on the context in which field surveys are conducted. Nicol and Humphreys (1973) suggested that this effect could be the result of a feedback between the thermal sensation of subjects and their behaviour and that they consequently 'adapted' to the climatic conditions in which the field study was conducted.

Unlike laboratory experiments, measurements in the field include the effects of all the behaviours of normal subjects during their everyday lives. Some of the behavioural actions are concerned with the thermal environment and will therefore affect the relationship between thermal comfort and the environment. The adaptive approach seeks to explain the differences between the field measurements and those obtained in the laboratory by looking at the cumulative effect of behaviour in this relationship.

The corollary of the effect shown in Figure 8.2 and discussed above is that in field surveys the comfort temperature is closely correlated to the mean temperature measured. This was found to be the case in surveys conducted over a wide range of indoor climates (Figure 8.3a). A similar effect was found when data were collected in Pakistan (Nicol *et al*, 1999) and Europe (McCartney and Nicol, 2002) from the same group of subjects at monthly intervals throughout the year (Figure 8.3b). The variety of indoor temperatures, particularly in Pakistan, is remarkable. The strong relationship of comfort temperature with mean indoor temperature is clear.

8.3.3.2 Adaptive actions

Interest in the phenomenon outlined above has concentrated on the so-called adaptive approach to thermal comfort which attributes the effect to an accumulation of behaviours or other factors which taken together can be used to ensure comfort. In a defining paper on the approach, Humphreys and Nicol (1998) explained the meaning of adaptive actions in the following way:

> The set of conceivable adaptive actions in response to warmth or coolness may be classified into five categories:
>
> 1.   regulating the rate of internal heat generation
>
> 2.   regulating the rate of body heat loss
>
> 3.   regulating the thermal environment
>
> 4.   selecting a different thermal environment
>
> 5.   modifying the body's physiological comfort conditions.
>
> The actions vary in the extent to which they are consciously executed. Vasodilation and constriction, sweating and shivering [physiological responses – F.N.] are not under conscious control. Changes of posture or degree of physical activity may be either deliberate or unconscious acts. Even the overtly behavioural responses may have an unconscious component, as they may become 'second nature' in a particular society, culture or climate.

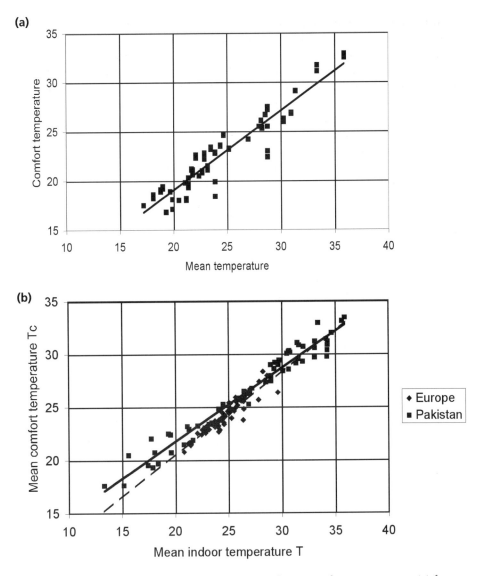

Figure 8.3 *The variation of comfort temperature with mean indoor temperature (a) from surveys throughout the world [from data presented in Humphreys (1976)] and (b) from within a particular set of climates [Europe (dashed line) and Pakistan] but at different times of year (from Nicol and Humphreys, 2002)*

Because there are very many conceivable adaptive actions, comfort is likely to be restored by means of a co-ordinated set of minor actions, rather than by means of a single mode of action. For example, a response to coldness might entail a slight increase in muscle tension, a barely perceptible vasoconstriction, a slightly 'tighter' posture, putting on a sweater and the desire for a cup of coffee. The effect of each might independently be small, but the joint effect can be large, not least because changes in heat flow and changes in thermal insulation are multiplicative in their effect on temperature differential. The more subtle adaptations are unlikely to be captured by questionnaire responses about clothing and activity and would therefore be 'invisible' to the usually recommended procedures for the evaluation of PMV and SET.

Adaptation can be regarded as a set of learning processes and therefore people may be expected to be well adapted to their usual environments. They will feel hot when the environment is hotter than 'usual' and cold when it is colder than 'usual'. The adaptive approach is therefore interested in the study of usual environments. In particular, what environments are 'usual', how does an environment become 'usual' and how does a person move from one 'usual' environment to another?

Not all researchers agree on the wide range of adaptive actions outlined by Humphreys and Nicol and there is generally a feeling that adaptation is concerned with behavioural, more or less conscious actions

As an example of how effectively adaptive actions can be used to achieve comfort, Figure 8.4 shows the actual proportion of subjects comfortable among office workers in Pakistan at different indoor temperatures. The data were collected over a period of a year in five Pakistani cities so the comfort temperature was continually changing, as

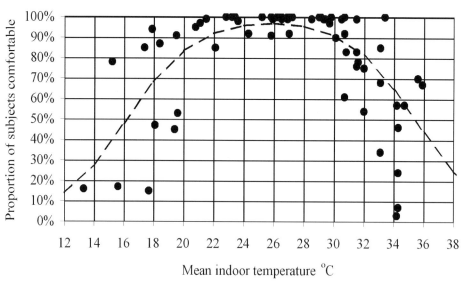

Figure 8.4 *Pakistan: the proportion of office workers who were comfortable at different indoor temperatures. Each point on the graph represents the results of one survey of about 20–25 people in a single office. It will be noticed that on many occasions the subjects recorded no discomfort. With a continually changing indoor temperature and comfort temperature, Pakistani buildings were found comfortable at temperatures ranging between 20 and 30°C with no cooling apart from fans (from Nicol et al, 1999)*

was the indoor temperature (Nicol *et al*, 1999). The major methods that these workers had to control their comfort were by changing their clothing and using air movement, fans being universally available in Pakistani offices. The curve shows the mean probability of comfort calculated using probit regression (Finney, 1964). Each point represents the proportion comfortable in a particular city in a particular month. Note that little discomfort is recorded at indoor temperatures between 20 and 30°C.

8.3.3.3 The adaptive principle

The fundamental assumption of the adaptive approach is expressed by the adaptive principle: *If a change occurs such as to produce discomfort, people react in ways which tend to restore their comfort.* This principle applies to field surveys conducted in a wide range of environments and thus legitimises meta-analyses of comfort surveys such as those of Humphreys (1976, 1978), Auliciems and deDear (1986) and deDear and Brager (1998, 2002). These meta-analyses have been used to generalize from the results of a number of individual thermal comfort surveys.

By linking the comfort vote to people's actions, the adaptive principle links the comfort temperature to the context in which subjects find themselves. The comfort temperature is a result of the interaction between the subjects and the building or other environment that they are occupying. The options for people to react will reflect their situation: those with more opportunities to adapt themselves to the environment or the environment to their own requirements will be less likely to suffer discomfort.

The prime contextual variable is the climate. Climate is an overarching influence on the culture and thermal attitudes of any group of people and on the design of the buildings they inhabit. Whilst the basic mechanisms of the human relationship with the thermal environment may not change with climate, there are a number of detailed ways in which people are influenced by the climate they live in and these play a cumulative part in their response to the indoor climate. The second major context of nearly all comfort surveys has been a building and the nature of the building and its services plays a part in defining the results from the survey. The third context is time. In a variable environment such as will occur in most buildings occupants will respond to changes in the environment. They will do this by taking actions to suit the environment to their liking or by changing themselves (for instance, by posture or clothing) to suit the environment. This implies that the comfort temperature is continually changing. The extent of these changes and the rate at which they occur is an important consideration if the conditions for comfort are to be properly specified.

8.3.3.4 The relationship with outdoor climate

Humphreys (1978) took the indoor comfort temperature determined in a number of surveys conducted world-wide and plotted them against the outdoor monthly mean temperature at the time of the survey. The results are shown in Figure 8.5. He found a clear division between people in buildings which were free-running (neither heated nor cooled) at the time of the survey and those in buildings that were climatized (heated or cooled) at the time of the survey. The relationship for the free-running buildings was closely linear. For climatized buildings the relationship is more complex.

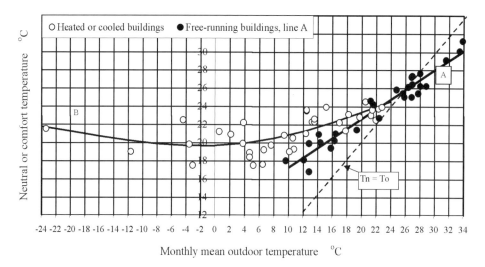

Figure 8.5 *The change in comfort temperature with monthly mean outdoor temperature. Each point represents the mean value for one survey. The buildings are divided between those that are climatized at the time of the survey and those that are free-running. Subsequent analysis of the ASHRAE database of comfort surveys (Humphreys and Nicol, 2000a) showed similar results (after Humphreys, 1978)*

deDear and Brager (1998) make a division between buildings which are centrally air conditioned and those which are NV. They argue that occupants of buildings which are air conditioned have different *expectations* than the occupants of NV buildings. It seems unlikely that people modify their responses to a building on the basis of their expectations of its building services. Nor is this distinction supported by evidence from the field (Humphreys and Nicol, 2002). Expectation does have a part to play, but more in defining the temperature people expect in a particular situation than in their attitude to the building services.

In a re-analysis of the data of deDear and Brager, Humphreys and Nicol (2000a) argue that using Humphreys' original distinction (between free-running and climatized buildings) increases the precision of the relationship both in free-running buildings and in those which are climatized.

It has been argued that using just the outdoor temperature to calculate comfort temperatures ignores many other factors such as the humidity and air movement. However, people's clothing insulation depends on outdoor temperature (Nicol *et al*, 1999), as does the use of building controls (Raja *et al*, 2001; Nicol, 2001). Raja and Nicol (1997) have shown posture to vary with temperature. Baker and Standeven (1995), Nicol and Humphreys (1973) and Fanger and Toftum (2002) have all suggested that the metabolic rate for a given activity may also vary with temperature or comfort vote.

The *feedback* between the climate and adaptive actions means that only the outdoor temperature need be considered in real situations in real buildings, though the relationship is an empirical 'black box' because the inter-relations are not all fully defined.

In a free-running building the indoor climate is linked by the building to outdoor conditions. When the building is being climatized the relationship changes, because the indoor climate is decoupled from outdoors.

8.3.3.5 People in buildings: adaptive opportunities

There are aspects of building services which affect the comfort of occupants. Leaman and Bordass (1997) have demonstrated that there is more 'forgiveness' of buildings where occupants have more access to building controls. By forgiveness they mean that the attitude of the occupants to the building is affected so that they will overlook short-comings in the thermal environment more readily. Variability is generally thought of as a 'bad thing' in centrally controlled buildings. A change in temperature makes occupants uncomfortable. In buildings where the occupant is in control, variability may result from people adjusting conditions to suit themselves. A certain amount of variability then becomes a 'good thing'. Where control is left to the building manager (through the HVAC system) there is a smaller envelope of acceptable conditions, comfort changes more quickly with temperature and the occupants appear less forgiving.

Baker and Standeven (1995) identify an 'adaptive opportunity' afforded by a building that will affect the comfort of its occupants. The premise is that the more opportunity occupants have to adapt the environment to their liking, the less likely are they to experience thermal stress and the wider will be the range of acceptable conditions. Adaptive opportunity is generally interpreted as the *ability* to open a window, draw a blind, use a fan and so on. It also includes dress code, working practices and other factors influencing the interaction between occupant and building.

Changes in clothing, activity and posture and the promotion of air movement change the comfort temperature. Other adaptive opportunities allow the occupants to change the indoor climate to suit themselves. Actual adaptive behaviour is an amalgam of these two types of action. The range of conditions considered comfortable is affected by the characteristics of the building and the opportunities for individual adaptation by occupants.

Nicol and McCartney (1999) found that it was difficult to quantify the adaptive opportunity in terms of the availability of building controls. Merely adding up the number of controls does not give a good measure of the success of a building or its adaptive opportunity. It would seem that in addition to the existence of a control a judgement is needed as to whether it is useful in the particular circumstances. In addition, the perceived usefulness of a particular control will change from time to time depending on conditions (Nicol and Kessler, 1998).

8.3.3.6 Time as a factor in specifying comfort conditions

When people take actions in response to a thermal environment, these actions take time to accomplish. There are a number of actions which can be taken: some, like opening a window, take little time, whereas others, such as the change of fashion from winter to summer clothes, take longer. The change is fast enough to keep up with the major fluctuations in the weather from season to season but not always fast enough to account for all the changes in the weather (Nicol, 2000). In his comparison between outdoor temperature and the comfort temperature indoors (see Figure 8.4), Humphreys (1978) used records of the monthly mean of the outdoor air temperature as the defining variable. deDear and Brager (2002) used the monthly mean of outdoor effective temperature. The weather can change dramatically within a month and both people and the buildings they inhabit change at a rate which will not be reflected by a monthly mean.

Nicol and Raja (1996) and McCartney and Nicol (2002) have tried to determine the rate of change of comfort temperature using comfort surveys conducted over a period of time. The exponentially weighted running mean of the temperature reflects fairly well the time dependence of the comfort temperature or clothing insulation.

The equation for the exponentially weighted running mean at time t is

$$T_{\text{rm}(t)} = (1 - \alpha)(T_{t-1} + \alpha T_{t-2} + \alpha^2 T_{t-3} \ldots) \tag{8.2}$$

where α is a constant such that $1 > \alpha \geq 0$, $T_{\text{rm}(t)}$ is the running mean temperature at time t, T_t is the mean temperature for a time t of a series at equal intervals (hours, days, etc.) and T_{t-n} is the instantaneous temperature at n time intervals previously. The time interval often used to calculate T_{rm} is a day. The time series gives a running mean temperature that is decreasingly affected by any particular temperature event as time passes. The rate at which the effect of any particular temperature dies away depends on α. Equation (8.2) simplifies to

$$T_{\text{rm}(t)} = (1 - \alpha)T_{\text{od}(t-1)} + \alpha T_{\text{rm}(t-1)} \tag{8.3}$$

where $T_{\text{od}(t-1)}$ and $T_{\text{rm}(t-1)}$ are the mean temperature and the running mean temperature for the previous day. Today's running mean can thus be simply calculated from yesterday's mean temperature and yesterday's running mean. The larger the value of α the more important are the effects of past temperatures.

The correlation of outdoor running mean temperature with comfort temperature rises gradually until α reaches about 0.8 and then starts to decrease. Although the peak in the correlation with comfort temperature is small, this is a real effect. The correlation with daily mean outdoor temperature T_{od} ($\alpha = 0$) and with the monthly mean of outdoor temperature ($\alpha \approx 0.95$) are both less than the correlation with T_{rm} where $\alpha = 0.8$. A similar effect has been found to apply to clothing insulation (Nicol and Raja, 1996; Morgan *et al*, 2002).

8.4 Recent developments and future directions

8.4.1 New research in thermal comfort

The conference Moving Thermal Comfort Standards into the 21st Century held in Windsor, UK, in April 2001 [selected papers are available in a Special Issue of *Energy and Buildings* (Nicol and Parsons, 2002)] revealed the breadth of research and the depth of controversy which continues to inspire interest in the study of thermal comfort. The conference set itself the following task:

The current international thermal comfort standard (ISO 7730) is based upon research conducted in the 1960s. The PMV/PPD thermal comfort index was developed from knowledge and thinking at that time...

With new knowledge and the proposed revision of ISO 7730, it is timely to review thoroughly what has been achieved in the past 30 years and integrate new knowledge and ideas into future standards...

The conference will present the thinking behind current international standards and debate the way in which they can be improved by the incorporation of new findings. Members of the relevant standards committees have been invited to attend the conference and will take an active part in the debates. At the same time, researchers will have an opportunity to present their results and take part in far-reaching scientific debates.

The conference was successful in bringing together the latest thinking in many fields related to thermal comfort and the areas of research which impinge upon it. In particular, a number of problems with the current thermal comfort standards were addressed and alternative methods presented by which new standards could be framed. Many of the international experts in thermal comfort and members of the relevant committees of the International Organization for Standardization (ISO) and the American Standards Institute, represented by ASHRAE, attended the conference. A key paper was that from Olesen and Parsons (2002) explaining the meaning of comfort standards and introducing the new ISO standard.

To allow for the errors in relating PMV to field measurements, Fanger and Toftum (2002) presented a correction to existing standards for warm climates where there is restricted contact with air-conditioned buildings. The authors suppose that 'The main reason [for the 'adaptive errors' in PMV – F.N.] is low expectations, but a metabolic rate that is estimated too high can also contribute to explaining the difference'. They do not present an extension for cold climates where similar 'errors' are also found (see Figure 8.1 and deDear and Brager, 2002).

Methods were presented for improving existing standards: through the improvement of the information on which the heat balance formula is based (Havenith *et al*, 2002), investigating the requirements of special groups (Parsons, 2002b) or assessing the interactions between different aspects of comfort (Toftum, 2002).

Other authors suggested new approaches to standards based on empirical evidence from field studies (deDear and Brager, 2002; Nicol and Humphreys, 2002). A particular concern of these authors was the issue of sustainability in the use of existing standards. In the case of deDear and Brager, a 'hybrid' standard was presented suggesting the use of existing PMV-based standards in air-conditioned buildings but an empirical standard for NV buildings. Nicol and Humphreys presented a case for an entirely empirical standard, backed by evidence (Humphreys and Nicol, 2002) that PMV is equally unreliable in air-conditioned buildings.

Given the complexities of the interactions between humans and the environments they inhabit, the empirical results of field studies are currently the most realistic option for the development of more sustainable standards, particularly for buildings. One result of the adaptive approach is that the conditions which people favour will be a function of the context.

8.4.2 Defining an adaptive standard for buildings

Most comfort studies have been conducted using subjects in buildings. There is consequently a large body of information relating to people in this context. Furthermore, the database can be added to relatively easily, so that new building contexts, building types and climates can be added relatively inexpensively. In this way a robust standard for comfort conditions within buildings could be relatively easily produced. Such a standard would overcome some of the shortcomings of existing models of thermal comfort arising from the steady-state nature of the underlying thermal models and the complexity of the behaviour which is included in the adaptive model. The empirical model is limited, however, by the database which is used to build it and cannot therefore be generalized beyond it.

Another possibility exists, which is to use the rapidly developing expertise in dynamic simulation, both of buildings and also of the physical/physiological system of the human. This possibility is explored in Section 8.4.3.

8.4.2.1 What kind of standards?

Standards can be divided into those which standardize a methodology and those which define good practice. An adaptive standard will most usefully be of the latter type. Adaptive practice is context dependent. A different standard may apply for different circumstances (e.g. buildings, outdoors or vehicles).

Here we outline the basis for a standard to define good practice in the definition of temperatures in buildings. Such a standard would indicate

- the indoor environments most likely to provide comfort
- the range of acceptable environments
- the rate of change of indoor environment which is acceptable to occupants.

The standard should help the designer make decisions about successful strategies in terms of the design of the building, the controls it provides and its services

8.4.2.2 The most likely comfort temperature

Evidence that the comfort temperature in free-running buildings depends on the outdoor temperature is shown in Figure 8.5. The equation for comfort temperature T_c is almost exactly

$$T_c = 13.5 + 0.54T_o \tag{8.4}$$

where T_o in this case is the monthly mean of the outdoor air temperature. Humphreys and Nicol (2000a) showed that this relationship between comfort temperature and outdoor temperature for free-running building is remarkably stable between Humphreys' (1978) data and deDear's (1998) ASHRAE database. The correlation coefficient r for the relationship was 0.97 for 1978 data and 0.95 for the ASHRAE database.

The relationship in buildings which are climatized is more complex and less stable. The indoor temperature is governed by the custom of the occupants (or their building services manager). A wide range of comfort temperatures for climatized buildings is shown in Figure 8.5. There is a difference of ~2°C in indoor comfort temperatures for climatized buildings between the two databases compiled in the 1970s and the 1990s (Humphreys and Nicol, 2000a). It is not clear whether this is due to a change in preference over time or to other factors, but the preferred indoor temperature may need to be determined from time to time or between one group of people and another. Note that this does not put the adaptive standard at a disadvantage vis-à-vis the rational indices: these also need to know clothing insulation and activity to calculate comfort temperatures.

8.4.2.3 The range of comfortable conditions

It is difficult to define the range of conditions which will be found comfortable. The adaptive approach tells us that variability in indoor temperatures can be caused by actions taken to reduce discomfort, in addition to those which are not controlled locally and hence are more likely to cause discomfort. Adaptive thermal comfort is therefore a function of the possibilities for change as well as the actual temperatures achieved. The width of the comfort 'zone', if measured purely in physical terms, will therefore depend on the balance between these two types of action. In a situation where there was no possibility of changing clothing or activity and where air movement cannot be used, the comfort zone may be as narrow as ±2°C. In situations where these adaptive opportunities are available and appropriate, the comfort zone may be considerably wider.

8.4.2.4 Using the standard to design buildings and their services

The adaptive relationship between comfort temperature and the outdoor temperature can be used to help design comfortable buildings. An example is shown in Figure 8.6. Here the indoor comfort temperature (T_c) is calculated from the mean outdoor temperature (T_o) and plotted on a monthly basis together with the monthly mean of the daily maximum (T_{omax}), minimum (T_{omin}) and mean outdoor air temperatures. Such a diagram helps the designer to judge whether passive heating and/or cooling is a possibility in the climate under consideration. The relationship between the comfort temperature and the range of outdoor temperatures shows whether, for instance, night cooling is likely to be a viable way to keep the building comfortable during the day in summer or to calculate whether passive solar heating will be enough in winter. This method has been used to define comfort indoors in a recent book (Roaf *et al*, 2001).

8.4.2.5 The case of climatized buildings – the adaptive algorithm

The comfort temperature in climatized buildings is a matter of custom but so long as the change is sufficiently slow, people will adapt to a range of temperatures. The indoor comfort temperature will naturally change with the seasons as people adjust their clothing to the weather. Thus the idea of an 'adaptive algorithm' (Humphreys and Nicol, 1995) to define a variable indoor temperature in terms of the running mean of the outdoor temperature is attractive. A crude form of such an algorithm is already used in ASHRAE Standard 55 (ASHRAE, 1992) which has different indoor set points for 'summer' and 'winter'. These seasonal set-points are based on crude assumptions about the seasonal change in clothing insulation. The adaptive algorithm changes

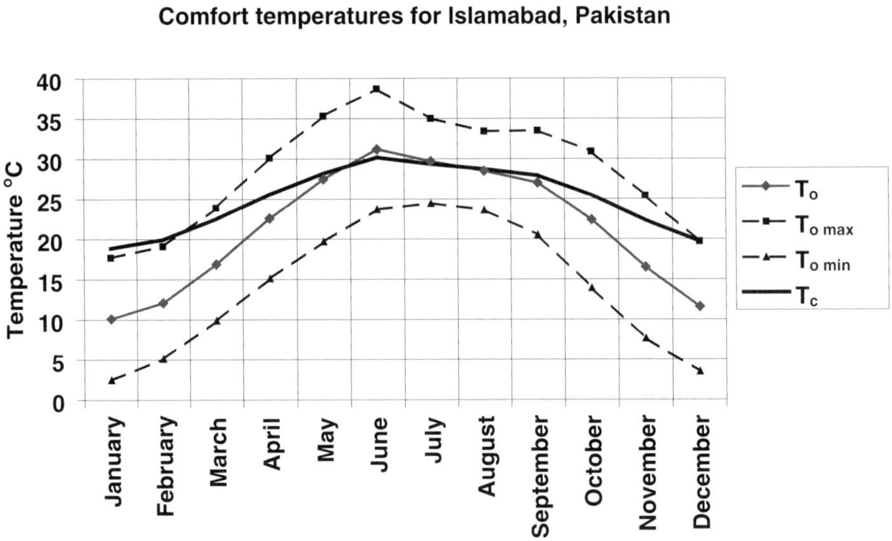

Comfort temperatures for Islamabad, Pakistan

Figure 8.6 *The seasonal changes in mean comfort temperature, T_c, in Islamabad, Pakistan, and its relation to mean daily maximum, minimum and mean outdoor temperatures, T_o. The relationship used to calculate comfort temperature from outdoor temperature is from Humphreys (1978) for free-running buildings*

continuously in line with results from comfort surveys: it does not rely on the vague – and often meaningless – description of 'season' but relates the set-point directly to the running mean of the current outdoor air temperature. A recent project (McCartney and Nicol, 2002) suggests that such a variable indoor standard does not increase occupant discomfort compared with a constant indoor temperature, yet does significantly reduce energy use by the cooling system.

8.4.2.6 Sustainable comfort standards

There is an advantage, when presented with two otherwise equal possible standards, in preferring the more sustainable one. A number of attempts have been made through simulation (Milne, 1995; Wilkins, 1995; Hensen and Centnerova, 2001) to predict the changes in energy use which will result from the use of a variable indoor set-point temperature in air-conditioned buildings, and most have suggested that energy savings will result. The extent of energy savings has been estimated in the region of 10% of the cooling load in UK conditions. In a recent European project, Stoops *et al* (2000) estimated that energy savings were in the region of 18% above that using a constant indoor temperature.

Whilst NV buildings use about half the energy of ones which are air conditioned (Kolokotroni *et al*, 1996) the temperatures in NV buildings are constantly changing. A constant-temperature standard therefore militates against the use of natural ventilation. A variable indoor temperature standard will help save energy by encouraging the use of NV buildings. Note that, although it will save energy in an air-conditioned building, a 'seasonal' temperature change such as is suggested by ASHRAE 55 (ASHRAE, 1992) may be almost as hard to achieve in a free-running building as a single constant temperature throughout the year.

Before such a standard could be developed, a programme of field surveys would be necessary in different climates and building types. Current information, although covering a wide range of climates, derives largely from office workers. More information from residences, schools, etc., would be needed if the standard were intended to cover those building types.

8.4.3 Developing a new dynamic approach to predicting thermal comfort in buildings

8.4.3.1 The relevance of a new approach

There are a number of dynamic physical/physiological simulation models of the human body (e.g. Fiala *et al*, 1999; Tanabe *et al*, 2002). These models have been developed and validated using numerous physiological experiments and are beginning to address the problem of providing a psychophysical simulation of thermal comfort responses. At the same time there are numerous dynamic thermal simulation packages for buildings. These simulations are increasingly sophisticated, but their treatment of occupant behaviour is generally unsatisfactory. Behaviour is generally (1) assumed to be optimal or (2) set according to some preconception of 'normal' behaviour or (3) used experimentally – to test the results of different patterns of behaviour. Despite their dynamic potential, building simulations currently treat the occupant as being represented by an algorithm based on steady-state conditions such as PMV. Likewise, physiological models often treat the environment as a constant or as undergoing a gradual or step change.

The problem is how to link the physiological model to the building model. Olesen and de Carli (2002) explored the implications for predicted indoor comfort, using PMV and measurements of indoor conditions, of allowing changes in clothing to occur as necessary. Boerstra *et al* (2002) used an adaptive upper limit to the maximum indoor temperature as a way of predicting the risk of discomfort in buildings. These new approaches demonstrate the need for more information about the use of building controls in particular and the overall occupant–building interaction in general. The transient interactions are mediated by the use of clothing (and possibly activity) on the one hand and the use of building controls on the other. The actual way in which these interactions occur has been observed in a number of field studies (see Section 8.4.3.2). The results of these can be used to inform and calibrate computer simulation.

The future of thermal comfort research must be to build the understanding of adaptive behaviour through computer modelling of the occupant–building system. An understanding of this occupant behaviour should be built through the developments in the computer modelling of buildings. These should take account of existing empirical knowledge of behavioural use of control systems for indoor temperature (Nicol, 2001). This calls for a 'vertical' approach to understanding indoor climate in buildings, combining the skills of physiologists, field researchers, building simulation and so on. Behavioural control of indoor conditions has been considered to be a weakness of NV buildings because the actions of building occupants are beyond the control of building designers or managers. It is felt that there is a danger that controls will not be used optimally from an energy standpoint (Bruant *et al*, 1996).

Simulations are normally used to produce precise predictions of indoor conditions from a known sequence of circumstances. This is in effect predicting the effect of known inputs, which must therefore be in the past and not the unknown inputs which will occur in the future. The aim here must be to *predict* the *risk* of discomfort by predicting the behaviour of the building in the future. An exact set of conditions will not be available, but a predicted distribution of conditions can be developed. Such an approach might develop empirical, stochastic algorithms to characterize occupant use of controls as suggested by Nicol (2001). These will then be used together with statistical information about the variation of external conditions (the weather) to provide a distribution of indoor conditions from which the risk of discomfort can be deduced.

8.4.3.2 Linking thermal comfort to a stochastic algorithm of the use of building controls

Some field studies of thermal comfort record the use of building controls. Patterns of behaviour have emerged in the way controls are used by building occupants. The use of controls is clearly influenced by physical conditions, but their use tends to be governed by a stochastic rather than a precise relationship (Nicol, 2001; Reinhart, 2001). Hence there is not a precise temperature at which everyone opens a window, but as the temperature rises there is an increased likelihood that they will have done so (Nicol *et al*, 1999; Raja *et al*, 2001).

The data collected about the use of controls in these studies is essentially binary – windows open or closed, blind up or down, etc. The likelihood that any particular control is being used can be said to depend on the thermal environment and in particular the temperature. Thus, as the indoor or outdoor temperature increases so does the likelihood that a window is opened or a fan switched on (Nicol, 2001). One method used to analyse such processes is probit analysis (Finney, 1964). This analysis assumes that the likelihood of an event occurring increases as the 'intensity' of the stimulus increases. The probability p $(0 < p < 1)$ of an event having happened can be defined according to the 'logit function':

$$\log[p/(1-p)] = a + bx \qquad (8.5)$$

where a and b are constants and x is the stimulus variable (in this case temperature or a thermal index). The values of a and b can be determined by a weighted linear regression analysis of the logit function against the thermal index (commonly used statistical packages such as SPSS can be used to calculate the values of a and b). Once the values of the constants are known, a curve can be constructed linking the index, and the probability p, using the equation

$$p = e^{(a + bx)}/[1 + e^{(a + bx)}] \qquad (8.6)$$

The form of the resulting curve for p is illustrated in Figure 8.7.

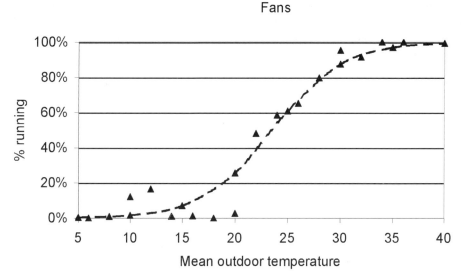

Figure 8.7 *Use of probit analysis to illustrate how the proportion of people who use fans in Pakistani offices changes with outdoor temperature. With increasing temperature, the proportion of people who use fans increases (▲). The probit line represents the best-fit line to the points using the curve in Equation (8.6) (from Nicol, 2001)*

In Equation (8.6), the variable x is some measure of the environment, either indoors or out. It may be a simple measure such as the temperature or the solar intensity. It is reasonable to assume that a combination of physical variables will make the subject respond by using the control. Whilst the variations in the use of some controls are best correlated with the outdoor temperature or an index of indoor conditions, others, for instance blinds or lights, may be better correlated with solar intensity. In addition, the use of one control may change depending on the use of another.

8.4.3.3 Building the algorithm into computer models

A model which is going to simulate the effect of controls must also allow for the effect of changes in wind speed, wind direction, cloud cover and solar intensity. Information is available about changes in these variables and it will be necessary to produce distributions of ventilation rate and solar heat gain for given seasons and sites and given control configurations. The effect of time lags in the responses both of the building and the occupants (Nicol, 2000) must also be considered.

The aim is to suggest a distribution of indoor temperatures rather than an exact value. A method using repeated simulations under different conditions can be used to predict the distribution of indoor conditions resulting from this combination of factors. It will itself have a distribution and being the combination of other distributions it will probably approximate to a normal distribution. This is generally in line with experience but needs to be checked.

The development of a stochastic approach to indoor temperature and air movement in occupied buildings will help to make building simulation useful to those who wish to design acceptable comfortable buildings for the future. In particular, the probabilistic approach will allow the *risk* of discomfort to be assessed.

8.4.3.4 How can the new approach be achieved and by whom?

At present, the main thrust of building simulation is directed towards the forecasting of energy use by buildings and their services and, less importantly, to the prediction of precise indoor environments. These criteria for simulation are not appropriate for the evaluation of NV buildings where the risk of discomfort rather than the energy consumption is the key point of concern for a building and its occupants and owners. Discomfort is the key because dissatisfaction with the building will affect productivity (McCartney and Humphreys, 2002) and the perceived indoor air quality (Humphreys *et al*, 2002). Discomfort can also lead to high-energy responses which are not sustainable.

This is an ambitious target, attempting to take two developed and validated technologies – simulations of the human thermoregulatory system and building simulations – and integrate them to produce a quantitatively and qualitatively different technology. Innovative aspects include

- the use of data from field surveys to define thermal dissatisfaction from the thermo-physiological states of the human body

- the use of field study results to develop algorithms for the dynamic behaviour of building occupants in respect of the frequency of use of building controls, clothing level, etc.

- the characterization of indoor climate and energy use as a distribution of values over time arising from a number of stochastic processes (use of controls, meteorological conditions, thermal response of occupants) rather than a precise value

- using this output to assess the risk of dissatisfaction rather than providing a specified comfort condition arising from a specific set of conditions.

The resulting occupant/building simulations will raise the possibility of developing methods to test the viability of different ventilation strategies and building control designs, in particular the design of window openings.

The importance of this work cannot be overestimated. Not only is the potential for the estimation of energy use by occupied NV buildings particularly important, but so also is the possibility of the risk assessment of dissatisfaction with the building. It is clear that the necessary expertise can now be found, not only in simulation but also in the conduct and interpretation of field surveys of thermal comfort and the use of controls. This will be an important step towards the rational use of energy, particularly in the definition and realization of low-energy buildings. The simulations and methodologies developed will also lead in the long run to the development of improved sustainable international standards for temperatures in buildings.

8.4.3.5 The necessary research effort

The research effort needed to realize the potential of the suggested methodology is unlikely to be possible without a major research effort from a network of researchers and research teams. It would be impossible at this stage to detail the exact nature and timetable for the research and development effort. Critical stages of the research effort are as follows:

- select a dynamic, multi-node simulation model for predicting human thermo-physiological responses to the physical environment
- extend the physiological model to predict the psychophysical response in terms of the comfort vote and thermal acceptability levels
- determine the dependence of clothing insulation and metabolic rate on comfort vote and indoor temperature in the field
- analyse empirical data about the use made of controls by building occupants
- develop ways to characterize weather data input for building simulations in stochastic terms
- select a suitable dynamic building simulation that can be modified to accept input parameters which are specified according to a stochastic algorithm
- apply the output from such simulations to the dynamic body simulation created from the first three points to enable the research team to carry out a sensitivity analysis and assess the risk of discomfort in the building
- use the resulting methodology to predict the likely success of any building, not in terms of expected indoor temperatures, but in terms of expected dissatisfaction
- use the methodology to assess the distribution of energy use resulting from the design of a building and occupant access to building controls
- the resulting building–occupant simulation will allow designers to choose an optimum building design strategy and to optimize the design and specification of controls.

8.4.3.6 Expected outcomes of the research

- The programme of research outlined above will develop methods for evaluation of the indoor comfort potentials of NV buildings which are under the whole or partial control of occupants.
- The simulation will allow realistic estimates to be made of the energy use by occupied NV buildings. This will feed in to legislation designed to monitor energy use by buildings.
- Lessons can be drawn for the design of buildings and building control systems for the ventilation and climatization of NV buildings. The application of the results to Building Energy Management Systems will also be an important output.
- Lessons will be drawn for the design of future sustainable thermal standards for buildings.
- Lessons can also be drawn for the education of building designers through the imaginative dissemination of the results of the research, e.g. through multimedia presentations, specialized teaching packs and so on.

8.5 References

ASHRAE, 1992, *Thermal Environment Conditions for Human Occupancy*, ASHRAE Standard 55, American Society of Heating Refrigeration and Air-conditioning Engineers, Atlanta, GA.

Auliciems, A and deDear, R, 1986, 'Air conditioning in Australia I: Human thermal factors', in *Architectural Science Review*, 29, 67–75.

Baker, N V and Standeven, M A, 1995, 'A behavioural approach to thermal comfort assessment in naturally ventilated buildings', in *Proceedings of CIBSE National Conference, Eastbourne*, London, Chartered Institution of Building Services Engineers, 76–84.

Bedford, T, 1936, *The Warmth Factor in Comfort at Work*, MRC Industrial Health Board Report No. 76, London, HMSO.

Boerstra, A C, Kurvers, S R and van der Linden, A C, 2002, 'Thermal comfort in real live buildings: proposal for a new Dutch guideline', in H Levin (ed), *Proceedings of the 9th International Conference on Indoor Air, 2002*, Vol. 4, *Indoor Air*, Santa Cruz, USA, 629–634.

Bruant, M, Guarracino, G, Michel, P, Santamouris, M and Voeltzel, A, 1996, 'Impact of a global control of bioclimatic buildings in terms of energy consumption and building performance', in *4th European Conference on Solar Energy in Architecture and Urban Planning, Berlin*, 537–540.

CEN/ISO, 1994, *Moderate Thermal Environments – Determination of the PMV and PPD Indices and Specification of the Conditions for Thermal Comfort*, CEN/ISO 7730, Geneva, International Organization for Standardization.

deDear, R J, 1998, 'A global database of thermal comfort field experiments', in *ASHRAE Transactions*, 104(1b), 1141–1152.

deDear, R J and Brager, G S, 1998, 'Developing and adaptive model of thermal comfort and preference', in *ASHRAE Transactions*, 104(1), 145–167.

deDear, R J and Brager, G S, 2002, 'Thermal comfort in naturally ventilated buildings: revisions to ASHRAE Standard 55', in *Energy and Buildings*, 34(6), 549–561.

Fanger, P O, 1970, *Thermal Comfort*, Copenhagen, Danish Technical Press.

Fanger, P O and Toftum, J, 2002, 'Extension of the PMV model to non-air-conditioned buildings in warm climates', in *Energy and Buildings*, 34(6), 533–536.

Fiala, D, Lomas, K J and Stohrer, M A, 1999, 'Computer model of human thermoregulation for a wide range of environmental conditions: the passive system', in *Journal of Applied Physiology*, 87(5), 1957–1972.

Finney, D J, 1964, *Probit Analysis*, Cambridge, Cambridge University Press.

Havenith, G, Holmer, I and Parsons, K, 2002, 'Personal factors in thermal comfort assessment: clothing properties and metabolic heat production', in *Energy and Buildings*, 34(6), 581–591.

Hensen, J L M and Centnerova, L, 2001, 'Energy simulations of traditional versus adaptive thermal comfort for two moderate climate regions', in *Proceedings of the Conference: Moving Comfort Standards into the 21st Century*, Oxford Brookes University, UK, 78–91.

Hopkinson, R G, 1963, *Architectural Physics: Lighting*, London, HMSO.

Humphreys, M A, 1976, 'Field studies of thermal comfort compared and applied', in *Journal of the Institution of Heating and Ventilating Engineers*, 44, 5–27.

Humphreys, M A, 1978, 'Outdoor temperatures and comfort indoors', in *Building Research and Practice*, 6(2), 92–105.

Humphreys, M A. and Nicol, J F, 1995, 'An adaptive guideline for UK office temperatures', in J F Nicol, M A Humphreys, O Sykes and S Roaf (eds), *Standards for Thermal Comfort: Indoor Air Temperature Standards for the 21st Century*, London, E & FN Spon, 190–195.

Humphreys, M A and Nicol, J F, 1996, 'Conflicting criteria for thermal sensation within the Fanger Predicted Mean Vote equation', in *Proceedings of the CIBSE/ASHRAE Joint National Conference 1996, Harrogate, Part 1*, London, Chartered Institution of Building Services Engineers, 153–158.

Humphreys, M A and Nicol, J F, 1998, 'Understanding the adaptive approach to thermal comfort', in *ASHRAE Transactions*, 104(1), 991–1004.

Humphreys, M A and Nicol, J F, 2000a, 'Outdoor temperature and indoor thermal comfort: raising the precision of the relationship for the 1998 ASHRAE database of field studies', in *ASHRAE Transactions*, 206(2), 485–492.

Humphreys, M A and Nicol, J F, 2000b, 'The effects of measurement and formulation error on thermal comfort indices in the ASHRAE database of field studies', in *ASHRAE Transactions*, 206(2), 493–502.

Humphreys, M A and Nicol, J F, 2002, 'The validity of ISO-PMV for predicting comfort votes in every-day thermal environments', in *Energy and Buildings*, 34(6), 667–684.

Humphreys, M A, Nicol, J F and McCartney, K J, 2002, 'An analysis of some subjective assessments of indoor air quality in five European countries', in H Levin (ed), *Proceedings of the 9th International Conference on Indoor Air, 2002*, Vol. 3, *Indoor Air*, Santa Cruz, USA, 86–91.

Kolokotroni, M, Kukadia, V and Perera, MDAES, 1996, 'NATVENT – European project on overcoming technical barriers to low-energy natural ventilation', in *Proceedings of the CIBSE/ASHRAE Joint National Conference 1996, Part 2*, London, Chartered Institution of Building Services Engineers, 36–41.

Leaman, A J and Bordass, W T, 1997, 'Productivity in buildings: the "killer" variables', presented at the Workplace Comfort Forum, London.

McCartney, K J and Humphreys, M A, 2002, 'Thermal comfort and productivity', in H Levin (ed), *Proceedings of the 9th International Conference on Indoor Air, 2002*, Vol. 1, *Indoor Air*, Santa Cruz, USA, 822–827.

McCartney, K J and Nicol, J F, 2002, 'Developing an adaptive control algorithm for Europe: results of the SCATS project', in *Energy and Buildings*, 34(6), 623–635.

McIntyre, D A, 1980, *Indoor Climate*, Barking, Applied Science Publishers.

Miller, G, 1956, 'The magic number seven, plus or minus 2', in *Psychological Review*, 67, 81–97.

Milne, G R, 1995, 'The energy implications of a climate-based indoor air temperature standard', in J F Nicol, M A Humphreys, O Sykes and S Roaf (eds), *Standards for Thermal Comfort: Indoor Air Temperature Standards for the 21st Century*, London, E & FN Spon, 182–189.

Morgan, C A, deDear, R J and Brager, G, 2002, 'Climate, clothing and adaptation in the built environment', in H Levin (ed), *Proceedings of the 9th International Conference on Indoor Air, 2002*, Vol. 5, *Indoor Air*, Santa Cruz, USA, 98–103.

Nevins, R and Gagge, P, 1972, 'The new ASHRAE comfort chart', in *ASHRAE Journal*, 14, 41–43.

Nicol, J F, 2000, 'Time and thermal comfort, evidence from the field', in A Sayigh (ed), *Renewables: the Energy for the 21st Century, WREC VI, Brighton, 2000, Part 1*, 477–482, Oxford, Pergamon Press.

Nicol, J F, 2001, 'Characterising occupant behaviour in buildings: towards a stochastic model of occupant use of windows, lights, blinds, heaters and fans', in *Proceedings of the Seventh International IBPSA Conference, Rio, Part 2*, International Building Performance Simulation Association, UK, 1073–1078.

Nicol, J F and Humphreys, M A, 1973, 'Thermal comfort as part of a self-regulating system', in *Building Research and Practice*, 6(3), 191–197.

Nicol, J F and Humphreys, M A, 2002, 'Adaptive thermal comfort and sustainable thermal standards for buildings', in *Energy and Buildings*, 34(6), 563–572.

Nicol, J F and Kessler, M R B, 1998, 'Perception of comfort in relation to weather and adaptive opportunities', in *ASHRAE Transactions*, 104(1), 1005–1017.

Nicol, J F and McCartney, K J, 1999, 'Assessing adaptive opportunities in buildings', in *Proceedings of the CIBSE National Conference*, London, Chartered Institution of Building Services Engineers, 219–229.

Nicol J F and Parsons, K C (eds), 2002, *Energy and Buildings*, 34(6), Special Issue on Thermal Comfort Standards.

Nicol, J F and Raja, I A, 1996, *Thermal Comfort, Time and Posture: Exploratory Studies in the Nature of Adaptive Thermal Comfort*, Oxford, School of Architecture, Oxford Brookes University.

Nicol, J F, Raja, I A, Allaudin, A and Jamy, G N, 1999, 'Climatic variations in comfort temperatures: the Pakistan projects', in *Energy and Buildings*, 30, 261–279.

Olesen, B W and de Carli, M, 2002, 'Long term evaluation of the general thermal comfort conditions', in H Levin (ed), *Proceedings of the 9th International Conference on Indoor Air, 2002*, Vol. 4, *Indoor Air*, Santa Cruz, USA, 1066–1071.

Olesen, B W and Parsons, K C, 2002, 'Introduction to thermal comfort standards and to the proposed new version of EN ISO 7730', in *Energy and Buildings*, 34(6), 537–548.

Parsons, K C, 2002a, *Human Thermal Environments*, 2nd edn, Oxford, Blackwell Scientific.

Parsons, K C, 2002b, 'The effects of gender, acclimation state, the opportunity to adjust clothing and physical disability on requirements for thermal comfort', in *Energy and Buildings*, 34(6), 593–599.

Parsons, K C, Webb, L H, McCartney, K J, Humphreys, M A and Nicol, J F, 1997, 'A climatic chamber study into the validity of Fanger's PMV/PPD thermal comfort index for subjects wearing different levels of clothing insulation', in *Proceedings of CIBSE National Conference, Part 1*, London, Chartered Institution of Building Services Engineers, 193–205.

Raja, I A and Nicol, J F, 1997, 'A technique for postural recording and analysis for thermal comfort research', in *Applied Ergonomics*, 27(3), 221–225.

Raja, I A, Nicol, J F and McCartney, K J, 2001, 'The significance of controls for achieving thermal comfort in naturally ventilated buildings', in *Energy and Buildings*, 33, 235–244.

Reinhart, C F, 2001, 'Daylight availability and manual lighting control in office buildings, simulation studies and analysis of measurements', *PhD Thesis*, University of Karlsruhe.

Roaf, S C, Fuentes, M and Taylor, S, 2001, *The Eco-house Design Guide*, London, Architectural Press.

Santamouris, M and Wouters, P, 1994, 'Energy and indoor climate in Europe – past and present', in G. Guarracino (ed), *Proceedings of European Conference on Energy Performance and Indoor Climate in Buildings, Part 1*, Ecole Nationale des Travaux Publics de l'Etat, Lyon, 1–17.

Sharma, M R and Ali, S, 1986, 'Tropical summer index – a study of thermal comfort in Indian subjects', in *Building and Environment*, 21(1), 11–24.

Stevens, S S, 1975, *Psychophysics: Introduction to its Perceptual, Neural and Social Prospects*, New York, Wiley.

Stoops, J, Pavlou, C, Santamouris, M and Tsangrassoulis, A, 2000, *Report to Task 5 of the SCATS Project (Estimation of Energy Saving Potential of the Adaptive Algorithm)*, Brussels, European Commission.

Tanabe, S-I, Kabayashi, K, Nakano, J, Ozeki, Y and Konishi, M, 2002, 'Evaluation of thermal comfort using multi-node thermoregulation (65MN) and radiation models and computational fluid dynamics', in *Energy and Buildings*, 34(6), 637–646.

Toftum, J, 2002, 'Human response to combined indoor exposures', in *Energy and Buildings*, 34(6), 601–606.

Wilkins, J, 1995, 'Adaptive comfort control for conditioned buildings', in *Proceedings of CIBSE National Conference, Eastbourne, Part 2*, London, Chartered Institution of Building Services Engineers, 9–16.

9   Passive cooling

Samuel Hassid

Environmental and Water Resources Engineering, Technion – Israel Institute of Technology, Haifa 32000, Israel

9.1 Introduction

What is *passive* cooling?

The term 'cooling' is obvious – it refers to the need to reduce temperature (and, often, humidity) during the cooling season – which differs from place to place.

The term 'passive' is taken from the corresponding counter-discipline, passive heating, which had attracted great interest during the years following the 1973 energy crisis. It implies a reduction in the use of fossil fuels.

In the case of passive heating, the main energy source is the sun. In the case of passive cooling, there are several possibilities for heat sinks.

From where does interest in passive cooling stem?

Passive solar heating has been the subject of many investigations. It is a fact that the largest part of the 'civilized' world lives in places where winter heating is the primary concern of people and the major consumer of energy resources. In fact, in many of those places, cooling used to be a minor concern, until recently.

In addition, passive *heating* is a relatively 'benign' problem, involving mainly two quantities, losses through the envelope of the building and solar heat gains through the openings. In the relatively cold climates of most of the northern countries of the EU, it could be safely assumed that optimizing the solar heating performance during the heating season could result in no significant detrimental effects during the cooling season.

Passive cooling, on the other hand, turns out to be no less important, especially in the Mediterranean climates, where summers are uncomfortably hot, to different degrees. Cooling increasingly became a consideration during the early 1990s in those countries, for the following reasons.

- Increased demand in comfort standards led to an 'explosion' in the number of air-conditioning (AC) machines (in Israel, for example, the majority of households now have some kind of AC device, whereas as late as the mid-1980s AC was still considered a luxury for most buildings). AC results in a dramatic increase in energy demand and energy peaks. In addition, the CFC coolants of AC devices based on the Carnot cycle are connected with the widening of the hole in the ozone layer (adsorption air conditioning is much less common).

- Many Mediterranean countries have been hit by heat waves, often resulting in great loss of life and disruption.

- Passive heating was discovered to be sometimes much less attractive than in the Northern EU. Overheating is often an issue with several passive solar buildings during the summer and transition periods.

9.2 Cooling versus heating problems

Cooling problems are far less benign than heating problems, for the following reasons.

- Cooling depends much more strongly on climatic factors other than temperature, e.g. humidity, air speed, etc.

- Internal loads act in addition to envelope conduction loads and are often the major energy consumption factor.

- In contrast to the single heat *source*, there are several heat *sinks*: the ground, the sky, the air (sensible and latent heat).

- Analysis of passive cooling is more complex than for the corresponding heating problem. In addition, some data often necessary for passive cooling calculations were not always available, whereas the focus on passive cooling in building energy simulation codes was rather small about 10 years ago.

9.3 PASCOOL programme

A major step towards introducing an awareness of passive cooling issues into energy-conscious building design was the European project PASCOOL (Santamouris and Argyriou, 1997a), which was in a way a continuation of the previous project PASSYS, but focused on passive cooling with emphasis mainly on Southern European (Mediterranean) countries. Prior to that, passive cooling, as a systematic discipline, had been the subject of a book which was rather too 'American' (Cook, 1989), whereas applications in other parts of the world existed, but were fragmented (Antinucci *et al*, 1992; Givoni, 1994).

After the end of PASCOOL, there were several other follow-up programs, such as URBVENT and POLIS, focusing mainly on specific aspects of passive cooling (Santamouris and Asimakopoulos, 1996).

In the remainder of this chapter, we shall follow to a large extent the methodology of PASCOOL, with complementary material where more novel aspects are to be described.

9.4 Essential features of passive cooling

The essentials of passive cooling are as follows:

- prevention of (or protection from) heat gains
- modulation of heat flows
- utilization of heat sinks.

9.4.1 Prevention of heat gains

Prevention of heat gains can be achieved through the following approaches.

- Use of outdoor and semi-outdoor spacing.
- Solar control and shading of openings.
- Thermal insulation (essential for both summer and winter). Note that in this case an increase in thermal insulation may not always be desirable for all building elements.
- Control of internal gains, mainly through daylight utilization. Daylight utilization may sometimes result in conflicting requirements with solar control, but has to be addressed.

9.4.2 Modulation of heat by internal (mainly) thermal mass

As in the case of passive solar heating, passive solar cooling requires thermal mass: in both cases, the source or sink is not available at the time that the heating/cooling demand is maximum, making it necessary to store heat/'coolness' during part of the day.

Thermal mass in this case is *internal* mass – its optimization depending on many parameters: climatic conditions, occupancy patterns, building orientation and the use of auxiliary heating/cooling.

Thermal mass in its interaction with the other building elements is still not a closed subject in building research, and the effect of appropriate positioning of thermal mass might be very important.

It is also important whether the surface of the mass is convectively or radiatively cooled.

9.4.3 Heat sinks

When one speaks of passive cooling, one mainly refers to *heat sinks*.

Heat sinks, which are intended to absorb (dissipate) excess heat, depend on (a) the availability of an appropriate environmental heat sink and (b) the appropriate thermal coupling and sufficient temperature differences for the transfers of heat from indoor spaces to sink.

The main dissipation techniques and heat sinks are as follows:

- radiative cooling – the heat sink being the sky and the heat transfer mode radiation

- ground cooling – the main heat sink being the earth and the heat transfer mode (within the heat sink) conduction

- evaporative cooling – the heat sink being air (the wet bulb depression) and the heat transfer mode evaporation

- ventilative cooling – the heat sink being the air and the heat transfer mode convection.

9.4.3.1 Radiative cooling

The sink in radiative cooling is the sky temperature, which can be up to 20°C lower than the actual temperature. As a result, a horizontal exposed surface (a roof) is subject to heat loss. The difference between the sky temperature and the atmospheric temperature decreases with the humidity of the atmosphere (the dew point temperature) and with the cloud cover.

The simplest radiative cooling technique is painting the roof white, but the performance is rather poor. However, in Mediterranean countries painting the roof white is very common.

In some cases, movable insulation can be used. This is not applicable to multi-storey buildings. Movable mass is also conceivable.

The *flat plate cooler* is the most common device using radiative cooling – in a way, it is the opposite of the solar collector. A problem is, of course, that some of the loss by radiation is balanced by a gain by convection. Therefore, a screening device is required.

This method is not suitable for humid areas. The related technology is not always simple and may be expensive.

Generally, the potential for its use is rather limited; it should be used simultaneously with other methods.

9.4.3.2 Ground cooling (earth coupling)

During the cooling season, the temperature in the soil is lower than the air temperature by several degrees, and, no less important, the daily swing of temperature is smaller than that of the air (the opposite is true during the heating season). This makes the ground a suitable energy sink that can be used to cool dwellings.

There are two main concepts for ground cooling: direct contact and earth-to-air heat exchangers.

Direct contact

The use of the thermal mass of the earth to mitigate the effect of higher air temperature has been used traditionally from time immemorial in cave dwellings.

Earth-integrated homes are integral parts of vernacular architecture in many places in the world. In many cases, part of the building facade is buried or semi-buried (integrated in the slope of a mountain or a hill), whereas in other cases the building is totally buried, including the roof.

Despite their energy-related benefits, earth-integrated buildings have some limitations: structural (roofs may have to bear much larger loads), daylighting (which is eliminated for those facades of the building which are earth-integrated) and the possibility of condensation, which can be dealt with, but at the expense of the energy savings.

Earth-to-air heat exchangers

It is possible to take advantage of the lower (or higher, during the heating season) temperature of the ground by circulating air through buried pipes. It is possible to use an open- or a closed-loop circuit. The pipes may be plastic, metallic or concrete. Detailed calculations are needed to optimize the system.

It is important to check control, as well as indoor air quality problems (humidity).

9.4.3.3 Evaporative cooling

In evaporative cooling, the effect of evaporation is used as a natural heat sink: the air is cooled by evaporating water, which reduces the sensible heat of the air by increasing the latent heat of the liquid water which is transformed into a vapour.

Evaporative cooling has its origins thousands of years ago, and was used in Ancient Egypt and Persia. In its more modern form, it had been rediscovered in the early 20th century in the USA, but was of limited use during times of cheap AC.

Evaporative cooling systems can be classified in several ways:

- *direct* or *indirect* evaporative cooling – depending on whether the air of the dwelling is directly cooled by the water or this is done through a secondary air loop

- *passive* or *hybrid* evaporative cooling – depending on whether evaporation occurs naturally or is due to air circulated by ventilators.

Passive direct systems include vegetation for evapo-transpiration, fountains, pools and ponds, in addition to the use of volume and tower water techniques.

Passive indirect systems include roof sprinkling, roof ponds and moving water films.

Direct hybrid air coolers consist of a porous material saturated with water, with air circulating through the porous pad by means of a ventilator.

Indirect evaporative coolers are based on a heat exchange, with air being cooled through evaporation on the primary loop and air in the second loop being cooled through the heat exchanger (it is important that that the outdoor wet bulb temperature is lower than the indoor dry-bulb temperature).

9.4.3.4 Ventilative cooling

Ventilation (either natural or mechanical) is a subject by itself and its importance far exceeds the cooling – it is related first of all to the indoor air quality of a building. Ventilation can be wind-driven, thermal-driven (stack effect) or fan-forced.

Ventilative cooling is the most common mode of passive cooling, especially for the Mediterranean climate.

There are several ways in which ventilation can be used for cooling:

- by increasing the convective loss from the human body, through a higher ambient air velocity (human or comfort ventilation), even if this sometimes means a slightly higher temperature or humidity

- by nocturnal ventilative cooling, whereby the building structure is cooled to the low night temperature, and by minimizing ventilation, one keeps the coolness stored during the day.

Nocturnal ventilation presupposes a relatively large temperature swing between day and night. The dwellings should have an adequate thermal mass, to store the 'night coolness'.

9.5 Future research needs in passive cooling

As a follow-up to the results of the PASCOOL programme, Santamouris and Argyriou (1997b) proposed the following priorities for future research.

9.5.1 Microclimate around buildings

It is necessary to understand better the microclimate around buildings, and particularly the urban microclimate. The use of outside air for cooling becomes problematic, in view of the deterioration of outdoor air.

The urban heat island effect results in much higher thermal loads in urban environments, as opposed to rural environments at the same attitude and topography. Increased urbanization has exacerbated the effect: on the one hand the population density increases and on the other open spaces per capita decrease. In addition, the ventilation potential decreases, as a result of the slowing of wind speeds in urban canyons. It is reported that there is a very strong correlation between the city size and the heat island intensity, which can reach a maximum value of 8 K in cities of ~3 million inhabitants. In many cases, although it is difficult to observe an increase in mean temperature, heat waves are observed during the summer – or the spring in the case of Israel.

Relevant research actions should be aimed mainly at improving the urban environment by integrating passive heating, daylighting and cooling. To achieve this goal, solar and microclimatic aspects of urban planning should be compiled in such a way that they can be used by urban planners. For major cities, it is necessary to use climatic data characteristic of the central (or other) parts of city, which may be considerably different from those obtained in open-space climatic stations. Also, more attention should be paid to the extreme situation during heat waves – after all, they are the times when the public at large passes judgement on energy-saving methods.

9.5.2 Ventilation and air quality aspects

Inadequate ventilation may be the primary cause of poor indoor air quality of buildings. This is reflected by the increase in the recommended ventilation rates in newer versions of ASHRAE ventilation standards, and also the decrease in upper concentration limits of CO_2.

Demand control ventilation techniques are based on the control of specific pollutants (mainly CO_2). These systems contribute to both air quality and energy efficiency, especially in transiently occupied buildings. The link between energy efficiency and indoor environment should be the subject of further research – in the case of ventilative night cooling, there might be a conflict between the two: during the day, the buildings whose cooling strategy is based on night ventilation may require minimization of daytime ventilation, but this may be unacceptable from the point of view of indoor air quality.

9.5.3 New thermal comfort standards

Thermal comfort standards – especially those focusing on air-conditioned environments – relate to steady-state conditions. These are rarely encountered, especially for passively cooled buildings. The only methods available to investigate thermal comfort under unsteady conditions are semi-empirical thermal comfort experiments, some of which point to considerable discrepancies from Fanger's results (Fanger, 1970). It was also shown during the PASCOOL programme that the perceived comfort conditions are totally different in passively cooled and in AC buildings and that people are comfortable at temperatures much higher than expected. In fact, they adapt themselves by moving to cooler parts of the same room or by modifying their clothing or their metabolic rate.

New thermal assessment models are required to take into account those two effects: the effect of changing climatic conditions and the difference between the perceived thermal comfort in air-conditioned and in non-air-conditioned rooms.

9.5.4 Natural ventilation and air flow in urban environments

In the PASCOOL programme, algorithms for natural single and cross-ventilation experiments were developed. It is necessary to adapt these algorithms to account for the urban environment, which significantly affects the pressure coefficients in the envelopes of buildings. In this sense, it is necessary to use a methodology including computational fluid dynamics (CFD) calculations, measurements using small-scale models in wind tunnels and measurements in actual buildings, for different wind speeds and directions. In addition, studies of the air flow distribution inside buildings are necessary. There is a need for tools for studying the combined thermal and flow effects in buildings – the convective heat transfer coefficients used are not always appropriate.

9.5.5 Research on natural cooling techniques

During PASCOOL, a European Atlas for the potential of radiative, evaporative and ground cooling was produced. One important issue, however, is the combination of those techniques with conventional AC – which is becoming very common in most countries. Research on this issue should include control devices based on fuzzy logic. Needless to say, the combined use of the mechanical AC with passive cooling techniques somehow reduces the advantages of the passive cooling techniques if the different expectations of thermal comfort are not taken advantage of.

It is essential to establish detailed guidelines for the integration of these systems in buildings: lack of knowledge concerning their performance is the major barrier to their dissemination.

For the case of evaporative cooling, which is appropriate for places with low relative humidity, one has to consider the appropriateness of the technique from the point of view of the use of water resources, which are becoming more and more scarce, especially in the Middle East.

9.5.6 Advanced solar control modelling and development of new components

As solar heat gains are the main heat loads in buildings, solar control devices are essential for passive cooling: reduction of solar loads is far more effective than the use of heat sinks. Solar control devices should be assessed not only on the basis of their thermal and visual impact, but also for their impact on natural ventilation of a space, which might sometimes be adversely influenced. Standardization of solar control devices is also necessary and should be developed.

9.5.7 Integration actions

In most European countries, including those in the South and the Mediterranean, heating problems still predominate, since measures that may lead to a cooler building during the summer may lead to an increase in heat energy consumption during the winter. It is therefore necessary to promote techniques that use an integrated approach to energy consumption for all end-uses: mainly heating, cooling and daylighting. Rating systems are required to address the issues of how a non-air-conditioned building should be compared with a building in which AC is used. Finally, it is also necessary to incorporate in rating systems the effect of energy-saving measures on peak loads and not only on energy – especially in places where the electrical grid is insular.

9.5.8 Seasonal storage

Seasonal heat (or cool) storage is also an issue that will eventually have to be addressed. Storing in underground location the heat (or 'coolness') to be used in the next heating/cooling season can be a very effective way to reduce fossil fuel consumption – provided that it can be made cost-effective. There is some interest in this field by the International Energy Agency. The problem is one of cost-effectiveness rather than one of techniques.

9.5.9 Non-conventional AC techniques

Although absorption AC and desiccant cooling are not, strictly speaking, passive cooling techniques, since they involve fossil energy consumption, they should also be considered, because they are more environmentally friendly. Absorption AC can be combined in many cases with solar heat, which is abundant during the summer.

Absorption has the advantage that no hexafluorides – with their adverse effects on the ozone layer – are required and that it can be used to reduce peak electricity demand during the summer. Desiccant cooling may be appropriate in situations where the humidity is high (and the temperature relatively low) or the latent load is high, and can be combined with other passive cooling techniques to cancel the effect of high humidity.

9.6 Conclusion

The penetration of AC in Southern European – and other Mediterranean – countries makes it imperative to address passive cooling techniques, be it through heat gain reduction or through the use of natural sinks.

Research should be concentrated on the study of the microclimate around buildings (especially under urban conditions), redefining thermal comfort under transient conditions, improving air quality aspects and developing alternative cooling systems.

9.7 References

Antinucci, M, Asiain, D, Fleury, D, Lopez, J, Maldonaldo, E, Santamouris, M, Tombazis, A and Yannas, S, 1992, 'Passive and hybrid cooling of buildings – state of the art', in *International Journal of Solar Energy*, 11, 251–271.

Cook, J (ed), 1989, *Passive Cooling*, Cambridge, MA, MIT Press.

Fanger, P O, 1970, *Thermal Comfort: Analysis and Applications in Environmental Engineering*, New York, McGraw-Hill.

Givoni, B, 1994, *Passive and Low Energy Cooling of Buildings*, New York, Van Nostrand Reinhold.

Santamouris, M and Argyriou, A, 1997a, 'Passive cooling of buildings – results of the PASCOOL program', *International Journal of Solar Energy*, 19, 3–19.

Santamouris, M and Argyriou, A, 1997b, 'Future research actions in passive cooling' *International Journal of Solar Energy*, 19, 199–211.

Santamouris, M and Asimakopoulos, D, 1996, *Passive Cooling of Buildings*, London, James & James.

10 Solar and energy efficiency as an option for sustainable urban built environments

Matheos Santamouris

Group Building Environmental Studies, Physics Department, University of Athens, Athens, Greece
E-mail: msantam@cc.uoa.gr

10.1 Introduction

Cities or urban areas are defined as the physical environment that it is composed by 'a complex mix of natural elements including air, water, land, climate, flora and fauna and the built environment that is constructed or modified for human habitation and activity, encompassing buildings, infrastructure and urban open spaces' (Hardy *et al*, 2001).

The quality of urban agglomerations is mainly defined by the type and strength of the anthropogenic activities, the existing infrastructures and the resources used, the wastes and emissions generated and the corresponding environmental impact, and by the efficiency and quality of the local institutions and governments.

The second half of the last century was a period of the most intensive urbanization that our planet has ever experienced. The urban population increased from 160 million to about 3 billion in just 100 years and it is expected to increase to about 5 billion by 2025. Transfer of people to cities has mainly happened and will continue to happen in the so-called less developed countries as the result of increased opportunities offered in the urban environment and the degradation of rural economies and societies.

Urban citizens, in developed countries, have benefited from the huge technological developments offered by the industrial revolution. Major problems of the 19th century have been solved, and economic developments have permitted life standards to be improved both qualitatively and quantitatively. The social pressures and higher income associated with the urban lifestyle have increased the capacity and the tendency of urban citizens to consume. It is characteristic that the wealthiest 25% of the human population consumes almost 80% of the world's economic output (WCED, 1987). However, such over-consumption has an important impact on both the city and the global environments. Approximately 64% of the world's economic production/consumption and pollution is associated with cities in rich countries, while other environmental problems such as heat islands and indoor air quality have an important impact on the overall environmental quality of cities and the health of city dwellers (Santamouris, 2001a)

Urbanization in less developed nations, where cities have received a population tidal wave, followed a completely different pattern. The tremendous increase in the population, lack of resources and small or zero development have resulted in poverty and major inequalities. The expectations of higher incomes and better life quality in urban areas were seldom realized and a tremendous number of city dwellers are actually living in totally unacceptable conditions. It has been estimated that almost 600 million urban citizens in the less developed countries live in shelters and neighbourhoods 'where their lives and health were continually threatened because of the inadequate provision of safe, sufficient water supplies, sanitation, removal of solid and liquid wastes and health care and emergency services' (Cainross *et al*, 1990).

The widely agreed set of priorities to improve cities define an agenda of actions that usually is called the 'agenda of sustainable cities'. However, the term is misleading as there is no agreed and clear definition of what the term 'sustainable cities' means. In parallel, as cities are systems that just import energy and material from their immediate and host environment and then export back degraded energy, waste and pollution, they cannot be 'sustainable' by definition. Despite that, cities have to meet human needs in settlements without depleting environmental capital, and poverty, inequalities and the very important depletion of the environmental capital are emerging problems that require immediate actions.

Appropriate strategies aimed at reducing over-consumption, increasing the use of renewable resources and reducing the production of wastes and of degraded energy up to a level not exceeding the assimilative capacity of local ecosystems or the ecosphere seem to be the greatest priorities in cities of the developed world.

In parallel, sustainable strategies for cities in less developed regions are focused mainly on the provision of basic human needs, such as appropriate dwellings, energy and water supply, sanitation systems, education and health care services (Devuyst, 2001).

Energy is one of the most important factors that define the quality of urban life and the global environmental quality of cities. The urbanization process dramatically affects energy consumption. A recent analysis (World Bank, 2003) showed that a 1% increase in the per capita GNP leads to an almost equal (factor 1.03) increase in energy consumption. However, as reported, an increase in the urban population by 1% increases energy consumption by 2.2%, i.e. the rate of change in energy use is twice the rate of change in urbanization. Increases in energy efficiency, use of renewable resources to supply cities, improvement of the urban thermal microclimate and adoption of sustainable consumption policies seem to be the main tools to reduce energy consumption in cities of the developed world.

This chapter [which is an extended version of an earlier paper (Santamouris, 2002)] discusses the main environmental problems of world cities, defines the main priorities of the sustainable agenda and discusses extensively the energy problems of cities in the developed world. Emphasis is given to the energy consumption of urban buildings. Some of the more interesting and promising ideas and solutions to reduce the energy consumption of urban buildings and improve sustainability issues in the urban built environment are presented.

10.2 Urbanization at the end of the 20th century

10.2.1 Increase of the urban population

The planet's population is increasing rapidly. More than 80 million of people are added every year and while the total world population was in 1987 close to 5 billion, it passed 6 billion in 2000 and according to the United Nations will continue to grow until the middle of the present century (UNFPA, 1998).

Most of the population growth is in cities. The urban population is growing much faster than the rural population; almost 80% of the world's population growth between 1990 and 2010 will be in urban areas and most probably will be in Africa, Asia and Latin America (United Nations, 1998). This means, simply, that there is a current addition of 60 million urban citizens per year which, as mentioned by UNEPTIE (2002), 'is the equivalent of adding another Paris, Beijing or Cairo every other month'.

In fact, at the beginning of the last century, just one tenth of the world population, 160 million, were city dwellers (O'Meara, 1999), whereas in 1950 the figure passed 200 million. In contrast, just after the start of this century, half of the world's population lives in cities, a 20-fold increase (O'Meara, 1999). Statistics show that the real boom in urbanization happened in the 1990s. During the last decade of the century, the urban population grew from about 2 to 3 billion, an increase of about 50% (Rees, 2001). Future scenarios for the next 15 years, predict a growth rate of about 2% per year (United Nations, 2002), while UN projects indicate that 61% of the world's population or about 5.1 billion people will live in cities by 2025, i.e. an increase of 70% in the first quarter of the century (United Nations, 1994; UNDP, 1998; Devuyst, 2001). Table 10.1 reports on the urbanization trends in the major areas of the planet (United Nations, 1998).

Table 10.1 *Trends and projections in urban populations by regions, 1950–2010 (United Nations, 1998)*

Region	1950	1965	1980	1995	2010
Urban population (million of inhabitants)					
Africa	33	66	130	251	458
Asia	244	426	706	1192	1816
Latin America and the Caribbean	69	133	233	350	463
Rest of the world	404	559	685	781	849
Percentage of population living in urban areas					
Africa	14.6	20.7	27.3	34.9	43.6
Asia	17.4	22.4	26.7	34.7	43.6
Latin America and the Caribbean	41.4	53.4	64.9	73.4	78.6
Rest of the world	55.3	64.1	70.5	74.2	78.0

In Europe, the level of urbanization is close to 75%, and between 1980 and 1995 the urban population increased by 9%. According to Stanners and Bourdeau (1995), in Europe, 2% of agricultural land is lost to urbanization every 10 years. Hahn and Simonis (1991) reported that during the last century, the surface of urban land per capita in Europe has increased 10-fold. The expected annual growth for the next 15 years is close to 0.3% and it is expected that Europe will stabilize at a level of urbanization close to 82% (UNCHS, 1996)

In fact, urbanization occurs mainly in Africa, Asia and Latin American countries as a result of the increased opportunities and services offered in cities (Figure 10.1). Fifteen years ago the urban growth rate in these areas was close to 3.8%, almost four times higher that of the developed countries (0.8%) (UNCHS, 2001). Urbanization rates of less developed nations are striking: between 1975 and 2000 1.2 billion people moved to cities and during the next 30 years it is expected that more than 2 billion people will become city dwellers. Intensification of agriculture that decreases job opportunities in the country, local conflicts, relative increase of the rural population, exhaustion of natural resources, land degradation and increased opportunities for jobs, education and health care in cities are the main driving forces of urbanization in less developed countries.

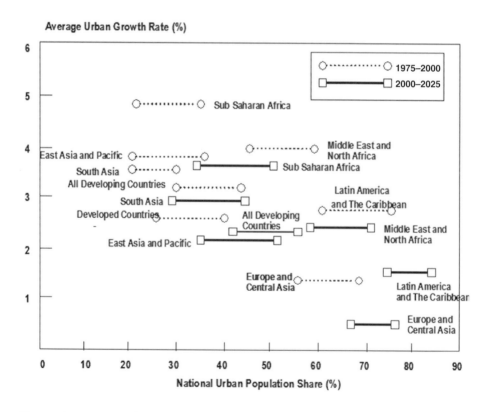

Figure 10.1 *Average urban growth as a function of the national urban population share (from World Bank, 2003)*

As a result of the rapid urban growth, important environmental, social, political, economic, institutional, demographic and cultural problems have appeared Poverty, environmental degradation, lack of sanitary and other urban services, lack of access to land and adequate shelters are among the more serious issues demanding attention.

10.2.2 The size of the world's cities

As a result of the rapid urbanization, the size of the world's urban agglomerations has grown dramatically. As mentioned by the United Nations (UNCHS, 2001), our planet hosts 19 cities with 10 million or more people, 22 cities with 5–10 million people, 370 cities with 1–5 million people and 433 cities with 0.5–1 million people.

To demonstrate the dramatic growth of city sizes, it can be mentioned that over the last 200 years, the average size of the 100 largest cities has increased from 200,000 to about 5 million inhabitants (Hardy *et al*, 2001). Recent data and future predictions show that by 2015, there will be around 560 cities with more than 1 million people (Devuyst, 2001), while the number of mega cities – cities with a population exceeding 8 million has increased from two in 1950 (London and New York) to 21 in 1990, 16 of them in less developed countries; in 2015 there are expected to be 33, 27 of them in the developing world (Carlson, 1996; UNCHS, 1996; WRI, 1996). In parallel, it is expected that by 2015 there will be 71 cities with more than 5 million people where almost 17% of urban citizens are expected to live (UNDP, 1998).

In fact most of the urban growth occurs and will continue to occur in less developed countries where 114 cities of over 4 million people are projected to exist by 2025, up from 35 cities in 1980 (Table 10.2). However, it should be pointed out that most of the urban population, in less developed countries, lives in cities with less than 1 million citizens, and almost 50% of the urban population lives in cities with less than 100,000 inhabitants (Hardy *et al*, 2001). As concerns Europe, it should be mentioned that half of the population lives in cities of 1000–50,000 people, 25% in medium-sized cities of 50,000–250,000 citizens and the remaining 25% in cities with more than 250,000 people.

Table 10.2 *The distribution of large cities by region, 1800–1990 (United Nations, 1994)*

Region	1800	1900	1950	1990
	Number of cities with a population of over 1 million			
Africa	–	–	2	27
Asia	1	4	26	126
Latin America and the Caribbean	0	0	7	38
Rest of the world	1	13	45	102
	Number of the world's 100 largest cities			
Africa	4	2	3	6
Asia	64	22	32	44
Latin America and the Caribbean	3	5	8	16
Rest of the world	29	71	57	34
	Average size of the world's 100 largest cities			
Number of inhabitants	187,000	724,000	2.1 million	5.3 million

10.3 Urban environmental problems

Environment is the one of the three pillars of sustainable development. Human activity has accumulated problems that have left increased pollutants in the atmosphere, vast areas of land resources degraded, depleted and degraded forests, biodiversity under threat, increasingly inadequate freshwater resources of deteriorating quality and seriously depleted marine resources (United Nations, 2002).

Cities contribute substantially to the above problems. In parallel, the other two pillars of sustainable development, social and economic, face extremely important problems, especially in less developed cities. In a general way, the urban environmental problems may be summarized in three main groups: the over-consumption of energy and resources that exceed their production by their nature, the production of degraded energy, waste and pollution more than the assimilative capacity of the ecosphere, and the lack of the necessary infrastructures to ensure the health and well being of all citizens in cities of less developed countries.

Over-consumption of resources, mainly energy, associated with increased air pollution mainly from motor vehicles, increases in the ambient temperature because of the positive heat balance in cities, heat islands, noise pollution and solid waste management seem to be the more important environmental problems in urban areas of developed countries. In parallel, poverty, increasing unemployment, environmental degradation, lack of urban services, overburdening of existing infrastructure and lack of access to land, finance and adequate shelter are among the more important environmental, social and economic problems in cities of less developed countries.

10.3.1 Cities in the developed world

10.3.1.1 Over-consumption of resources

Over-consumption of resources in cities of the developed world is well shown when the ecological footprint of cities is calculated and compared between cities. The ecological footprint of a population group is 'the area of land and water required to produce the resources consumed and to assimilate the wastes generated by the population on a continuous basis, wherever on earth that land is located' (Rees, 1996). Calculations have shown that there are only 1.5 ha of ecologically productive land and about 0.5 ha of truly productive ocean for every person on earth (Rees, 1996). However, the eco-footprints of average residents of high-income countries range as high as 5 and 6 ha per capita (Rees and Wackernagel, 1996; Wackernagel and Rees, 1996). Other analyses calculate the eco-footprint of wealthy countries as up to 10 ha per capita while people in the less developed countries have footprints of less than 1 ha (Wackernagel *et al*, 1997, 1999).

A British study has estimated that the ecological footprint of London for CO_2 assimilation, food and forest products is close to 120 times larger than the city's area or about nine-tenths the area of the entire country (Sustainable London Trust, 1996). Ecological footprint estimations for Canada have shown that in the Toronto region (Onisto *et al*, 1998) the per capita ecological footprint is close to 7.6 ha. Given that Toronto has 2,385,000 residents, the aggregate eco footprint is 18,126,000 ha, an area 288 times larger than the city's political area (63,000 ha). In a similar way, it is calculated

(Wackernagel *et al*, 1999) that the eco-footprint of Vancouver, Canada is 3,634,000 ha or 319 times its nominal area. In another study using region-specific data of the 29 largest cities of Baltic Europe (Folke *et al*, 1997), it is calculated that an area of forest, agricultural, marine and wetland ecosystems 565–1130 times larger than the area of the cities themselves is required. Concluding the analysis of eco-footprints, it must be pointed out that, as shown by Wackernagel and Rees (1996), the resources of the equivalent of three planet earths are required if the world's current population continues to live at the OECD average of today (Cainross *et al*, 1990). In parallel, as stated by Rees (1996), 'to raise the present world population to Canadian material standards using prevailing technologies would require nearly four earth-like planets'.

10.3.1.2 Thermal degradation of cities

Increasing urbanization has led to deterioration of the urban environment. Deficiencies in development control have important consequences on the urban climate and the environmental efficiency of buildings. The size of housing plots has been reduced, thus increasing densities. The increasing number of buildings has crowded out vegetation and trees. As reported (Environmental Protection Agency, 1992), New York has lost 175,000 trees or 20% of its urban forest in the previous 10 years.

As a consequence of heat balance, air temperatures in densely built urban areas are higher than the temperatures of the surrounding rural country. The phenomenon, known as 'heat island', is due to many factors, the more important of which were summarized by Oke *et al* (1991) and deal with (a) the canyon radiative geometry that contributes to the decrease in the long-wavelength radiation loss from within street canyons owing to the complex exchange between buildings and the screening of the skyline, (b) the thermal properties of materials that increase the storage of sensible heat in the fabric of the city, (c) the anthropogenic heat released from combustion of fuels and animal metabolism, (d) the urban greenhouse, that contributes to the increase in the incoming long-wavelength radiation from the polluted and warmer urban atmosphere, (e) the canyon radiative geometry decreasing the effective albedo of the system because of the multiple reflection of short-wavelength radiation between the canyon surfaces, (f) the reduction of evaporating surfaces in the city putting more energy into sensible and less energy into latent heat and (g) the reduced turbulent transfer of heat from within streets.

Urban heat island studies usually refer to the 'urban heat island intensity', which is the maximum temperature difference between the city and the surrounding area. Data compiled from various sources (Santamouris, 2001a) show that heat island intensity can be as high as 15°C. Extensive studies on the heat island intensity in Athens involving more than 30 urban stations showed that urban stations present higher temperatures of between 5 and 15°C compared with reference suburban stations.

Heat island data in some North American cities have been reported (Environmental Protection Agency, 1992). The importance of the temperature increase becomes more apparent when the cooling degree-days corresponding to urban and rural stations are compared. Taha (1997) gave the increase in the cooling and heating degree-days due to urbanization and heat island effects for selected North American locations (Tables 10.3 and 10.4). As shown, the difference in the cooling degree-days can be as high as 92%, while the minimum difference is close to 10%. Regarding the heating degree-days, the maximum difference is close to 32% and the minimum is close to 3%. An increase in the cooling degree-days has a tremendous impact on the energy consumption of buildings for cooling.

Table 10.3 *Increase in the cooling degree-days due to urbanization and heat island effects: averages for selected locations for the period 1941–70 (source: Taha, 1997)*

Location	Urban	Airport	Difference (%)
Los Angeles	368	191	92
Washington, DC	440	361	21
St. Louis	510	459	11
New York	333	268	24
Baltimore	464	344	35
Seattle	111	72	54
Detroit	416	366	14
Chicago	463	372	24
Denver	416	350	19

Table 10.4 *Increase in the heating degree-days due to urbanization and heat island effects: averages for selected locations for the period 1941–70 (source: Taha, 1997)*

Location	Urban	Airport	Difference (%)
Los Angeles	384	562	–32
Washington, DC	1300	1370	–6
St. Louis	1384	1466	–6
New York	1496	1600	–7
Baltimore	1266	1459	–14
Seattle	2493	2881	–13
Detroit	3460	3556	–3
Chicago	3371	3609	–7
Denver	3058	3342	–8

Higher urban temperatures have a serious impact on the electricity demand for air conditioning of buildings. Increased smog production contributes to increased emission of pollutants from power plants, including sulphur dioxide, carbon monoxide, nitrous oxides and suspended particulates. The heat island effect in warm to hot climates exacerbates cooling energy use in summer. As reported (Environmental Protection Agency, 1992), for US cities with populations larger than 100,000 the peak electricity load will increase by 1.5–2% for every 1°F increase in temperature. Taking into account that urban temperatures during summer afternoons in the USA have increased by 2–4°F during the last 40 years, it can be assumed that 3–8% of the current urban electricity demand is used to compensate for the heat island effect alone.

Comparisons of high ambient temperatures with utility loads for the Los Angeles area have shown that an important correlation exists. It is found that the net rate of increase of the electricity demand is almost 300 MW per °F. Taking into account that there has been a 5°F increase in the peak temperature in Los Angeles since 1940, this is translated into an added electricity demand of 1.5 GW due to the heat island effect. A similar correlation between temperature and electricity demand has been established for selected utility districts in the USA. Based on the above rates of increase, it has been calculated that for the USA the electricity costs for summer heat islands alone could be as much as $1 million per hour or over $1 billion per year (Environmental Protection Agency, 1992). Computer studies have shown for the whole country the possible increase in the peak cooling electricity load due to the heat island effect could range from 0.5 to 3% for each 1°F rise in temperature.

Studies in the Tokyo area reported by Ojima (1990–91) indicated that during the period between 1965 and 1975, the cooling load of existing buildings increased by 10–20% on average because of the heat island phenomenon. It is concluded that if it continued to increase at the same rate, it would result in more than a 50% increment in 2000.

Calculations of the spatial cooling load distribution in the major Athens area, based on experimental data from 20 stations, have been reported (Santamouris, 1997) (Figure 10.2). It is found that the cooling load of reference buildings at the centre of the city is about the double that in the surrounding Athens area. It is also reported that high ambient temperatures increase peak electricity loads and place serious demands on the local utilities. Almost a double peak-cooling load has been calculated for the central Athens area compared with the surroundings of the city. Finally, a very important decrease in the efficiency of conventional air conditioners, because of the temperature increase, is reported. It is found that the minimum Coefficient of Performance (COP values) are lower by about 25% in central Athens, obliging designers to increase the size of the installed air-conditioning systems, thus intensifying

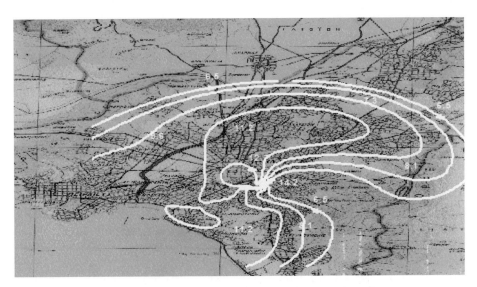

Figure 10.2 *Iso-cooling load lines for the reference building in Athens for August 1996 and for 26°C set-point temperature*

peak electricity problems and energy consumption for cooling (Hassid *et al*, 2000; Santamouris *et al*, 2001).

10.3.1.3 Air pollution and noise

In addition to increased energy demand for cooling, increased urban temperatures affect the concentration and distribution of urban pollution because heat accelerates the chemical reactions in the atmosphere that lead to high ozone concentrations. Other sources such as transport, industry, combustion processes, etc., contribute to increased pollution levels in urban areas. In Europe it is estimated that in 70–80% of European cities with more than 500,000 inhabitants, the levels of air pollution involving one or more pollutants exceeds the WHO standards at least once in a typical year (Stanners and Bourdeau, 1995)

Urban pollution is linked to climatic change, acidification and photochemical smog. Comparison of daily peak temperatures in Los Angeles and 13 cities in Texas with ozone concentrations show that as the temperature rises ozone concentrations can reach dangerous levels (Hahn and Simonis, 1991). Also, the number of polluted days may increase by 10% for each 5°F increase (Environmental Protection Agency, 1992). Urban geometry plays an important role in the transport and removal of pollutants. The roughness of urban buildings and landscapes increases air turbulence, thus enhancing the dispersion of pollutants. Also, if pollutants land in sheltered areas such as street canyons, they may reside longer than they would in a windy rural environment and reduce wind speeds, thus increasing pollutant concentrations. Increased industrialization and urbanization have created important pollution problems in urban areas. Sulphur dioxide, particulate matter, nitrogen oxides, carbon monoxide, etc., affect human health in a direct way and also affect historic monuments and buildings. It is calculated that the cost of damage by sulphur dioxide alone to buildings and construction materials might be of the order of 10 billion euros per year for the whole of Europe (Kucera *et al*, 1992).

Damage from increased pollutants is evident. Analysis of the relationship between hospital admissions and sulphur oxide levels in Athens (Plessas, 1980) found that a 'three-fold increase in air pollutants doubles hospital admissions for respiratory and cardiovascular disorders' and that 'acute respiratory illness shows the highest correlation for the SO_2 variable'. Levels of nitrogen oxide are particularly high in urban environments. NO_2 levels in San Francisco and New York exceed 200 $\mu g/m^3$ and in Athens the corresponding concentration is close to 160 $\mu g/m^3$ (OECD, 1983).

Health problems associated with the urban environment are mainly associated with the increased use of cars. This has been acknowledged recently by the British Medical Association (1997). Pollution from gasoline and petrol has been proved to be partly responsible for heart disease. Polionecki *et al* (1997) have shown that in London, one in 50 heart attacks treated in hospitals was strongly linked with carbon monoxide, which is mainly derived from motor vehicle exhausts.

The role in and the impact of outdoor conditions on the indoor climate and also the relation between outdoor and indoor pollution are obvious aspects of building physics and will not be repeated here. However, intensive urbanization and deterioration of the outdoor air observed during in recent years has created a new situation with serious consequences for indoor environmental quality. In fact, outdoor pollution is one of the sources of the so-called 'sick building syndrome', the other being related to indoor sources. Numerous studies reported in recent years show the serious impact of the outdoor environment on indoor air quality (Godish, 1989).

Outdoors pollution and inadequate ventilation may be the primary causes of poor indoor air quality in buildings. Monitoring of 356 public access buildings showed that in approximately 50% of the buildings an unsuitable ventilation rate was the primary cause of illness complaints and poor air quality (Wallingford and Carpenter, 1986). Increased outdoor concentrations seriously affect indoor concentrations of pollutants. Measurements of nitrogen oxide concentrations in a hospital in Athens (Argiriou *et al*, 1994) showed high concentrations for indoor standards, which rose between 33 and 67 $\mu g/m^3$.

Noise in the urban environment is a serious problem. According to Stanners and Bourdeau (1995), unacceptable noise levels of more than 65 dB(A) affect between 10 and 20% of urban inhabitants in most European cities. It is also reported that in cities included in the Dobris Assessment, unacceptable levels of noise affect between 10 and 50% of urban residences. The OECD (1991) has calculated that 130 million people in OECD countries are exposed to noise levels that are unacceptable. The same study reported that in the Netherlands during the decade 1977–87, the proportion of the population claiming moderate noise disturbance increased from 48 to 60%, and in France, between 1975 and 1985, the urban population exposed to noise levels between 55 and 65 dB(A) increased from 13 to 14 million. UBA (1988) reported that in the western part of Germany and in towns with up to 5000 inhabitants, 14–16% of the population are strongly annoyed by street noise. In towns with between 5000 and 20,000 inhabitants this proportion increases to 17–19%, in cities with between 20,000 and 100,000 inhabitants it is 19–25% and finally in cities with more than 100,000 inhabitants it rises to 22–33%.

10.3.2 Cities in the less developed world

As already stated, poverty, increasing unemployment, environmental degradation, lack of urban services, overburdening of existing infrastructure and lack of access to land, finance and adequate shelter are among the more important environmental, social and economic problems in cities in less developed countries.

10.3.2.1 Urban poverty

The growth of large cities in the less developed countries has been accompanied by an increase in urban poverty, mainly because of the increasing gap between incomes and land prices and the failure of markets to provide housing for low-income groups. As reported by the United Nations (2002), 'in cities of the less developed world, one out of every four households lives in poverty; 40% of African urban households and 25% of Latin American urban households are living below locally defined poverty lines'.

Poverty is mainly concentrated in specific social groups and in particular locations as the economic reality in these countries forces low-income groups to settle on deteriorated and marginal land in or around cities and without access to basic infrastructures and services.

Poverty is among the major reasons for environmental degradation and unfortunately urban poverty is on the increase. In fact, as reported by the World Health Organization (WHO), poverty and inequality are two of the most important contributory factors to poor environmental conditions and poor health. It is characteristic that in 1970, the richest 20% of the planet had almost 30 times more income than the poorest 20%. At the present time, this figure has doubled. The net income of the 358 richest people in the world is larger than the combined annual income of the poorest 45% of the world's population (Devuyst, 2001).

10.3.2.2 Housing

Perhaps the most important of the basic needs in poorer areas of cities in less developed countries is the use of 'affordable and decent housing, which contributes to ensure, health, security, development, empowerment, well-being and urban functional efficiency'.

As estimated by the United Nations (UNCHS, 2001), more than 1 billion urban citizens live in unsuitable housing mostly in squatter and slum settlements, while in most of cities in less developed countries between one and two thirds of the population live in poor-quality and overcrowded housing (Hardy *et al*, 2001), with insufficient water supply, inadequate or no sanitation, inefficient rubbish collection, no electricity or energy networks and under the risk of flooding and other environmental phenomena (Cairncross, 1990).

10.3.2.3 Energy and air quality

Electricity provision, the use of inappropriate fuels for heating, cooking and lighting and indoor air quality are major problems in cities of the less developed world. In low-income cities (less than US $750/person), only 70% of the population is connected to the grid, which provides electricity for just a few hours per day.

The income of the households defines the type of fuel used for thermal processes. Low-income households choose cheap fuels such as wood, kerosene or paraffin, whereas the higher the income the greater is the use of cleaner fuels, natural gas or electricity (Smith, 1990; Smith *et al*, 1994). As pointed out, this is a kind of an 'energy ladder' (Smith, 1990; Smith *et al*, 1994).

The use of open fires and of inappropriate fuels, in overcrowded houses, is an important source of poor indoor air quality that contributes to acute respiratory infections that kill 4 million people per year, mostly children under the age of 5 years (WRI, 1996). Existing studies suggest that indoor concentrations of total suspended particulates are 10–100 higher than the existing standards (Saksensa and Smith, 1999). As reported (Smith and Akbar, 1999), in South Asian countries, indoor air pollution from solid fuels burned in open fireplaces probably contributes to a higher total exposure than outdoor pollution sources (Smith and Akbar, 1999).

Regarding outdoor air quality, there are more than 1.5 billion urban dwellers who are exposed to levels of outdoor air pollution that are above the accepted maximum concentrations, and it is estimated that 400,000 additional deaths every year are attributable to outdoor air pollution.

10.3.2.4 Lack of infrastructures

Most cities in the less developed countries do not offer the necessary infrastructure in order to provide citizens with safe potable water, sanitation and waste collection and treatment.

Officially, it is estimated that as many as 25% of urban dwellers in the developing world do not have access to safe potable water supplies (Rees, 1996); however, the real number may be much higher.

Even those living in areas with piped supplies, reliability of the water network is a serious problem. Water supply has declined from 124 litres per day in 1967 to 64 litres per day in 1997. In 1967, almost all housings connected to the water network received a 24 hour service, whereas by 1997 the proportion had declined to only 56%, with almost 20% of households receiving water only for 1–5 hours per day (White *et al*, 1972; Thompson *et al*, 2000; Hardy *et al*, 2001).

Those not connected to the network either have to buy water from private vendors or must queue for hours each day at public standpipes and then carry more than 120 kg of water many kilometres. As there is a great shortage of taps, there are more than 500 citizens per tap waiting for more than 90 mins. In some cases, there are more than 1500, and there are even cases with more than 2500 inhabitants per standpipe (White *et al*, 1972; Development Workshop, 1995; Thompson *et al*, 2000; Hardy *et al*, 2001). However, as estimated by Briscoe (1986), more than 20–30% of the population in the less developed world have to buy water from private vendors, spending 5–30% of their total income on water (Cairncross, 1990; Azandossessi, 2000)

Concerning sanitation facilities, it is estimated that almost two thirds of the population of cities in less developed countries have no hygienic facilities for disposal of excreta and perhaps a higher percentage lack the necessary means to dispose of wastewaters (Sinnatamby, 1990). As mentioned by Hardy *et al* (2001), cities with more than 1 million of inhabitants have no sewer systems, and fewer than 35% of cities in the developing world have their wastewater treated (United Nations, 2002).

In parallel, between one third and half of the solid waste generated within most cities in less developed countries is not collected. As estimated by the World Bank, more than US $200 billion have to be invested each year in basic infrastructure in less developed countries, and in the period up to 2005, given the population growth and the additional demands on materials, '... it would be reasonable to expect the total volume of investment to reach six trillion US dollars by that time' (NRTEE, 1998).

10.4 Urban sustainability – an oxymoron or a realistic perspective?

Cities are systems that import energy and resources and produce degraded energy and matter that has to be assimilated by the surrounding area. Thus, when based on ecological and systemic definitions, it is difficult to consider cities as sustainable systems.

However, cities present important advantages and should not be considered as places that generate only environmental cost. They may provide high-quality living conditions with lower levels of energy use, waste, pollution and in general low environmental impact than the wealthy rural or suburban areas (Mitlin and Satterthwaite, 1996; UNCHS, 1996). In parallel, health services in cities are much better developed than in rural areas and this is well proven by international epidemiological and demographic studies that suggest much higher survival rates in cities (UNCHS, 1996). Economy of scale in cities decreases considerably the pressure on land and the cost of new infrastructure and services such as water treatment plants, energy and other networks, educational and health services, etc. Finally, benefits provided by cities to people outside their boundaries should not be neglected as the city's economic activities provide incomes by purchasing goods. Thus, cities may hold promise for sustainable development mainly when they are able to support a large number of people and limit their per capita impact on the natural environment.

According to Rees (1996), there are two basic criteria for ecological sustainability of cities:

- the consumption of renewable and replenishable energy and resources should not exceed their production in nature

- the production of degraded energy and matter by cities must not exceed the assimilative capacity of local ecosystems or the ecosphere.

To comply with the defined frame, cities have to satisfy five broad categories of environmental goals (Hardy *et al*, 2001):

- To provide the environmental conditions that can ensure the health of urban citizens and reduce the vulnerability of the population. This includes basic infrastructures and services such as adequate provision of water, sanitation, rubbish collection and drainage for all the urban area and its citizens.

- To reduce the risk of chemical and physical hazards in the everyday life of the city.

- To provide citizens with a high-quality urban environment that protects the natural and cultural heritage and to provide outdoor comfort and the necessary urban spaces for the well being of city dwellers (urban parks, public spaces, sport facilities, children's playgrounds, etc).

- To reduce as much as possible the shift of the environmental load and cost generated by the cities to the inhabitants and ecosystems surrounding the urban area.

- To ensure that the consumption of resources and goods and the corresponding generation of matter and degraded energy are compatible with the limits of the natural capital and do not transfer environmental load and cost to future generations or to other human groups.

The relative performance of urban systems with respect to the above goals defines the degree to which cities fulfil the needs of the people and protect the global environmental capital. It is evident that to satisfy such a complex set of goals, a very efficient institutional, political, social, economic and cultural regulatory framework is required.

10.5 We do not have 'solutions' but we have ideas

Working towards more sustainable cities, one has to define specific actions that may contribute to solving local environmental problems. It is clear that every city has its own characteristics and problems and there are no universal solutions that may be applied everywhere.

Thus, the aim of the present chapter is not to describe a comprehensive set of ideas to achieve urban sustainability. Such a goal is extremely ambitious and certainly outside the present objectives. What the present contribution aims to offer is a discussion of the ideas and possible solutions we have to foresee in order to decrease the energy consumption of buildings in cities of the developed world, reduce the environmental cost because of the energy use and improve environmental comfort in and around buildings. Such a goal may appear to be reduced, however, as buildings are the main consumers of energy in cities, and this contributes tremendously to achieving a more sustainable urban environment where the environmental cost is not transferred to future generations and to other human groups (IBGE, 1993; LRC, 1993; Flavin and Lenssen, 1995).

Certainly there is a long list of ideas on how to decrease the energy consumption of buildings in our cities. However, and in the author's opinion, the main concerns and technological ideas that may be well thought out in order of priority are as follows.

- Improve the urban microclimate, fight heat islands and reduce the energy needs for cooling.

- Use of sustainable energy supply systems for buildings based on the use of renewable sources such as solar and biomass district heating and cooling.

- Use of demand side management techniques to control and regulate the energy consumption of large consumers.

- Integration of passive and active solar systems in the envelope of new and existing buildings and use of high-energy performance supply and management equipment.

- Application of appropriate city planning techniques when new settlements are designed. The idea of a compact city, reducing the needs for transport and also the energy consumption of buildings, is gaining increasing acceptance. Ideas such as these developed by the New Urbanism movement (Calthorpe, 1993; Katz, 1994), based on mixed land uses, greater dependence on public transport, cycling and walking, decentralization of employment location, etc., may be further developed and applied to create a more sustainable urban environment.

In parallel, a series of institutional, economic and regulatory actions are foreseen as important. The more important of them may be the following.

- The development of a new, more efficient legislative frame on the energy performance of buildings. The development of the new European Directive on the Energy Performance of Buildings is a very good base to improve further the efficiency of urban buildings.

- Integration of the environmental cost in the price of goods and services.

- Adoption of the 'green consumption' principle by the urban citizens.

- Adoption of the principle of 'fair trade' by the citizens and their institutions in order to reduce the exploitation of people mainly in less developed countries.

- Application of new ecological principles on the production and management of energy-related systems and components, such as the principle of natural capitalism.

- Strengthen the involvement of local authorities in the production, maintenance and management of energy systems at the city level.

In the following some of the above ideas are further developed.

10.5.1 Improve the urban microclimate

Improvement of the ambient microclimate in the urban environment involving the use of more appropriate materials, increased use of green areas, use of cool sinks for heat dissipation, appropriate layout of urban canopies, etc., to counterbalance the effects of temperature increase, is among the more efficient measures.

An increase in the energy consumption in urban areas, because of the heat island effect, places great stress on utilities that have to supply the necessary additional load. Construction of new generating plants may solve the problem but it is an unsustainable solution, is expensive and takes a long time. Adoption of measures to decrease the energy demand in urban areas, such as the use of more appropriate materials, increased plantation, use of sinks, etc., seems to be a much more reasonable option. Such a strategy, adopted by the Sacramento Municipal Utility District (SMUD), has proved to be very effective and economically profitable (Flavin and Lenssen, 1995). It has been calculated that a megawatt of capacity is actually eight times more expensive to produce than to save. This is because energy-saving measures have low capital and no running costs, whereas the construction of new power plants involves high capital and running costs.

The optical characteristics of materials used in urban environments and especially the albedo to solar radiation and emissivity to long-wavelength radiation have a very important impact on the urban energy balance. Yap (1975) reported that systematic urban–rural differences in surface emissivity hold the potential to cause a portion of a heat island.

10.5.1.1 Use of cool materials

Use of high-albedo materials reduces the amount of solar radiation absorbed through building envelopes and urban structures and keeps their surfaces cooler. Materials with high emissivities are good emitters of long-wavelength energy and readily release the energy that has been absorbed as short-wavelength radiation. Lower surface temperatures contribute to decrease the temperature of the ambient air as the heat convection intensity from a cooler surface is lower. Such temperature reductions can have significant impacts on cooling energy consumption in urban areas, a fact of particular importance in hot climate cities.

The use of appropriate materials to reduce heat islands and improve the urban environment has attracted increasing interest in recent years. Many research studies have been carried out to identify the possible energy and environmental gains when light-coloured surfaces are used. Studies have investigated the impact of the materials' optical and thermal characteristics on the urban temperature and also the possible energy reduction during the summer period. A detailed guide on light-coloured surfaces has been published by the US EPA (Environmental Protection Agency, 1992). It has been shown that important energy gains are possible when light-coloured surfaces are used in combination with the planting of new trees. For example, computer simulations reported by Rosenfeld *et al* (1998) show that white roofs and shade trees in Los Angeles would lower the need for air conditioning by 18% or 1.04 billion kWh, equivalent to a financial gain of close to $100 million per year.

The author, using infrared thermography, has assessed the temperature of materials used in pavements and streets in the major Athens area during the summer period. A typical picture is shown in Figure 10.3. As shown, the temperature of non-shaded asphalt was close to 59°C, and the temperature of green areas was close to 31°C.

Extensive measurements of surface temperatures for more than 70 materials used for streets and pavements have been performed during a whole summer (Doulos, 2001). Instant temperature differences of more than 45°C were measured between asphalt and white cover materials.

Large-scale changes in urban albedo may have important direct and indirect effects on the urban scale. Measurements of the indirect energy savings from large-scale changes in urban albedo are almost impossible. However, using computer simulations the possible change in the urban climatic conditions can be evaluated. Taha *et al* (1997), using one-dimensional meteorological simulations, have shown that localized

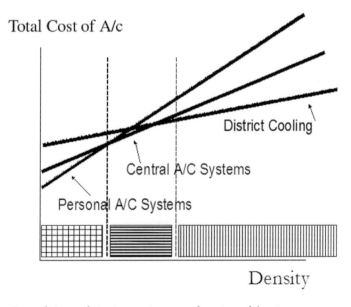

Figure 10.3 *Cost of air conditioning options as a function of density*

afternoon air temperatures on summer days can be lowered by us much as 4°C by changing the surface albedo from 0.25 to 0.40 in a typical mid-latitude warm climate. The same author (Taha, 1994), using three-dimensional mesoscale simulations, calculated the effects of large-scale albedo increases in Los Angeles. It was shown that an average decrease of 2°C and up to 4°C may be possible by increasing the albedo by 0.13 in urbanized areas. Further studies (Akbari *et al*, 1989) have shown that a temperature decrease of this magnitude could reduce the electricity load from air conditioning by 10%. Recent measurements in White Sands, New Mexico, indicated a similar relationship between naturally occurring albedo variations and measured ambient air temperatures. Taha (1997) analysed the atmospheric impacts of regional scale changes in building properties, paved surface characteristics and their micro-climates and discussed the possible meteorological and ozone air quality impacts of increases in surface albedo and urban trees in California's South Coast Air Basin. By using photochemical simulations it was found that implementing high-albedo materials would have a net effect of reducing ozone concentrations and that domain-wide population-weighted excess exposure to ozone above the local standards would be decreased by up to 12% during peak afternoon hours.

10.5.1.1 Use of vegetation

Trees and green spaces contribute significantly to cooling our cities and saving energy. Trees can provide solar protection to individual houses during the summer period while evapotranspiration from trees can reduce urban temperatures. Trees also help mitigate the greenhouse effect, filter pollutants, mask noise, prevent erosion and calm their human observers. As pointed out by the EPA (Environmental Protection Agency, 1992), 'the effectiveness of vegetation depends on its intensity, shape, dimensions and placement. But in general, any tree, even one bereft of leaves, can have a noticeable impact on energy use'.

The American Forestry Association in 1989 estimated that the value of an urban tree is close to $57,000 for a 50-year-old mature specimen. As indicated by the EPA (Environmental Protection Agency, 1992), the above estimate includes a mean annual value of $73 for air conditioning, $75 for soil benefits and erosion control, $50 for air pollution control and $75 for wildlife habitats.

Numerical studies trying to simulate the effect of additional vegetation on urban temperatures have been performed by various researchers and provide very useful information. Huang *et al* (1987) predicted that increasing the tree cover by 25% in Sacramento and Phoenix, USA, would decrease air temperatures at 2.00 p.m. in July by 6–10°F. Simulation results for Davis, California, using the URBMET PBL model reported by Taha (1988) show that the vegetation canopy produced daytime temperature depressions and night-time excesses compared with the bare surrounds. The factors behind temperature reduction are evaporative cooling and shading of the ground, whereas temperature increase during the night is the result of the reduced sky factor within the canopy. Results of the simulations show that a vegetative cover of 30% could produce a noontime oasis of up to 6°C, in favourable conditions, and a night time heat island of 2°C.

The impact of trees on the energy consumption of buildings is very important. As reported by the US National Academy of Sciences (1991), the planting of 100 million trees combined with the implementation of light surfacing programmes could reduce electricity use by 50 billion kWh per year, which is equivalent to 2% of the annual electricity use in the USA, and reduce the amount of CO_2 dumped in the atmosphere by as much as 35 million tons per year.

Urban agriculture, growing vegetables and fruits, in and around cities, can help to improve the urban microclimate and provide essential food to people. In fact, one seventh of the planet's food supply is grown in cities and there are 800 million urban farmers in the world (van Wijngaarden, 2001).

In Europe, almost 72% of all urban households in the Russian Federation grow food and Berlin has more than 80,000 urban farmers (Cainross *et al*, 1990). In St. Petersburg, the Urban Gardening Club has very efficiently promoted roof-top gardening. Estimations show that in just one district, it is possible to grow 2000 tonnes of vegetables per season from 500 roof-tops.

In Chicago, the local environment department promotes the construction of gardens on top of several city buildings as part of a US EPA program studying ways to help cool cities and reduce smog. In Canada, the city of Vancouver in collaboration with City Farmer, a non-profit association, promotes urban food production and environmental conservation. This has resulted in a new public garden which demonstrates conservation methods 'such as contouring of the ground, soil conditioning using compost, collection of rain water and the use of native plants' (City Farmer, 1998).

10.5.2 Use of sustainable energy supply systems

Sustainable energy supply systems and mainly the use of district heating and cooling systems based on the use of renewable energies such as solar and biomass or the use of waste heat, is the major tool to introduce clean and sustainable energy in cities. The energy produced may supply the residential sector, industry, urban agriculture and any other sector requiring hot or cold water. District heating and cooling brings heat or cool into the buildings (by way of chilled water) and avoids a number of distributed air conditioners with poor performance and high cost. It pays for itself in economies of scale but brings large energy and environmental advantages. It provides opportunities to reduce significantly electrical consumption and thus pollutant emissions. District systems have gained increasing acceptance. In some countries, particularly Denmark, Finland and Sweden, market penetration in relation to total space heating needs is very high (up to 50%).

In the 1980s, the total installed heat production capacity for district heating in the International Energy Agency (IEA) region was close to 122,000 MWth, mostly concentrated in Denmark, Finland, Germany, Sweden and the USA. Installed capacity in Europe was 82,000 MWth, together with 40,000 MWth in the USA. Combined production linked to district heating systems was very prevalent in Europe and accounted for 36% of installed heat capacity. During the 1990s, installed heat production capacity in Europe increased and was close to 110,000 MWth. For the USA, installed capacity almost doubled to 80,000 MWth. Thus, the total installed capacity is close to 250,000 MWth in the IEA region. This was the result of a total additional investment in district heating and combined heat and power of about US $38 billion, assuming a global cost of US $300 per kWth.

Nowadays, district heating is supplied to over 22 million people in Europe and 100 million people in Greater Europe. The maximum heat output capacity in European Union countries is close to 141,000 MWth (Euroheat and Power, 2001), 45,000 MWth of which is installed in Germany and 29,000 MWth in Sweden. The use of district heating systems results in significant energy savings, of close to 10 M of primary energy per year. This represents 0.5% of the total primary energy supply or import savings of about US $2 billion annually.

District cooling systems (DCS) have mainly been developed in the USA and present a number of very important advantages. In recent years, important district cooling networks have been installed in Europe (Figure 10.4) (Adnot and Lopes, 2000). The maximum district cooling capacity installed in European Union countries is close to 762 MW cooling, mainly installed in Northern European countries such as Sweden, Germany, France and the UK (Vadrot and Delbes, 1995). The main characteristics of some European DCS are given in Table 10.5 (Adnot and Lopes, 2000).

In Japan, district cooling represents a major source for supply of cooling in buildings. The installed capacity exceeds 723 MWc, whereas in the USA the installed capacity exceeds 1900 MWc (Vadrot and Delbes, 1995).

The most important advantage has to do with the dramatic decrease in peak electricity load. As buildings served by the district cooling network do not present peak cooling demands at the same time, the peak load line of district cooling systems is much smoother and therefore there is no need to over-design the cooling capacity of the network. This results in substantial reductions in the capital and operational costs. In parallel, room and central air-conditioning systems are designed to meet the peak cooling conditions. Thus, more than 90% of the operation period performs outside the nominal conditions and their efficiency is reduced. A good example is given in Figure 10.5, where the reduction in the peak electricity load in Cleveland is shown prior to

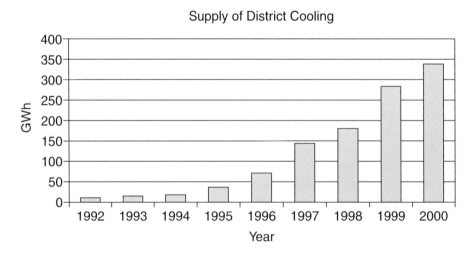

Figure 10.4 *Evolution of district cooling networks in Sweden (Swedish District Heating and Cooling Association, 1999)*

Table 10.5. *Main characteristics of some district cooling systems in Europe*

Site	L (km)	P (MW)	P/L (KW/m)	Energy (MWh)	Energy/power (h)
Central Paris	40	125	3	154,000	1200
Gothenburg	–	12	–	n.a.	n.a.
Stockholm	10	60	6	40,000	670
La Defense, Paris	10	123	12.3	145,000	1200
Lyon	10	36	3.6	n.a.	n.a.
Lisbon	20	60	3	n.a.	n.a.
Small Swedish projects	1–5	3–16	3	n.a.	n.a.
Small French projects	2–12	12–36	3–6	n.a.	n.a.

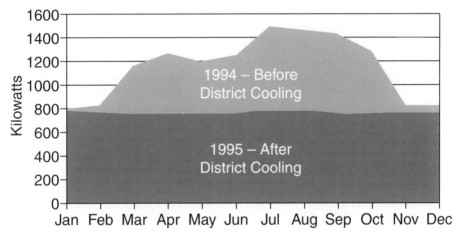

Figure 10.5 *Decrease in the peak electricity load in Cleveland because of the introduction of district cooling techniques*

and after the integration of a district cooling system in the city (information obtained from the website of the International District Energy Association, 2002). However, the overall economics of district cooling systems are highly dependent on the density of the area that they have to supply. Such a study, comparing room air conditioners (RAC) and central air conditioners (CAC) with district cooling systems, has been performed in the frame of the URBACOOL project (Adnot and Lopes, 2000). As shown in Figure 10.6, district cooling techniques present much lower costs than CAC and RAC for increased urban densities.

District cooling has gained increasing acceptance in Sweden, where the first Swedish district cooling network started in 1992. By the end of 2000, 25 district cooling networks were in operation. During 2000 the networks supplied around 340 GWh of district cooling (Figure 10.7) (data taken from the website of the Swedish District Heating and Cooling Association, 2002).

District energy systems are very efficient as they operate at high efficiencies, can increase effective building space, decrease operational, maintenance and capital costs

Figure 10.6 *Surface temperatures in Athens, (Summer 2001)*

of the user and can improve indoor air quality as they do not generate any chemical or biological pollution in the building. In parallel, district heating and cooling techniques, when operated by municipalities and community authorities, may be the source of important of revenues for the local society. In Europe, most hot water district heating systems operate at temperatures of 90–150°C (temperature of primary supply line). Higher temperatures, up to 175°C, are common in the USA. At temperatures above 150°C, heat exchangers are always required.

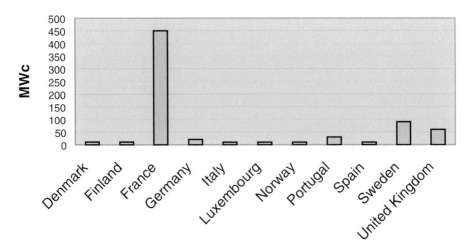

Figure 10.7 *Installed capacity of district cooling systems in Europe*

District heating and cooling installations using renewable energies are constantly increasing in number in Europe. The annual energy growth of the renewable's contribution is close to 10–15% (Euroheat and Power, 2001). Figure 10.8 shows the distribution of the primary energy used in the European Union for district heat and CHP production (Euroheat and Power, 2001). As shown, renewables contribute almost 9.5% of the primary energy, and waste heat offers almost 12% (Euroheat and Power, 2001). In many European countries the potential for district heating systems is very high, while the number of settlements supplied by district heating networks is continuously increasing. Table 10.6 reports the energy delivered and the type of fuel used in Sweden for district heating applications. As shown, more than 50% of the energy is delivered by waste heat and renewable energy sources (data taken from the website of the Swedish District Heating and Cooling Association, 2002).

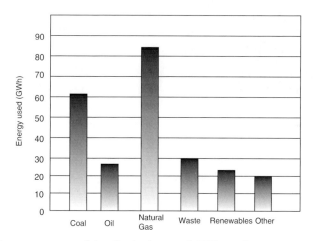

Figure 10.8 *Primary energy used for district heat and CHP production in EU countries, 1999*

Solar district heating systems with a diurnal storage system have been developed in Europe, at total costs of between €200/m² and €600/m² of collector area (Fisch *et al*, 1998; Reinhard, 2002). As stated (European Large Scale Solar Heating Plants Network, 2002), under favourable cases, investment costs may be down to €250/m² of collector, resulting in a solar heat cost of €0.06/kWh, for typical conditions. Examples with more than 100 m² of solar collectors have been developed in Austria, Denmark, Germany, Greece, Italy, Sweden and the Netherlands. District heating systems based on solar energy with a seasonal storage facility of about 1500 m³ may cover more than 50% of the overall heating demand, i.e. space heating and domestic hot water. When solar district heating systems are combined with waste heat or biomass they may become very competitive from the economic point of view.

Actually in the European Union countries there are 65 plants of more than 500 m² of solar collectors in operation, making altogether 110,000 m² and 50 MWth of thermal output (European Large Scale Solar Heating Plants Network, 2002). The number of solar-assisted plants is increasing rapidly and more than 48 new plants have been put into operation since the beginning of 1995 (European Large Scale Solar

Table 10.6 *Energy delivered and type of fuel used in district heating systems in Sweden (data taken from the website of the Swedish District Heating and Cooling Association, 2002)*

	2000	*1999*	*1998*
Thermal energy delivered (TWh)	41.4	43.3	43.0
Thermal power ordered (GW)	24.2	23.3	23.5
Net production of thermal energy (TWh)	3.7	4.5	4.7
Installed electrical energy (GW)	2.0	1.9	2.0
Use of fuel, etc. (TWh)	51.1	53.8	56.6
– oil	3.0	5.8	6.8
– coal	3.7	4.4	5.2
– firewood	13.9	14.8	15.1
– pine oil	1.5	1.5	
– refuse	5.5	5.4	5.5
– industrial waste heat	3.5	3.7	3.4
– electric boilers	1.8	1.4	1.5
– production from heat pumps	7.1	7.0	7.1
– peat	2.4	1.9	2.3
– natural gas	3.0	3.5	3.5
– other fuel, high-temperature water, etc.	5.8	4.5	6.1
Length of distribution net (km)	12,020	11,180	10,721
Efficiency (%)	85	87	83

Heating Plants Network, 2002). Most of the solar plants are installed in Sweden (23), and Germany is increasing rapidly its number of solar installations.

The potential of district heating and cooling systems when combined with CHP is very high. A recent analysis by Euroheat and Power (2000) determined that the existing DHC/CHP systems decrease EU carbon emissions by 6%. It is also estimated that 'expanding DHC and doubling the share of CHP production, according to the Community goal, will further reduce EU carbon emissions 8% by 2010'.

10.5.3 Use of demand side management techniques

Demand side management techniques may be the most appropriate tools to reduce the peak and total energy demand in cities. During recent years, some forms of demand side management techniques have been extensively used by European utilities.

Apart of the use of sustainable district heating and cooling systems, five types of demand side management actions can be identified:

● DSM1. Use of more energy-efficient air conditioners and heating devices, which implies better performance and better design and integration to the building.

● DSM2. Application of advanced control systems such as inverters and fuzzy logic in order to take into account the operational profiles of urban buildings, like the highly intermittent occupation of residential and commercial buildings in urban areas.

- DSM3. Direct load control such as remote cycling by the utilities in cooling usage as in other usage. This technique is widely applied during peak periods on several million room air conditioners in the USA. By limiting the available duty cycle during peak periods, utilities can reduce the peak demand significantly. Attention has to be given to consumers' comfort.

- DSM4. Improvements to the building design to decrease their heating and cooling load. This may involve actions on heat and solar protection, heat modulation and dissipation of excess heat in a lower temperature environmental sink.

- DSM5. Use of co-generation techniques. This type of distributed generation of electricity, possibly plus cold/hot water or steam, can reduce peak transportation costs and use of fuel.

10.5.4 Use of passive and active solar systems in urban buildings

The adaptation of urban buildings to the specific environmental conditions of cities in order to incorporate efficiently solar and energy-saving measures and counterbalance the radical changes and transformations of the radiative, thermal, moisture and aero-dynamic characteristics of the urban environment is a major priority. This incorporates appropriate sizing and placing of the building openings, to promote solar energy utilization, enhance air flow and natural ventilation and improve daylight availability, integration of photovoltaics and also the use of passive cooling techniques to decrease cooling energy consumption and improve thermal comfort.

Passive solar heating, cooling and lighting techniques have reached a high degree of technical maturity. Large-scale applications, especially in new settlements, have shown that very high energy gains can be achieved while the thermal and visual comfort and indoor air quality are very satisfactory (IEA, 1997). Further penetration and use of solar technologies are associated with their adaptation to the new conditions almost imposed by the specific social, economic and technical trends dominating the overall sector of the built environment.

Retrofitting of existing buildings provides by far the greatest potential for the incorporation of solar technologies and energy efficiency measures into urban buildings. Within many countries there is considerably more activity in retrofitting and re-using buildings than in constructing new ones. It has been mentioned (Santamouris, 1995) that more than 70% of building's related investments in Western Europe are channelled to urban renewal and building rehabilitation. In the tertiary sector, retrofitting of the post-War stock is seen in the property market as the major area of activity for the next few years and thus the incorporation of solar energy systems and components could be significant.

Retrofitting of existing urban buildings offers an opportunity to implement solar energy and energy efficiency measures. Application of passive solar techniques coupled with energy efficiency systems leads to important energy and environmental benefits

(Santamouris, 1995), such as more attractive, daylit interiors, less dependence upon mechanical systems and avoiding ozone-depleting refrigerants, lower energy and maintenance costs, a good long-term investment with less dependence on supplies of delivered energy, less overheating, more comfort and, debatably, a healthier internal environment and opportunities for straightforward personal control, particularly in cellular offices.

New design methodologies and tools and more advanced materials and components permit the building community to design and construct more efficient urban buildings. Designers may now select more advanced windows and better insulation materials, solar cells and collectors, heat pumps, daylighting, integrated lighting and shading control systems, free nocturnal air cooling, pre-heaters such as air heat recovery and air-to-ground heat exchangers for preheating in winter and cooling in summer, etc.

In particular, the development of the glazing industry has been spectacular in recent years. New advanced glazing elements such as low-e coated windows, holographic optical glazing, electrochromic materials and glazing units with a filling of aerosilica gel granules provide new efficient materials and opportunities for retrofitting of urban buildings. Simple low-e glazing contributes to reducing the heating and cooling needs associated with windows by more than 50% and contributes to satisfying daylight requirements.

Estimations by the European glazing industry (GEPVP, 2001) show that in Europe there is some 1.303 million m^2 of single-glazed windows and a similar number of simple double-glazed windows. Their replacement with low e-glass may contribute an energy conservation of 26 Mt per year or M€14,264/year. In parallel, the corresponding CO_2 reductions are estimated to be close to 82.4 Mt/year. Advanced glazing materials have already penetrated well into the European market. In Germany, low-e glass holds a market share of about 90% (Figure 10.9) (Reinhard, 2002).

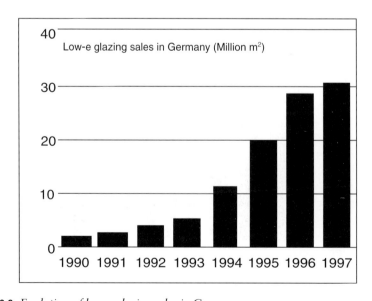

Figure 10.9 *Evolution of low-e glazing sales in Germany*

Lighting is one of the largest electrical loads, especially in commercial buildings. Efficient lighting design can displace up to the 70% of lighting energy requirements in office buildings. Use of new advanced lighting and daylighting systems can contribute, in the USA, to a saving of up to 50% of the annual lighting energy use, equal to US $20 billion/year. In Europe, estimations of EUROACE have shown that the possible use of advanced lighting systems in buildings may contribute to saving more than 50 Mtonnes of CO_2 per year (EUROACE, 1998). The same study estimated that if improved insulation, advanced glazing and controls and improved lighting systems are used by 2010, the total possible energy gains for European buildings are between 430 and 452 Mt of CO_2.

10.5.5 Appropriate legislation for buildings

Legislation regulating the energy consumption of buildings is a major instrument in reducing the energy demand of buildings. Appropriate legislation may reduce gains through the envelope or ventilation, increase gains and contribute to making the energy systems of the building perform more efficiently. This is very clearly shown in a report (ADEME, 1998) where, using the national building codes of major European countries (Figure 10.10), the energy consumption for heating purposes has been calculated for a reference building (Figure 10.11), taking into account the local climatic data for each country. As shown, because of the inappropriate regulations, the heating demand of southern European countries exceeds the corresponding consumption of many northern states!

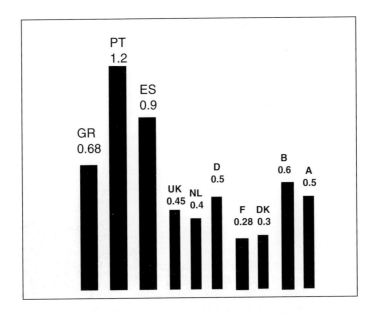

Figure 10.10 *Overall heat transfer coefficient, U, for outer walls in selected European countries*

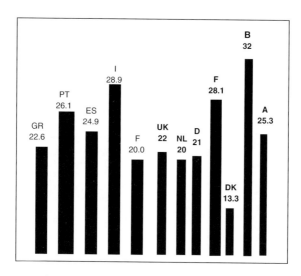

Figure 10.11 *Energy demand of a model house (kWh/m³/a) in selected European countries (ADEME, 1998)*

Recently, new energy performance regulations have been developed by many European countries. Most of them either define a maximum permitted energy consumption for the different types of buildings or are based on the principle of a 'reference building'. A very good compilation of the existing and proposed energy performance regulations of most European countries is given by Visier (2001). New regulations have to satisfy the requirements of the new European Directive on the Energy Performance of Buildings that defines a set of strict and intensive measures for existing and new buildings.

10.5.6 Towards more compact cities

The form of a city has a huge impact on its energy consumption. Higher densities mainly decrease the energy spent on transport. Comparison of the density of American, Canadian and European cities with the energy spend (Figures 10.12 and 10.13) clearly demonstrates such a conclusion (Skinner, 2000).

In general, the reconsideration of the architectural and planning priorities for the urban environment may contribute substantially to decreasing the energy consumption spent by urban citizens. It is widely accepted that by making our cities more compact, both energy and environmental factors improve. In particular, energy for transport may decrease considerably although there is an increased possibility of increasing heat island intensity, particularly in hot climates.

As stated by O'Meara (1999), changes in the layout of urban neighbourhoods can lower energy demands from transport by a factor of 10. In fact, this was shown by Browning *et al* (1998), who compared the modelled energy consumption of two contrasting households, one living in a high energy efficiency standards contracted house located in a typical suburban area and the other living in an old 'energy hog' house of 1988, located in a traditional urban area. Although the urban building used

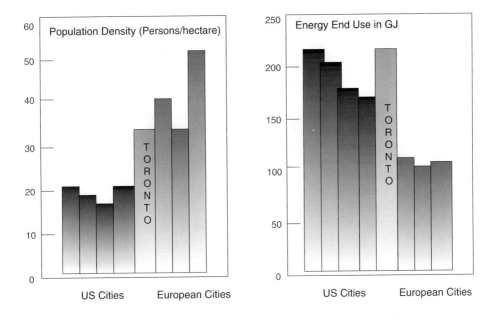

Figure 10.12 *Population density against energy use in the USA, Canada and Europe (Skinner, 2000)*

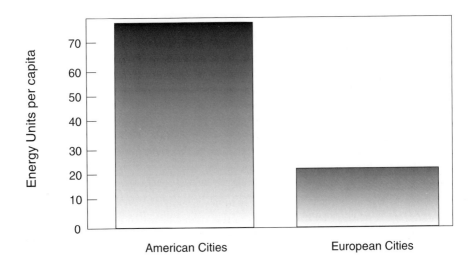

Figure 10.13 *Per capita energy consumption for transport in American and European cities (Skinner, 2000)*

more energy for heating, overall 10 times less energy was used because its use of an automobile was much lower, taking into account that the access to services was easier and the level of public transport was good. Similar results were reported by Goodacre (1998) for Lancaster in the UK.

Compact growth offers important economic benefits. Recent studies trying to quantify the benefits of compact design concluded that the State of New Jersey in the USA would save US $1.3 billion if a compact growth development option was followed instead of the usual sprawl type (O'Meara, 1999). In a similar way, another study for Maryland, USA, concluded that if the rapid suburban development in this state continues at its current pace, instead of a more compact development, the necessary additional infrastructure will be close to US $10 billion for the period 1995–2020 (O'Meara, 1999).

Although compact cities may provide important energy and environmental benefits, it is the dense cities that most people try to avoid for the location of their homes (Baker, 2001). Thus, new ideas such as those developed by the New Urbanism movement (Calthorpe, 1993; Katz, 1994), based on mixed land uses, greater dependence on public transport, cycling and walking, decentralization of employment location, etc., or the ideas of Bill Dunster for 'Hopetown' (Vadrot and Delbes, 1995), for a new building type which combines premises for living and working with food production, may be further developed and applied to create a more sustainable urban environment.

10.6 Conclusions

The energy consumption of the building sector is very high and is expected to increase further because of the improving standard of living and increase in the world population. To satisfy the increased energy needs, particularly in less developed countries, without compromising the atmospheric environment, clean and low-cost systems and techniques have to be employed. Passive and active solar techniques combined with advanced conservation technologies seem to be the most appropriate and efficient solution to this problem. In parallel, energy efficiency and advanced solar energy systems can contribute greatly, in conjunction with other measures, to make urban energy systems in developed countries more sustainable.

Appropriate future planning in cities should consider that the built environment is not just a collection of buildings, but is in fact the physical result of various economic, social and environmental processes strongly related to the standards and needs of society. Economic pressures related to the property and labour markets, investment and equity, household income and the production and distribution of goods, in combination with social aspects related to culture, security, identity, accessibility and basic needs, and finally, in association with environmental influences related to the use of land, energy and materials, define and determine the built environment in which we live and will also determine the future of solar technologies.

10.7 References

ADEME, 1998, *Final Report of the MURE Program*, Brussels, SAVE Program, European Commission, Directorate General for Energy and Transport.

Adnot, J and Lopes, C, 2000, 'Central solutions for city cooling', in M Santamouris (ed), *Urbacool Final Report*, Brussels, SAVE Program, European Commission, Directorate General for Energy and Transport.

Akbari, H, Rosenfeld, A and Taha, H, 1989, 'Recent developments in heat island studies: technical and policy', in *Proceedings of Workshop on Saving Energy and Reducing Atmospheric Pollution by Controlling Summer Heat Islands, Berkeley, CA, February 23–24 1989*, 14–20.

Argiriou, A, Asimakopoulos, D, Balaras, C, Daskalaki, E, Lagoudi, A, Loizidou, M, Santamouris, M and Tselepidaki, I, 1994, 'On the energy consumption and indoor air quality in office and hospital buildings in Athens, Greece', in *Journal of Energy Conversion and Management*, 35(5), 385–394.

Azandossessi, A, 2000, 'The struggle for water in urban poor areas of Nuakchott, Mauritania', in *Waterfrond*, Issue 13, January, New York, UNICEF.

Baker, N, 2001, 'The city as natural form: models of urban microclimates', in M Hewitt and S Hagan (eds), *City Fights*, London, James & James.

Briscoe, J, 1986, 'Selected primary health care revisited', in J S Tulchin (ed), *Health, Habitat and Development*, Boulder, CO, Lynne Reinner.

British Medical Association, 1997, *Road Transport and Health*, London, British Medical Association.

Browning, R, Helou, M and Larocque, P A, 1998, 'The impact of transportation on household energy consumption', in *World Transport Policy and Practice*, 4, 1.

Caincross, S, 1990, 'Water supply and the urban poor', in J E Hardoy *et al* (eds), *The Poor Die Young: Housing and Health in Third World Cities*, London, Earthscan.

Cairnross, S, Hardoy, J E and Satterthwaite, D, 1990, 'The urban context', in J E Hardoy, S Cainross and D Satterthwaite (eds), *The Poor Die Young: Housing and Health in Third World Cities*, London, Earthscan, 1–24.

Calthorpe, P, 1993, *The Next American Metropolis*, New York, Princeton Architectural Press.

Carlson, E, 1996, *The Legacy of Habitat II, The Urban Age 4, 2*, Washington, DC, World Bank Group.

City Farmer, 1998, *Urban Agriculture Notes*, newsletter.

Development Workshop, 1995, *Water Supply and Sanitation and its Urban Constraints. Beneficiary Assessment for Luanda*, World Bank.

Devuyst D, 2001, 'Sustainable development at the local level: the North–South context', in D Devuyst, L Hens and W de Lannoy (eds), *How Green is the City*, New York, Columbia University Press.

Doulos, L, 2001, 'Comparative study of almost 70 different materials for streets and pavements', *MSc Final Report*, Department of Physics, University of Athens.

Environmental Protection Agency, 1992, *Cooling Our Communities. A Guidebook on Tree Planting and Light Colored Surfacing*, Washington, DC, Environmental Protection Agency.

EUROACE, 1998, *Report on Assessment of Potential for the Saving of Carbon Dioxide Emissions in European Building Stock*, Brussels, EUROACE.

Euroheat and Power, 2000, *Comments on Green Paper on Greenhouse Gas Emissions Trading Within the European Union*, Brussels, The International Association for District Heating, District Cooling and Combined Heat and Power.

Euroheat and Power, 2001, *District Heat in Europe*, Brussels, Euroheat and Power.

European Large Scale Solar Heating Plants Network, 2002, *www.chalmers.se*.

Fisch, M N, Guigas, M and Dalenbäck, J O, 1998, 'A review of large-scale solar heating systems in Europe', in *Solar Energy*, 63(6), 355–366.

Flavin and Lenssen, 1995, *Power Surge: a Guide to the Coming Energy Revolution*', London Earthscan.

Folke, C, Jansson, A, Larsson, J and Costanza, R, 1997, 'Ecosystem appropriation by cities', in *Ambio*, 26, 167–172.

GEPVP, 2001, *Low-e Glass in Buildings, Impact on the Environment and Energy Savings*, Brussels, Short Brochure, Groupement Européan des Producteurs de Verre Plat.

Godish, T, 1989, *Indoor Air Pollution Control*, Chelsea, MI, Lewis Publishers.

Goodacre, C, 1998, 'An evaluation of household activities and their effect on end-user energy consumption at a social scale', *PhD Thesis*, Geography Department, Lancaster University.

Hahn, E and Simonis, U E, 1991, 'Ecological urban restructuring', in *Ekistics*, 58(348/349), May–June/July–August.

Hardy, J E, Mitlin, D and Satterthwaite, D, 2001, *Environmental Problems in an Urbanizing World*, London, Earthscan.

Hassid, S, Santamouris, M, Papanikolaou, N, Linardi, A and Klitsikas, N, 2000, 'The effect of the heat island on air conditioning load', in *Journal of Energy and Buildings*, 32, 131–141.

Huang, Y J, Akbari, H, Taha, H and Rosenfeld, A H, 1987, 'The potential of vegetation in reducing cooling loads in residential buildings', in *Journal of Climate and Applied Meteorology*, 26, 1103–1116.

IBGE, 1993, 'Constitution d'un système d'éco-géo-information urbain pour la région Bruxelloise intégrant l'énergie et l'air', Convention Institut Wallon et Mens en Ruimte, Brussels, Institut Bruxellois pour la Gestion de l'Environment.

IEA, 1997, in A G Hestnes, R Hastings and B Saxhof (eds), *Solar Energy Houses, Strategies, Technologies, Examples*, London, James & James.

International District Energy Association, 2002, *www.districtenergy.com*

Katz, P, 1994, *The New Urbanism: Toward an Architecture of Community*, New York, McGraw-Hill.

Kucera, V, Henriksen, J F, Knotkova, D and Sjostrom, C, 1992, 'Model for calculations of corrosion cost caused by air pollution and its application in 3 cities', Paper 084, 10th European Corrosion Congress, Barcelona, 5–8 July 1993.

LRC, 1993, *London Energy Study Report*, London, London Research Centre.

Mitlin and Satterthwaite, 1996, 'Sustainable development and cities', in C Pough (ed), *Sustainability, the Environment and Urbanization*, London, Earthscan, 23–61.

National Academy of Science, 1991, *Policy Implications of Greenhouse Warming*, Report of the Mitigation Panel, Washington, DC, National Academy Press.

NRTEE, 1998, 'Canada offers sustainable cities solutions for the world', discussion paper for a workshop, Ottawa, National Round Table on the Environment and the Economy.

O'Meara, M, 1999, 'Exploring a new vision for cities', in L Brown, C Flavin and H F French (eds), *State of the World, 1999. A Worldwatch Institute Report on Progress Toward a Sustainable Society*, New York, W. W. Norton.

OECD, 1983, *Control Technology for Nitrogen Oxides in the Atmosphere*, Paris, OECD.

OECD, 1991, *Fighting Noise in the 1990s*, Paris, OECD.

Ojima, T, 1990–91, 'Changing Tokyo metropolitan area and its heat island model', in *Energy and Buildings*, 15–16, 191–203.

Oke, T R, Johnson, G T, Steyn, D G and Watson, I D, 1991, 'Simulation of surface urban heat islands under "ideal" conditions at night – Part 2: Diagnosis and causation', in *Boundary Layer Meteorology*, 56, 339–358.

Onisto, L, Krause, E and Wackernagel, M, 1998, *How Big is Toronto's Ecological Footprint?* Toronto, Centre for Sustainable Studies and City of Toronto.

Plessas, D, 1980, *The Social Cost of Air Pollution in the Greater Athens Region*, Athens, KEPE.

Polionecki, J D, Atkinson, R W, de Leon, A P and Anderson, H R, 1997, 'Daily time series for cardiovascular hospital admissions and previous days air pollution in London, UK', in *Occupational and Environmental Medicine*, 54, 535–540.

Rees, W, 1996, 'Global change, ecological footprints and urban sustainability, in D Devuyst, L Hens and W de Lannoy (eds), *How Green is the City*, New York, Columbia University Press.

Rees, W, 2001, 'The conundrum of urban sustainability', in D Devuyst, L Hens and W de Lannoy (eds), *How Green is the City*, New York, Columbia University Press.

Rees, W E and Wackernagel, M, 1996, 'Urban ecological footprints: why cities cannot be sustainable and why they are a key to sustainability', in *EIA Review*, 16, 223–248.

Reinhard, C F, 2002, 'Energy efficient solar buildings', in *EUREC Position Papers*, London, James & James.

Rosenfeld, A, Romm, J, Akbari, H and Lioyd, A, 1998, 'Painting the town white and green', paper available through the web site of Lawrence Berkeley Laboratory, *www.lbl.gov*

Saksensa and Smith, 1999, 'Indoor air pollution', in G McGranahan and F Murray (eds), *Health and Air Pollution in Rapidly Developing Countries*, Stockholm, Stockholm Environment Institute.

Santamouris, M, 1995, *Energy Retrofitting of Office Buildings – Energy Efficiency and Retrofit Measures for Offices*, SAVE Program, Final Report, Brussels, European Commission, Directorate General for Energy.

Santamouris, M, 1997, *Passive Cooling and Urban Layout*, Interim Report, POLIS Research Project, Brussels, European Commission, Directorate General for Science, Research and Development (available from the author).

Santamouris, M (ed), 2001, *Energy in the Urban Built Environment*, London, James & James.

Santamouris, M, 2002, 'Sustainable cities – realistic targets for an Utopian subject', paper presented at the Green Cities Conference, Westerloo, Belgium.

Santamouris, M, Papanikolaou, N, Livada, I, Koronakis, I, Georgakis, C, and Assimakopoulos, D N, 2001, 'On the impact of urban climate on the energy consumption of buildings', in *Solar Energy*, 70 (3) 201–216.

Sinnatamby G, 1990, 'Low cost sanitation', in J E Hardoy *et al* (eds), *The Poor Die Young: Housing and Health in Third World Cities*, London, Earthscan.

Skinner, N, 2000, 'Energy management in practice: communities acting to protect the climate', in *UNEP Industry and Environment*, January–June, 43–48.

Smith, 1990, 'Dialectics of improved stoves', in L Kristoferson *et al* (eds), *Bioenergy, Contribution to Environmentally Sustainable Development*, Stockholm, Stockholm Environment Institute.

Smith and Akbar, 1999, 'Health-damaging air pollution: a matter of scale', in Gordon McGranahan and Frank Murray (eds), *Health and Air Pollution in Rapidly Developing Countries*, Stockholm, Stockholm Environment Institute.

Smith *et al*, 1994, 'Air pollution and the energy ladder in Asian cities', in *Energy*, 19(5), 587–600.

Stanners D and Bourdeau P (eds), 1995, *Europe's Environment – The Dobris Assessment*, Copenhagen, Denmark, European Environmental Agency.

Sustainable London Trust, 1996, *Sustainable London*, London, Sustainable London Trust.

Swedish District Heating and Cooling Association, 2002, *www.districtenergy.se*

Taha, H, 1988, 'Site specific heat island simulations: model development and application to microclimate conditions', LBL Report No. 26105, *MGeogr Thesis*, University of California, Berkeley, CA.

Taha, H, 1994, 'Meteorological and photochemical simulations of the south coast air basin', in H Taha (ed), *Analysis of Energy Efficiency of Air Quality in the South Coast Air Basin – Phase II*, Report No. LBL-35728, Berkeley, CA, Lawrence Berkeley Laboratory, Ch. 6, 161–218.

Taha, H, 1997, 'Urban climates and heat islands: albedo, evapotranspiration and anthropogenic heat', in *Energy and Buildings*, 25, 99–103.

Taha, H, Douglas, S and Haney, J, 1997, 'Mesoscale meteorological and air quality impacts of increased urban albedo and vegetation', in *Energy and Buildings*, 25, 169–177.

Thompson *et al*, 2000, 'Waiting at the tap: changes in urban water use in East Africa over three decades', in *Environment and Urbanization*, 12(2), 37–52.

UBA, 1988, *Larmbekampfung 88, Tendenzen, Probleme, Lasungen*, Berlin, Umweldbundesamt.

UNCHS, 1996, United Nations Council for Human Settlements, *An Urbanizing World, Global Report on Human Settlements, 1996*, Oxford, Oxford University Press.

UNCHS, 2001, United Nations Council for Human Settlements, *The State of the World Cities*, New York, United Nations.

UNDP, 1998, *United Nations Development Programme: Urban Transition in Developing Countries*, New York, United Nations Development Programme.

UNEPTIE, 2002, *Tomorrow's Market: Global Trends and Their Implications for Business*.

UNFPA, 1998, *The State of World Population 1998*, New York, United Nations Population Fund.

United Nations, 1994, *World Urbanization Prospects: the 1994 Revision*, New York, United Nations.

United Nations, 1998, *World Urbanization Prospects: the 1996 Revision*, New York, Population Division, United Nations.

United Nations, 2002, *United Nations Environmental Program: Global Environmental Outlook*, New York, United Nations.

Vadrot, A and Delbes, J, 1995, *District Cooling Handbook*, 2nd edn, Brussels, Thermie Program, European Commission, Directorate General for Energy.

van Wijngaarden, T, 2001, 'An example of eco-city development: urban agriculture', in D Devuyst, L Hens and W de Lannoy (eds), *How Green is the City*, New York, Columbia University Press.

Visier, J C, 2001, *Final Report of WP1*, Brussels, ENPER–TEBUC SAVE Program, European Commission, Directorate General for Energy and Transport.

Wackernagel, M and Rees, W E, 1996, *Our Ecological Footprint: Reducing Human Impact on the Earth*, Gabriola Island, BC and New Haven, CT, New Society Publishers.

Wackernagel, M, Onisto, L, Linares, A C, Falfan, I S L, Garcia, J M, Guerrero, A I S and Guerrero, M G S, 1997, *Ecological Footprints of Nations. Report to the Earth Council, Costa Rica*, New York, United Nations.

Wackernagel, M, Onisto, L, Bello, P, Linares, A C, Falfan, I S L, Garcia, J M, Guerrero, A I S and Guerrero, M G S, 1999, 'National natural capital accounting with the ecological footprint concept', in *Ecological Economics*, 29, 375–390.

Wallingford, K M and Carpenter, J, 1986, 'Field experience overview: investigating sources of indoor air quality problems in office buildings', in *Proceedings of IAQ 86*, Atlanta, GA, ASHRAE.

WCED, 1987, *Our Common Future. Report of the UN World Commission on Environment and Development*, Oxford, Oxford University Press.

White *et al*, 1972, *Drawers of Water: Domestic Water Use in East Africa*, Chicago, University of Chicago Press.

World Bank, 2003, *World Development Report, 2003*, New York, World Bank.

WRI, 1996, World Resource Institute, *World Resources, 1996–1997. The Urban Environment*, Oxford, Oxford University Press.

Yap, D, 1975, 'Seasonal excess urban energy and the nocturnal heat island – Toronto', in *Archives of Meteorol. Geoph. Bioklima., Series B*, 23, 68–80.

Index